4-

-09

/ —

THE NEW COMPLETE
Pembroke Welsh Corgi

Ch. Vangard Jenelle   Ch. Vangard Mister Ski Bum
      Ch. Schaferhaus Danielle   *Courtesy of Robert L. Simpson*

THE NEW COMPLETE
Pembroke
Welsh Corgi

Deborah S. Harper

HOWELL
BOOK HOUSE
New York

Howell Book House
A Prentice Hall Macmillan Company
15 Columbus Circle
New York, NY 10023

MACMILLAN is a registered trademark of Macmillan, Inc.

Library of Congress Cataloging-in-Publication Data
Harper, Deborah S.
 The new complete Pembroke Welsh corgi / Deborah S. Harper.
  p. cm.
 Rev. ed. of: The complete Pembroke Welsh corgi / by Mary Gay
Sargent and Deborah S. Harper. 1979.
 Includes bibliographical references.
 ISBN 0-87605-249-9
 1. Pembroke Welsh corgi. I. Sargent, Mary Gay. Complete
Pembroke Welsh corgi. II. Title.
SF429.P33H37 1994
636.7'37—dc20   93-51047
                              CIP

Manufactured in the United States of America

10 9 8 7 6 5 4 3 2 1

Contents

About the Author

DEBORAH S. HARPER believes in the value of positive contributions. That belief has punctuated her participation in the Pembroke Welsh Corgi fancy since she acquired her first Corgi in 1960. Her long list of achievements on behalf of the breed over three decades proves that she follows up on her beliefs with action.

Mrs. Harper has served the Pembroke Welsh Corgi Club of America as its Secretary from 1970 to 1983. She has judged Specialty matches and Sweepstakes for many Pembroke Clubs. In 1991 she had the highly coveted honor of judging the Sweepstakes for the National Specialty. She has also worked on a wide variety of committees for the PWCCA and for the local Mayflower Club.

A highly respected breeder, Mrs. Harper's Walborah prefix appears on the names of many fine animals despite the limited nature of the breeding program. Once named PWCCA Breeder of the Year, Mrs. Harper has produced numerous champions but never breeds more than one or two litters a year. Her house dogs are show dogs and her show dogs are house dogs—eloquent testimonial that the two are not mutually exclusive. She has also met with success in obedience as well as conformation competition.

As this book goes to press, a dog of her breeding is the top-winning male Pembroke in history with an impressive record, which includes forty-four Bests in Show.

Her collaboration on the original edition of this book, *The Complete Pembroke Welsh Corgi*, quickly succeeded in making her name a household word everywhere around the world the breed is appreciated. Now, with the publication of the second edition, *The New Complete Pembroke Welsh Corgi*, Mrs. Harper's ongoing positive contribution to her breed extends to yet another generation of Pembroke enthusiasts.

This endearing breed is fortunate to enjoy the allegiance of so dedicated an individual. Her energy, integrity and devotion to detail have served the Pembroke well in many ways. These qualities, combined with her evident scholarship have made this book the most important single contribution to the literature of the breed ever published. What follows on these pages is for you to share and treasure just as you do your Pembrokes.

Preface

OVER FIFTEEN YEARS have passed since the publication of the first edition of *The Complete Pembroke Welsh Corgi*. The major portion of the original book was researched and written by Mary Gay Sargent. I was glad to be able to come in toward the end and help finish up the project.

During the last few years we both were urged by the publisher and interested members of the Corgi community to revise and update the book. Clearly, as time went by the need for a new book became more pressing. In the winter of 1992, with the promise of support, I agreed to undertake a 50 percent revision. Unfortunately, Gay was not available as before to spearhead the work. It became a fascinating and challenging year.

A great deal has happened in the Pembroke Welsh Corgi world and in the sphere of purebred dogs in general. Additional bloodlines have become prominent, new records have been set, and Corgis have become active in several new fields of endeavor. The object has been to introduce all the new material and at the same time retain much of the old so that this edition is able to stand alone—complete.

The most difficult task has been to adhere to the restrictions placed by the publisher. The new book has to remain the same size as the old. Moreover, the overall number of photographs must be reduced by 30 percent. It has been most disheartening to have to eliminate many old favorites and set aside plans to illustrate how selected bloodlines have bred on through several generations. An appendix lists the page in the old edition where to find the pictures of the important dogs that had to be omitted. And, as before, many people and their fine dogs have had to go unmentioned.

New and perhaps unfamiliar titles appear after the dogs' names throughout the book. The new Obedience Championship (OTCH), Herding titles (HC, HT, PT, HS, HI, HX, H.Ch.), and Versatility awards (VC, VCX) are explained in the chapter on Performance Activities. Of course, Companion Dog (CD), Companion Dog Excellent (CDX), Utility Dog (UD), Tracking Dog (TD) and Tracking Dog Excellent (TDX) remain the standard Obedience and Tracking titles.

In 1990 the Pembroke Welsh Corgi Club of America, Inc., initiated a Register of Merit (ROM) and Register of Merit Excellent (ROMX) for dogs and bitches who have produced a certain number of American champion offspring. For example, a male must have sired fifteen champions and a bitch produced ten champions to be given the designation ROMX. (At last count there were fifty-four ROMX Pembrokes, eight of which are bitches.) These titles now appear and are a measure of the animal's ability to produce offspring of quality.

Of major significance to the entire dog fancy was the splitting of the Working Group into two sections in 1983. On the first of January that year the Cardigan and Pembroke Welsh Corgis were assigned to the new Herding Group. Consequently, Group placements after that date represent competition with about half the number of other breeds as before the split. Obviously, the chances for a placement are now twice as good.

With all this in mind, I sincerely hope the standard set by the first edition has been upheld in *The New Complete Pembroke Welsh Corgi*.

DEBORAH S. HARPER

Acknowledgments

WITH ANY UNDERTAKING of this magnitude, many people rally around and contribute a good deal of time and ideas. This marvelous support has made it possible to gather the material and present it in book form for others to enjoy. It has been both educational and a pleasure to hear from many people in all corners of the Corgi world. I regret that space does not allow mention of every individual whose help has been most generously given.

For the material brought over from the original book, thanks must go to Phyl Young and Barbara Spengler, who worked with Mary Gay Sargent to provide many of the photographs. Mrs. Gladys Orlowski made available Mr. Orlowski's Corgi scrapbooks, which provided much information on the early days of the breed in America. The Welsh Corgi League Handbooks and the Pembroke Welsh Corgi Club of America's *Pembroke Welsh Corgi Newsletter*, *Pembroke Welsh Corgis in America* handboooks and *An Illustrated Study of the Pembroke Welsh Corgi Standard*, all have been utilized in the preparation of both books. Permission to draw from these publications by the two organizations was greatly appreciated. In the first edition Mrs. Barbara Ludowici sent information on Australia, and Mrs. Lilian Timmins prepared a scrapbook of Canadian dogs. Tasha Tudor's drawing enhances the chapter on Corgi grooming. The permission granted by the Lisa Studios, Ltd., for the inclusion of the two photographs of members of the British royal family with their Corgis is again acknowledged.

The impetus behind the preparation of *The New Complete Pembroke Welsh Corgi* certainly has been Sally Howe of Howbout Kennels in Campbell, California. Right from the beginning she has provided encouragement, invaluble expertise and editorial assistance. Many of her points of view were well taken and have been incorporated into the text. Her professional skills have eased tangled sentences and typos. Thank you, Sally, for your consistent willingness to help and many hours of work.

Special mention must be made of Bonnie Hansen, who put together a tremendous amount of data on Pembroke Welsh Corgis that have earned titles in Obedience and Tracking. Phyllis Lambert, keeper of records for the PWCCA, compiled the listing of ROMX and ROM dogs, which was in constant use. Kristen Frantzen Orr provided a head drawing and overlay for the chapter on the Standard. From Australia Helen Thompson and Diane Baillie sent reams of fascinating and well-organized material on the dogs of their country, more inviting than a travelogue.

And to all of you who responded to my request for pictures and biographical material on your dogs with abundance, I am truly grateful.

There were enough pictures to fill three books. To my great dismay, far too many had to be returned unused.

Finally, the whole project promptly would have been deemed impossible without the unfailing assistance of my good friend Thomas C. Cooper, Jr., computer expert extraodinaire. He has graciously spent countless hours setting up, fixing up and finishing up all of my work at the keyboard and monitor. Tom deserves the biggest "thank you" of all.

1

Origins of the Pembroke Welsh Corgi

JUST HOW or when the Pembroke Welsh Corgi and its northern cousin, the Cardigan Welsh Corgi, came to be no one knows. Welsh people know the sturdy little Corgi has been a familiar sight watching over the cattle and guarding the homestead in Wales for many centuries.

With the Corgi seeming to have been in existence in Wales forever, it is natural that many legends and fireside stories about Corgis passed from one generation of Welshmen to the next.

One such legend provides a charming tale for the curious of how the Corgi came to live in the hills of southwestern Wales. According to the legend, two young children out tending the family's cattle on the king's land found a pair of puppies, which they thought were little foxes. When the children took the puppies home, they were told by the menfolk that the little dogs were a gift from the fairies. The "wee folk" of Welsh legend used the small dogs either to pull their carriages or as fairy steeds. As the foxlike puppies grew, they learned to help their human companions watch over the cattle, a task that was to be the duty of their Corgi descendants for many centuries thereafter. Should anyone doubt the truth of the legend, the present-day Welsh Corgi still bears the marks over his shoulders of the little saddle used by his fairy riders.

This diagrammatic map of England and Wales is correlated with the early history of the Welsh Corgi. Note the distance of Lancaster, the area where the Lancashire Heeler has existed for many years, from Pembrokeshire and Cardiganshire. Also of interest is the great distance traveled by Welsh farmers and their Corgis when they drove cattle to London.

POSSIBLE ORIGIN

Numerous breeds have, at some time, had their ancestry traced to the dogs of ancient Egypt, and the Corgi is no exception. It has been claimed by the occasional zealous writer that dogs portrayed in the decorations of Egyptian tombs are clearly of Welsh Corgi type. And though most breed authorities have dismissed this theory, it has been written that the small, short-coated dogs with prick ears and pointed muzzles depicted on the famous statue of Anubis, the Egyptian God of the Setting Sun, were direct ancestors of the Welsh Corgi.

What has been considered to be more plausible evidence of the Corgi's antiquity is found in the Laws of Hywel Dda, or Howell the Good, King of South Wales. The laws were codified in about A.D. 920 from earlier, unwritten Welsh law. Among the ancient laws was one that placed a value on the various types of dogs according to the work they performed. No, not for taxation yet, but rather for purposes of redress should an animal be killed or stolen. The shepherd's or herdsman's cur was said to be of the same value as an ox, providing it was proven to be a genuine herder or drover, making it of more value than either the watch cur or the house cur.

Whether or not the herdsman's cur and the Corgi were one and the same is open to speculation. Those who contend that the Corgi was, indeed, the herdsman's cur base their conclusion on the belief that the Corgi is the only breed of cattle dog to have been established in Wales.

The tenth-century homesteader in the unyielding Welsh hills had to struggle to secure what at best would be a meager existence for his family. Most likely the poorer farmers could not afford to maintain a number of dogs, each with a specialized function. Whatever dog the farmer kept, whether bred primarily as a bird dog, a ratter or a cattle dog, had to be a jack of all trades.

Demonstrating the frugality of Welsh farmers even in modern times are the dogs of the various sporting breeds, which were pressed into use as general-purpose farm dogs in Wales. Reports are not uncommon of the Welsh Springer Spaniel, an excellent field dog, and of the fine terrier breeds of Wales, successfully working livestock.

While it is entirely possible that the early ancestors of the Welsh Corgi were included in the classification of herdsman's cur, the term itself probably referred to any dog who was a useful cattle dog, regardless of type or heritage. Tempting though it may be, we cannot look to the Laws of Hywel Dda for valid evidence of the antiquity of the Corgi breeds.

LLOYD-THOMAS'S THEORY OF SEPARATE ORIGIN

Popular opinion maintains that the Pembroke and Cardigan Welsh Corgi originated as two entirely separate and unrelated breeds, the Pembroke being a member of the large Spitz family and the Cardigan evolving from the Dachshund or Tekel class. Members of the Spitz family, such as the Schipperke, the Pomeranian, the Keeshond and the Samoyed, are characterized by prick ears, a pointed muzzle and (in most) a curly tail. The Tekel group, which includes the Dachshund and the Basset Hound, are essentially long-bodied, deep-chested, short-legged dogs, heavier in muzzle than typical Spitz types.

The probable source of the separate origin theory seems to be a series of articles written by W. Lloyd-Thomas on the Cardigan Welsh Corgi, which appeared in issues of *Pure-Bred Dogs—American Kennel Gazette* in the fall of 1935. Lloyd-Thomas, a native of Cardiganshire, South Wales, and a recognized authority on Welsh farm dogs, theorized that ancestors of the Cardigan Corgi were brought into Wales from central Europe by invading Celtic tribes about 1200 B.C.

Satisfied that the early Pembroke Corgi possessed none of the identifying Tekel characteristics of the Cardigan, but instead strongly resembled the members of the Spitz family, Lloyd-Thomas concurred with what he termed the "tradition" that the Pembroke Corgi was introduced into Wales by Flemish weavers in A.D. 1107.

Eventually a striking physical similarity between the two Corgi breeds developed. Lloyd-Thomas attributed the development of stockier, lower-to-ground, heavier-headed Pembroke strains to occasional crossings of the Pembroke with the "original" Corgi, as he preferred to call the Corgi from Cardiganshire. He tells us that Corgi puppies brought down by enterprising young lads from Bronant, a district in the heart of the Cardiganshire hills, were sold for pocket money to the farmers in South Wales. And it was the influence of these dogs that brought about the change in Pembroke type.

Lloyd-Thomas stoutly maintained that the Corgi traffic never went in reverse. That is, the early Pembrokeshire Corgis were never seen in the Cardiganshire hills. In fact, we are told no dog other than the original Corgi was known in the Bronant district until at least the late 1850s.

The Cardigan Corgi's gradual refinement and somewhat diminished size from that of the original Corgi, along with a change of ear carriage from a drooping ear to an erect, slightly hooded ear, plus changes in coat quality, all supposedly were brought about by the influence of breeds other than the Pembroke Corgi, breeds that began to appear on Cardiganshire farms during the last quarter of the nineteenth century.

Until about 1875, Welsh farmers grazed their cattle on unfenced Crown or common land. Over the years families came to regard certain areas of the common grazing land as being theirs, and other farmers' cattle on the particular parcel of land were trespassers. Mr. Lloyd-Thomas believed that the original Corgi was not a herding dog but rather was a "courser" used to chase trespassing cattle out of a claimed grazing area. Anyone who has watched a modern Corgi on a dead run chase after a squirrel trespassing at the bird feeder will be able to picture exactly how a coursing Corgi set off about his task. The original Corgi's failure to adapt as a herding dog was said to be his undoing, for once the grazing land was fenced, the Welsh farmer needed a dog to take the cattle to and from pasture, not a dog whose only talent was to scare off trespassing stock.

Farmers in the Cardiganshire hills soon looked to Collies and Herders to help them manage their cattle. And it was through subsequent crossings of the original Corgi with herding dogs, such as the Red Herder, the Brindle Herder, the Scotch Collie and the early Pomeranian that the Corgi, of which Lloyd-Thomas writes, changed in appearance. Thus the breed came to resemble more closely the Corgi of southwestern Wales, the Pembroke Corgi.

Unfortunately, what could only be theory about the separate origins of the two Welsh Corgi breeds has become accepted as established fact, especially here in America. While Lloyd-Thomas wrote convincingly about the history of the Corgi, it should be noted that his observations were based on his own memories and on the recollections of the aged Cardiganshire hillmen with whom he conversed. At no point in his *Gazette* articles did he substantiate his claims with references to earlier source material. At best his theory was based on actual observation of the Corgi breeds over an eighty-year period, with stories and descriptions passed on by succeeding generations of Bronant crofters. The time span involved covered but a very short period of the Corgi's history, if the original Corgi was introduced into Wales in 1200 B.C.

The many unanswered questions and unresolved discrepancies raised by the separate origin theory make its acceptance difficult, if not impossible, for many Corgi enthusiasts.

HUBBARD'S THEORY OF SCANDINAVIAN AND FLEMISH INFLUENCE

Clifford Hubbard, well known for his in-depth study of the two Corgi breeds, proposed a rather different theory of origin for the Pembroke. He dates the beginnings of the breed back to the ninth and tenth centuries, when Scandinavian Vikings invaded coastal regions of Wales from Anglesey to the south of Pembrokeshire. According to Hubbard's theory, the Vikings, who eventually settled in South Wales, brought with them a Swedish cattle dog known as the Vallhund or Vastergotland Spitz. The Vallhund, remarkably similar in appearance to the Pembroke Corgi, was probably crossed with the native Welsh herd dog, the Corgi. It was perhaps at this point in time that two distinctly different Corgi types began to develop: the original short-legged, long-bodied, deep-chested dog with droopy ears remained as the Cardiganshire Corgi, while the Corgi of the Pembrokeshire region took on many of the Spitzlike characteristics of the Vallhund.

Hubbard further postulated that the Spitz characteristics seen in the Pembroke Corgi as a result of the Vallhund influence were subsequently accentuated by crosses with dogs thought to be either Schipperkes or early Pomeranians. These came to South Wales with Flemish weavers, when they settled in Pembrokeshire in about A.D. 1107, during the reign of Henry I.

Although they came to Pembrokeshire as craftsmen, the Flemish weavers were agrarian by nature and set about establishing small farms patterned after those left behind in their homeland. It is not unreasonable to assume that farm dogs accompanied the livestock known to have been brought into Wales by the Flemish immigrants.

The Flemish dogs probably descended from small Spitz dogs developed during the Stone Age by Neolithic dwellers in the lake settlements of Switzerland, Hungary and parts of Russia. The northern Spitz breeds were noted for being clever, capable herding dogs. If the Pembrokeshire farmers found the offspring of outcrosses between native Corgis and the newly introduced Flemish dogs to be proficient cattle dogs as well as bright, attractive companions with their foxy faces and erect ears, it is not surprising that the new strain was purposely continued.

Hubbard himself recognized the difficulties involved in the theory of the influence of the Vallhund on the development of the Pembroke Corgi—not the least of which is the fact that the present-day Vallhund, commonly found in the southwestern provinces of Sweden, is virtually unknown in Norway or Denmark, where the invading Norsemen originated.

Another point referred to by Hubbard is color. The Vallhund is typically wolf-gray, a color found in other Spitz breeds such as the Keeshond and the Norwegian Elkhound but not the Corgi. While claiming that the dominant red or sable colors of the Flemish dogs obliterated the Vallhund coloring in the Pembroke Corgi, Mr. Hubbard overlooked the matter of color when he used the Lancashire Heeler as another example of a Spitzlike heeling dog that he considered closely related to the Swedish Vallhund.

The Lancashire Heeler, a small black and tan cattle dog quite similar in appearance to the Corgi, has existed for centuries in northern England. It is said to still persist in the Ormskirk district of Lancashire. The late Miss Eve Forsyth-Forrest, whose Corgis carried the Helarian prefix, believed the existence of the Lancashire Heeler substantiated her theory that the Corgi was the original native dog of Britain. Accordingly, at the time of the Saxon invasions some Britons fled into the depths of the Forest of Elmet, and it was there a pocket of their

This Swedish Vallhund bitch, Litton of Duncliffe of Ormareon, a winner in the English show ring, shows the similarity to the Pembroke Corgi. The Vallhund can have a natural bobtail.

Corgilike Lancashire Heelers survived the passing centuries. The suggestion that the early Corgis, both Pembroke and Cardigan, were commonly black and tan in color strengthens the theory of a probable link between the Corgi breeds and the Lancashire Heeler.

The pronounced similarity in appearance, as well as in the instinctive guarding and herding capabilities shared by the Pembroke Corgi and the Swedish Vallhund, leaves little doubt that their paths have crossed. Just when and where will most likely remain another matter of conjecture.

COMBE'S THEORY

Yet another piece of the puzzle has recently come to light from a different direction. In 1987 Iris Combe, who combines an extensive research background and a fascination with pastoral breeds, published a small book, *Herding Dogs, Their Origins and Development in Britain*. Her theory concerning the Pembroke Welsh Corgi compliments that of Clifford Hubbard but with an added dimension.

Back in the early history of the British Isles, Stone Age people first inhabited the coastal areas, where they kept a few domestic animals for pagan rituals, but subsisted mostly on what they could pull from the sea. In the northwestern section of the land countless seabird colonies covered the cliff faces and provided a ready supply of flesh and eggs to vary the diet. Local wild canids were adapted to take advantage of these birds, so early man began to utilize them for their skills.

When the Celtic tribes migrated from mainland Europe, they too pressed to the western shores of both Britain and Scandinavia. Greyhoundlike hunting dogs that they had with them along the way died out or mixed with other local dogs of the regions they populated. One can only guess what these early hybrids looked like.

However, to this day on a remote island off the coast of Norway there remains in isolation a breed unchanged for thousands of years. It is the Lundehund or Puffin dog, and it has been used for centuries for wildfowling.

The Spitzlike Lundehund bears a resemblance, especially in the head, to a long-legged, tailed Corgi. Its prick ears can fold back to close the ear canal to the elements. It also has an extremely flexible neck and shoulders, which enabled it to work its way through the jagged jumble of rocks protecting the Puffin burrows. Further unusual features of this unique breed are extra toes to give the dog traction and the effect of a webbed foot. In color it is red and white, with light sable markings on its face and back.

Mrs. Combe, working with Nordic canine researchers, points out that the trade in feathers, meat and oils from various seabirds became important to the Scandinavian economy. In the eighth century Vikings were known to have made annual spring trips to the British offshore islands as far south as Anglesey in northern Wales in search of these valuable commodities. Presumably the travelers brought with them dogs that had proven themselves to be useful in this endeavor. Later during the Viking invasions the Norsemen settled the coastline and imported some of the farm animals and dogs as described by Clifford Hubbard.

It is interesting to note that if Nordic wildfowling dogs were comparable to the Lundehund, as opposed to the Vallhund, and if they interbred with indigenous dogs, the color dilemma of Hubbard's theory of Viking influence on early Corgis is resolved. Also, the point of emigration for Lundhunde types was the Viking's Norway, not Sweden, where the Vallhund evolved.

In any case, according to Mrs. Combe's studies, Corgis remained a factor in the flourishing feather and fowl trade of later centuries. As guardians of the homestead, Corgis rounded up stray poultry, penned them for the night and protected their charges from predators. Some of the flocks of geese became tremendous, and the only way of getting them to the market was to drive them there. The Corgi's ability to herd came to fore. Several dogs at a time would take charge and urge the birds to the appointed destination. It must have been quite a sight.

Indeed, the Corgis were used around the farm on cattle and other livestock as well. As a drover, however, Mrs. Combe contends their trips were of short duration, to the local markets or butchers' yards, where they came in handy with their darting, heel-nipping ways. In later years the Welsh dogs were invaluable in moving Irish cattle off the boats and onto railroad cars bound for the English interior.

DERIVATION OF THE NAME

What knowledge of the Pembroke Welsh Corgi's earliest history that time itself has not buried, the very name Corgi has. Not only is the true meaning of the word "Corgi" unknown, but it is often impossible to discern, even in present-day writings, whether the references being made are to Pembroke or Cardigan Corgis. The ambiguity makes any effort to trace the history of either breed just that much more frustrating.

Some breed historians believe the term "corgi" is derived from the word *cur*, meaning "to watch over." This definition is certainly appropriate for a little dog whose duty for centuries was to watch over the livestock on Welsh homesteads. Others believe that *corgi* was the Celtic word for "dog," and that at the time of the Norman Conquest, *corgi* or *curgi* took on the connotation of "cur" or mongrel, as the Normans disdainfully considered all local dogs to be mongrels. In Wales the name evolved to mean simply any small cattle dog.

In an attempt to uncover the anglicized meaning of *corgi*, Clifford Hubbard's own laborious search through sources made available to him at the National Library of Wales and the Dictionary Department of the Board of Celtic Studies led him to agree that the word *corgi* actually meant "cur" or "cur dog." Hubbard found this meaning for *Korgi ne gostoc* in one of the earliest dictionaries, Wyllam Salesbury's *A Dictionary in Englyshe and Welshe* (London, 1574), and a similar definition of "cur" in Spurrell's *Geiriadur Cynaniaethol Seisoneg A Chymraeg* (Caerfyrddin, 1872).

The three types of curs referred to in the ancient Welsh laws, the watch cur, the house cur and the shepherd's or herdsman's cur, suggest that while *corgi* can be interpreted as meaning "cur dog," the term "cur" was not used explicitly to designate the Corgi.

Though the "cur dog" meaning of the word *corgi* seems to be most widely accepted, other possible meanings have been proposed. One such popular interpretation is that *cor* is Welsh for "dwarf," and *gi* is a form of the Welsh word *ci* meaning "dog." Freeman Lloyd, a well-known breed authority and an honorary president of the Welsh Corgi Club of America in the Club's formative years, made good use of the "dwarf dog" theory. He postulated that the Corgi is a miniature of the Welsh Sheepdog, common to the mountainous parts of Wales; or if of mixed descent, the Corgi evolved from a cross of Welsh Sheepdogs and some kind of terrier.

Turning the "dwarf dog" interpretation around slightly, others have suggested perhaps it is just as the Welsh legends tell it, and that *corgi* means "dog of the dwarfs."

In the south of Wales, a common endearment, *Y Corgi Bach*, means "you little rascal." Knowing how the Corgi delights in being a lovable, little rascal, it is not surprising that "corgi" and "rascal" came to be colloquial synonyms.

The English name Heeler, which was applied to both the Cardigan and the Pembroke Corgi, originated from the Corgi's habit of hurrying cattle to and from pasture by nipping at their heels. The Welsh verb meaning "to heel" is *sodli*, and the Welsh farmers frequently referred to the Pembrokeshire Corgi as *Ci Sodli*, or in northern Wales, *Ci Sodlu*.

Just when the name Corgi came into widespread use is not clear. Despite the references to Corgis in early literature, the name was supposedly known to very few people even as late as the 1800s. The familiar, short-legged, long-backed cattle dog was known as the Welsh Cur, and it was under the classification of *Cwn Sodli* (plural of *Ci Sodli*), Curs or Heelers, that the Corgi was first exhibited at agricultural shows in Wales at the close of the nineteenth century.

Through common usage Corgis has now become the accepted plural of Corgi, though what is thought by many to be the proper plural form, *corgwyn*, is still seen occasionally. As it is claimed by some Welsh people that the singular and plural forms are one and the same, Corgi, it is possible the use of the different plural forms varied with the district in Wales. The plural spelled with an "e," Corgies, is simply a misspelling and has never been considered to be a correct plural form. The "shire" has been dropped from the names of both Corgi breeds, and in many Corgi circles today we hear the breeds referred to as Pems and Cardis.

Although uncertainties about the derivation and use of the name Corgi are unlikely to be resolved, perhaps future archaeological findings, such as the discovery of a complete dog skeleton and skeletal remains of other dogs unearthed during excavations of the Windmill Hill neolithic site in Wiltshire, England, will reveal the true origin of the Pembroke Welsh Corgi. Maybe then we will learn of the actual relationship between the two Corgi types and, in turn, their connection with the seemingly related Vallhund of Sweden and the Lancashire Heeler of northern England.

Left to right: Eng. Ch. Rozavel Golden Girl, unknown, Eng. Ch. Bowhit Bisco, Eng. Ch. Crymmych President and Eng. Ch. Shan Fach, the first English Pembroke champion.

2

Early Recorded History

BY THE NINETEENTH CENTURY, with working Welsh farm dogs being tax exempt, the popularity of the Corgi burgeoned. Scores of Corgis, or Welsh Curs, as they were commonly called, were seen at market places and livestock fairs, especially in the Maenclochog, Pembrokeshire district of South Wales. There were said to be one or two Corgis on every farm in the district at the turn of the century.

Despite the popularity the Pembroke Welsh Corgi enjoyed in his native locale, he was unknown to the outside world until the early part of this century. The advent of classes for Cwn Sodli, Heelers or Curs at early shows combined with the interest taken in the breed by a number of dedicated dog fanciers in the Pembrokeshire area was the beginning of a new era for the breed. It was an era in which successful efforts would be made to standardize Pembroke type; and the little Corgis would leave their homeland to take up residence at Buckingham Palace and in new homes around the world.

FIRST SHOWS

In a diligent search through Welsh journals and newspapers dating back to the 1890s, Clifford Hubbard uncovered what appears to be the earliest record of classes offered for Curs at an agricultural show. The show was held by the Bancyfelin Horticultural and Agricultural Society at Bancyfelin, Carmarthenshire, in 1892. Mr. Hubbard listed the prize winners as being ''first—Mr. J.

Thomas, Cwmcoch; second—Mr. J. Thomas, Castellwaun; commended—Mr. D. Davies." Since the prizes were awarded in the name of the exhibitor, we do not know the names of the first Corgis to win in show competition.

It was not until the Royal Welsh agricultural show held at Carmarthen in August of 1925 that Corgi classes were held under official Kennel Club rules. Some of the Corgis that were prominent in early Pembroke pedigrees appeared at this important show. Buller, sire of the famous Caleb, won the Open Dog class, with Ted, the sire of Caleb's dam, taking second place. A Cardigan won the Open Bitch class, while Rose, the first Corgi to be registered with the Kennel Club, settled for third place.

THE CORGI CLUB

In December 1925 a giant step forward was taken when the Corgi Club was formed in Carmarthen. The majority of the members of the newly formed club resided in the Pembrokeshire area. It was not surprising that it was the Pembroke type to which they gave their allegiance.

To counteract the spreading influence of the Pembroke fanciers, in 1926 Cardigan supporters formed their own society, eventually named the Cardigan Welsh Corgi Association.

The original officers and eighteen-member committee of the Corgi Club included such early pillars of the breed as Captain Jack Howell, his brother Adrian, Mr. John John, Mr. D. T. Davies and Mr. W. Merchan Phillips. Captain Howell presided at the first annual meeting, held at the Castle Hotel in Haverfordwest. Captain Williams served as honorary secretary.

In 1926, in order to comply with a Kennel Club directive, the name of the club was changed to include "Welsh," and the Welsh Corgi Club was officially registered with the Kennel Club.

Still an active club in Wales, members of the Welsh Corgi Club celebrated its Golden Jubilee in 1975, marking a half century devoted to furthering the interests of the Pembroke Welsh Corgi.

In 1928, the labors of the Corgi's earliest supporters finally reaped deserved rewards. The Welsh Corgi was removed from the Kennel Club register of "Any Other Variety not Classified," and the breed was assigned to the Non-Sporting Group. Official recognition brought with it the granting of coveted Challenge Certificates for the Welsh Corgi, a tremendous encouragement for the breeders engaged in an uphill struggle to establish the Corgi as a worthy show dog.

Shan Fach, a red Pembroke bitch, whelped in 1928, was the first Corgi, either Pembroke or Cardigan, to become a champion. Her first two Challenge Certificates were won while she was owned by Mrs. G. Gwyn Jones. She gained her crowning CC in the ownership of Mr. Oliver Jones, of the Pantyblaidd prefix under judge Mr. Sid Bowler of Bowhit fame.

The first dog champion, also a Pembroke Corgi, was Bonny Gyp, bred by Mr. Bennett and owned by Mr. F. C. Davies.

It was the breed's good fortune to have numbered among its staunchest supporters in Pembrokeshire several experienced breeders of Sealyham Terriers. These Sealyham breeders who turned their attentions to the Pembrokeshire Corgi included Captain Jack Howell, master of the Pembrokeshire Fox Hounds and charter member of the Welsh Corgi Club. Also in this group were Captain Checkland Williams, another soldier and sportsman, breeder of the "Wern" Pembrokes and specialist judge; Mr. and Mrs. Sid Bowler, whose Bowhit Pembrokes had such an impact upon the breed it would be virtually impossible to find a Pembroke today that did not have some Bowhit blood many generations back; and Mrs. Victor Higgon, some of whose "of Sealy" Pembrokes were among the first of the breed to be exported to various parts of the world.

In spite of the advances made by the breeders of the 1920s, the Corgi scene remained just short of ruinous chaos for several years following the granting of championship status. Cardigans and Pembrokes were classified together as a single breed in the Kennel Club registry, and the two Corgi types, shown together, were judged by a single Standard.

Mongrelly-looking dogs of every description—heavy set, long and low, fine boned and terrierlike, straight fronted or crooked fronted, with or without tails—all appeared in the Corgi ring. The ancestry of the dogs being shown was an equally jumbled-up affair. Some dogs were of unknown and perhaps questionable ancestry, some of indeterminate mixture of Corgi types and some of properly pure Pembroke or Cardigan blood.

Chronic hard feelings between Cardigan and Pembroke fanciers erupted into open animosity, reaching the point where the supporters of one Corgi type would not exhibit their dogs under a judge who was even suspected of favoring the other type. The dispute probably originated when exhibitors showing the Cardigan type in the classes for Heelers at the early agricultural shows were indignant that the Pembrokeshire Corgi should also be allowed to compete as a Heeler.

As unpleasant as the situation was, it most likely prevented the development of one far worse, the merging of the two Corgi types into one and the loss of two valued separate breed types. While there was sporadic interbreeding of the Pembroke and Cardigan types, the disdain followers of one type held for dogs of the other type prevented the practice from becoming widespread.

The Kennel Club ruling in 1934, giving the Pembroke and Cardigan Corgis separate breed status, brought the disruptive controversy to an end. With the air cleared and the fences mended, breeders could settle down to the business at hand of building lines that would conform with a Standard specific for each breed. An additional Kennel Club ruling, made in 1934, which made tail docking permissible, aided breeders in their efforts to establish greater uniformity of appearance among Pembrokes.

When a new name in Pembrokes, Rozavel, first appeared in 1930, the spotlight on the breed's advancement began to shift from southern Wales to England, where the Pembroke was to meet with skyrocketing success. While her Rozavel Pembrokes were making an indelible impact upon the breed, Mrs. Thelma Gray (then Miss Thelma Evans) was dedicating her seemingly endless energies to the promotion of the breed both in England and abroad. Pembroke fanciers are greatly indebted to Mrs. Gray, not only for the contributions made by the Rozavel Corgis, but also for the detailed records of the early producers and show dogs provided in her books on the Welsh Corgi breeds.

Through Mrs. Gray's efforts, the Welsh Corgi League was founded in England in 1938. Over the years the League has remained a prominent force in the breed and currently enjoys a membership of approximately 1,300 home and overseas members.

FOUNDATION STOCK

In the late 1920s and early 1930s, three dogs emerged as the foundation on which many lines were subsequently built. The first of the triad was Ch. Bowhit Pepper, a rich red dog sired by Caleb out of Glandofan Fury. Pepper was the sire of six Pembroke champions, including the breed's first champion, Shan Fach.

Pepper was one of the few dogs of note who appeared in both Pembroke and Cardigan pedigrees. Apparently Pepper himself was from a litter of both Corgi types, for it is reported that at an early Cardiff show, Pepper won as a Pembroke while his litter sister, Jill, won at the same show, listed as a Cardigan.

Mated to Fancy, a daughter of Ch. Bonny Gyp, Pepper sired his seventh champion, the important Cardigan Ch. My Rockin Mawer. Ch. My Rockin Mawer, in turn, was to make his mark on the Pembroke breed by siring Defiant Girl of Merriedip, the Best of Breed Winner at the Pembroke Welsh Corgi Club of America's first Specialty show.

Pepper was a dog of intensely good type for his time and proved to be a prepotent stud. His offspring were especially noted for their charm and keen intelligence. In fact, Pepper was used so extensively that where to go with heavily-bred Pepper stock became a very real problem.

An answer to the dilemma appeared in 1929 with the arrival on the scene of an outcross dog, Ch. Crymmych President, a son of Newman Chatter out of Crymmych Beauty. After President was purchased by the Rozavel Kennels from his breeder, Mr. Oliver Jones, he quickly gained his title and proved himself a noteworthy sire, with seven of his offspring becoming champions. Despite the consistent quality he sired, President is chiefly remembered as the sire of a dog whom many consider to be the great progenitor of the breed, Ch. Rozavel Red Dragon.

Ch. Rozavel Red Dragon, bred by Mr. G. Jones in 1932, was purchased at six weeks of age by the Rozavel Kennels. The sire of eleven English champions and numerous other champions around the world, Dragon also made his mark as a spectacular show dog. Of the twelve Challenge Certificates won by Dragon, eleven were won under different specialist judges, and the last nine were taken in succession, with Dragon being undefeated in the breed each time. His last CC was won at the Welsh Corgi League show in May 1940, under Miss Pat Curties, owner of the world-famous Lees Kennels—Dragon's last show and the last Corgi Specialty show held in England until after the war.

Eng. Ch. Bowhit Pepper (Caleb ex Glandofan Fury), whelped in 1926.

Eng. Ch. Crymmych President (Newman Chatter ex Crymmych Beauty), whelped 1929,
sired eleven English champions including Ch. Rozavel Red Dragon.   *Fall*

15

Eng. Ch. Rozavel Red Dragon (Eng. Ch. Crymmych President ex Felcourt Flame), whelped in 1932. Winner of twelve Challenge Certificates and sire of eleven English champions, he exerted a profound influence on the breed.

At the time of his death, Mrs. Barbara Douglas-Redding wrote in the 1950 *Welsh Corgi League Handbook* of Red Dragon:

> As a youngster, from the word "go" he was obviously a "character" and a bit of a "card." He picked his friends carefully with the air of a connoisseur, and although he acknowledged them like the great gentleman he always was, one felt that he had conferred an honour on one as he answered a greeting remark. He was reserved without being in the least shy and kept his entire allegiance and great integrity for his owner and his adored guardians Mr. and Mrs. Sonley with whom he always lived. He was their first consideration and pride, and they were so obviously his in return. "Buster" shared their whole life. He was an honoured and welcome patron at the cinema when they went, and travelled about the countryside with joy and poise on the back of Mr. Sonley's motorcycle. He was never left out of anything.
>
> Mrs. Sonley always had his favorite dinner of spaghetti with cheese and tomato sauce ready for him on his return from the shows, and it was she who knitted him those beautifully-fitting emerald green coats that became his colouring so well when he went off to shows in cold weather.
>
> He was never off colour or dull. Always on his toes whether in the ring or out of it. He loved to play ball and would retrieve and work seriously as well. A more brilliant vital personality in the canine world either as a showman or a stud force it would be hard to find. He went "all out" in the ring. A dynamic small figure right on its toes. Rich flaming red and white; impossible to overlook; he won literally everywhere under everybody. They just couldn't do anything else.

Dragon died at the remarkable age of seventeen years and five months, with his type and stamina, as well as the intelligence and personality of a glorious dog, thoroughly ingrained in the breed for generations to come.

3

New Beginnings in America

IT WAS IN LONDON's Paddington Station in 1933 that Mrs. Lewis Roesler (later Mrs. Edward Renner) first saw and fell in love with Little Madam. Little Madam, a Bowhit Pepper daughter, was on her way to a show with her owner, Mrs. Lewis of Fishguard, Wales. Captivated by Little Madam's charm, Mrs. Roesler purchased her on the spot for a total of twelve pounds.

FIRST RECORDED IMPORTS

Before returning home to her Merriedip Kennels, Mrs. Roesler visited a number of Corgi kennels in Wales, and a Pembroke named Captain William Lewis after one of Mrs. Roesler's own Welsh ancestors was selected to accompany Little Madam on her journey to America in the spring of 1934.

The Merriedip Kennels, then located in the Berkshire Hills of Massachusetts, were already well established as a leading force in Old English Sheepdogs when the new Corgi immigrants arrived. Mrs. Roesler attributed the success of her Merriedip Old English line to its strong foundation consisting of the best imports Mrs. Roesler could locate during her numerous trips abroad. Intent upon achieving a similar success with her Corgis, Mrs. Roesler continued over the years to seek out the best available Pembroke stock to build a broad base of bloodlines from which she could establish her own strain.

When the Welsh Corgi received official recognition as a breed in the United

Ch. Little Madam of Merriedip, a Bowhit Pepper daughter, the first Pembroke Welsh Corgi to be registered with the American Kennel Club, in 1934.

States, Little Madam of Merriedip became the first Corgi to be registered with the American Kennel Club, and Captain William Lewis, the second registered. Their names appear in the August 1934 Stud Book under the listing Welsh Corgis, for then, as in England, Pembroke and Cardigan Corgis were not yet recognized as separate breeds.

Early records suggest that though Pembrokes were the first of the two Corgi types to be registered with the American Kennel Club, a pair of Cardigans were actually the first known Corgi imports to America. Born in the Bronant district of Wales, Cassie and a six-month-old companion, Cadno, arrived in Boston in June 1931. Sired by Mon, the last of the original Corgis of Bronant, Cassie is claimed by some to be the true ancestress of the Cardigan breed, for she heads nearly every successful strain in existence today.

The Merriedip imports are the first Pembrokes of which we have official record in the United States. There is, however, reason to believe others were brought to the country prior to the arrival of Little Madam and Captain William Lewis.

Mrs. Helen Bole Jones, a prominent Cardigan fancier, believes that her grandmother, Mrs. Patterson Bole, imported Pembrokes before 1934. Mrs. Jones's belief is substantiated by a column in the March 1935 issue of *Pure-Bred Dogs—American Kennel Gazette* in which Mrs. Harriet Price wrote that Mrs. Bole had been breeding both Corgi types since 1932, though her preference was for the Cardigans.

EARLY WEST COAST ACTIVITY

Early Corgi activity in this country was by no means restricted to the East Coast. Pembroke history was rapidly in the making in California as well.

The prominent figure behind the record-setting California Pembroke Corgis was Mr. E. M. Tidd of Oakland. The first Pembroke to be registered by Mr. Tidd was Toots, a bitch of Rozavel breeding. Toots was purchased from Ralph Gardener, the pioneer breeder of Pembrokes in Canada and was in whelp to Rozavel Gaiters when she arrived in the States. Her litter, whelped August 15, 1934, became the first Pembroke litter to be registered with the American Kennel Club. Puppies from this Canadian-bred litter were registered under the prefix Sierra.

Early in 1935 Mr. Tidd had the good fortune to buy Bowhit Pivot, an exciting young dog from the Bowhit Kennels in Wales. The late Sid Bowler had purchased Pivot for his wife at the Crufts show, where the dog had been shown under the name of Vipont Scamp by his breeder, Lord Hothfield.

Pivot is described as a dark red, nice-fronted, low-to-ground dog with a good head and intelligent expression. He completed his English championship in three straight shows, all in good company. Having already picked off the plum of being the first Pembroke Welsh Corgi to win Best in Show at a British all-breed Open show with his spectacular win at Carmarthen in May 1934, Bowhit Pivot continued to make Corgi history after arriving in California. The honor of

Eng. Am. Can. Ch. Sierra Bowhit Pivot (Eng. Ch. Crymmych President ex Chalcot Saucebox), whelped in 1933, the first American Pembroke champion.   *Ladin*

being the first American Pembroke champion as well as being the first imported English champion fell to Pivot. He also had the distinction of being the first Pembroke to win a Group placing in this country.

Pivot started off his American show career by winning the breed's first major. He became America's first Pembroke champion just one month before Little Madam was to complete her championship and become the country's first champion Pembroke bitch.

Bowhit Pivot's offspring followed in the history-making footsteps of their illustrious father. Before leaving England, Pivot had sired Robin Hood of Down East, who was imported for the Down East Kennels in Blue Hill, Maine, by the professional handler and, later, all-breed judge Percy Roberts. Robin Hood of Down East was a consistent winner for his owner, Elizabeth Anderson, and made his mark in canine history by being the first Corgi to win a Group placing at the Westminster show. The year was 1936, and the same show marked the official beginnings of the Pembroke Welsh Corgi Club of America.

As he was by Crymmych President out of Chalcot Saucebox, a double Bowhit Pepper granddaughter, Pivot carried the Pepper-President combination breeders in both England and America were finding so successful.

Mr. Tidd's Canadian bitch, Toots, was sired by a double Pepper grandson. Her dam was a half-sister to President. Thus the mating of Toots to Bowhit Pivot concentrated still more the Pepper-President combination in a litter whelped August 10, 1935, the first American-bred Pembroke litter on record.

Out of the first Pivot-Toots litter came Sierra Bruin. Purchased by Mr. C. B. Owen of Minneapolis, Bruin ultimately distinguished himself by becoming the first American-bred Pembroke dog champion. A repeat of the Pivot-Toots breeding produced the country's first American-bred Pembroke bitch champion, Sierra Vixen. Both Vixen and her older brother Bruin completed their championships early in the summer of 1937.

Derek Rayne, one of America's foremost all-breed judges and long-time Pembroke fancier, purchased Ch. Sierra Bruin from Mr. Owen in 1937. At that time, Mr. Rayne already owned three Pembrokes. The following year, the illustrious Bowhit Pivot was purchased from Mr. Tidd, and he joined his son, Bruin, in Mr. Rayne's Pemwelgi Kennels.

During this time, Mr. Rayne was the trainer at the Obedience Club of California, so it was only natural that Bruin soon entered Obedience competition. In short order, Bruin was not only the first American-bred Pembroke champion on record, but he also was the first American-bred Pembroke champion with a CD Obedience title.

Eng. Am. Ch. Sierra Bowhit Pivot continued to enjoy show ring successes in Mr. Rayne's ownership. At the close of his remarkable career Pivot had won Best of Breed at least forty times and sired five champions. Demonstrating the staying power of the breed, Pivot won the Working Group under Mrs. Beatrice Godsol at San Diego at the age seven and a half and went on to enjoy yet another ten years of good health.

THE SHOW SCENE IN THE 1930s

Corgi competition in the East did not build up as quickly as it did on the West Coast. Championship points were awarded to eastern Pembrokes for the first time at the Kennel Club of Philadelphia show, November 16 and 17, 1934. Four Cardigans and two Pembrokes were shown together. Little Madam, en route to Best of Breed, was Winners Bitch for her first two points. Mrs. Bole's Cardigan bitch, Megan, was Reserve. In dogs, Tip, another Cardigan owned by Mrs. Bole, took the dog points, and Mrs. Roesler's Captain William Lewis was Reserve.

Though unsuccessful at finding championship points at shows from July 1934 until the Philadelphia show in November, Little Madam won for herself and the breed many fast friends during her show ring appearances.

Perhaps it was due to the fact that Welsh Corgis were classified and shown as terriers at the time of Little Madam's first shows that a number of her admirers, who eventually became Pembroke breeders, were terrier people. In Wales a band of Sealyham Terrier breeders was instrumental in promoting the Pembroke as a show dog. In the United States a group of Cairn Terrier breeders was won over by Pembroke charm. Prefixes associated with the top Cairns of the day, such as Down East, Tapscot and Elphinstone, soon were carried by winning Pembrokes as well.

By the end of the summer of 1935, show entries in the breed were increasing. For the first time in the East, Pembroke exhibitors were able to muster up a three-point major entry, this at the Ox Ridge (Connecticut) show in August. The Best of Breed winner, Little Madam, went on to place fourth in the Working Group, the breed having been reassigned to that group early in the year.

On the weekend following the Ox Ridge event, Rozavel Gwenda, a newcomer owned by Katherine Irvine, won fourth in the Group at the Middletown, New York show. A Challenge Certificate winner in England, she followed her first Group placing here with two more, giving her three Group placings in three consecutive weekends.

Gwenda's breeding again demonstrated the high regard breeders held for the combination of Crymmych President and Bowhit Pepper lines. She was sired by Bowhit Pepper, and her dam, sired by Crymmych President, was out of a President daughter. When she was imported by Miss Irvine in 1934, Gwenda was in whelp to President. From the resulting litter, Gitana and her brother, Shan Coch, were shown some, but neither equaled their dam in her show ring successes.

Though just a point away from gaining her championship, Gwenda took a leave of absence from the show ring for maternal duties. Sadly for those who knew her and for the breed itself, Gwenda died shortly after whelping her litter in December 1935.

During 1936, enthusiasm for the breed continued to spread. New dogs were being imported at such a rate that Elizabeth Anderson was prompted to describe in one of her *Gazette* columns the great ship, the *Queen Mary*, as the "*Mayflower* of the Corgi pioneers."

The newly-formed Pembroke Welsh Corgi Club of America's first Specialty was held in conjunction with the prestigious Morris & Essex show in the spring of 1936. Robin Hood was Winners Dog for five points, and Mrs. Roesler's Defiant Girl of Merriedip went Winners Bitch and Best of Breed.

Another highlight of the year followed the Specialty in June, when Mrs. Thelma Gray, owner of the renowned Rozavel Kennels in England and breeder of many American imports, judged an entry of twelve Pembrokes at the Greenwich (Connecticut) show. Robin Hood was Best of Breed at that event, another five-point win for him, and Defiant Girl was Winners Bitch for three points.

Unfortunately, fate was to again take a promising bitch before her true contribution to the breed could be made. Defiant Girl, the daughter of the Cardigan, Ch. My Rockin Mawer, was struck by a truck and died, as did Rozavel Gwenda, a point or two away from being America's second bitch champion.

WASEEKA KENNELS

Of the kennels that started in the breed during the years 1936 to 1940, two rose rapidly to the foreground, their Corgis sharing prominence in the show ring with those from Merriedip.

The Waseeka Kennels in Ashland, Massachusetts, owned by Miss Elizabeth Loring (later Mrs. Davieson Power) were already known worldwide for the outstanding Newfoundlands bred there when Miss Loring, intrigued by the beguiling Little Madam, decided to add Pembrokes to her kennel.

Immediately after the purchase of a Rozavel Gwenda daughter, Lady Penrhyn, and upon the arrival of Tomboy of Sealy from England, Miss Loring set

Robin Hood of Down East, a Bowhit Pivot son, Winners Dog at the first Pembroke Welsh Corgi Club of America Specialty, in 1936.

22

about producing quality home-bred stock. The Waseeka Pembrokes were to dominate American-bred competition in the breed for some while to come.

The imports judiciously selected by Miss Loring played an important part in maintaining the high quality of the Waseeka Pembrokes. Tomboy, the first of the Waseeka Pembroke imports and a winner of nine Bests of Breed with six Group placings, was the sire of the first Pembroke homebred champion at Waseeka.

The most glamorous of the Waseeka imports was Eng. Am. Ch. Lisaye Rattle, imported in the summer of 1936. Rattle, described as being so close to perfection that she could safely serve as the model for the breed Standard, was undefeated in breed competition in England before coming to the States. Rattle had the honor of being the first Pembroke Welsh Corgi to win a Working Group in this country. She did this at the Brocton show in September of 1936. Rattle collected two more Group wins and half a dozen Group placings in her show career and amassed a total of thirty Best of Breed wins, which included top honors at two PWCCA Specialty shows.

Lisaye Rattle was a Red Dragon daughter out of a Crymmych President daughter and should have been useful as a dam. But, as has happened with some of the breed's loveliest bitches, Rattle simply was not a producer. And the hard luck that tested the mettle of other early Pembroke breeders struck again when Rattle, the outstanding winner of her day, met an untimely death when she was suffocated in a kennel fire.

ANDELYS KENNELS

Barbara Lowe Fallass was the force behind the success of the Pembrokes at the Andelys Kennels. Like Waseeka, Andelys rose quickly to the top in Corgi

Eng. Am. Ch. Lisaye Rattle (Eng. Ch. Rozavel Red Dragon ex Rozavel Juniper), the first Pembroke Welsh Corgi to win a Working Group in the United States and the winner of two PWCCA Specialty shows.

competition during the late thirties. Prior to moving to this country and settling in Cross River, New York, Mrs. Fallass lived in France, where the Andelys name, derived from *Les Andelys*, the name of her home in Normandy, was carried by her top winning Smooth Fox Terriers.

Mrs. Fallass first became acquainted with the Pembroke at the 1929 Crufts show. She subsequently watched the breed's progress with great interest. After determining that the Corgi's popularity was not just a passing fancy following the publicity the royal family's Corgis had been receiving, Mrs. Fallass purchased Torment of Sealy, an accomplished Obedience worker in England.

Torment arrived in the spring of 1937. In the summer of 1938 the Andelys Kennels imported Scarbo of Cogges, a Red Dragon daughter out of Tiffany of Cogges. Scarbo, who lacked but one ticket to make up her English championship, became the first Pembroke champion at the Andelys Kennels.

During the last half of 1938, Mrs. Fallass imported eight Pembroke Corgis. Were that to happen today, cries of "mass breeding" would resound throughout Corgi circles everywhere. Nonetheless, Mrs. Fallass brought to our shores some of the best Pembrokes England had to offer. Included at that time were two notable English champions, Eng. Am. Ch. Fitzdown Paul of Andely and Eng. Am. Ch. Rozavel Traveller's Joy.

The first with a Fitzdown prefix to come to this country, a prefix that is still well to the fore in England today, Fitzdown Paul had started his show career by winning Best of Breed at the 1936 Crufts show. He followed this win by collecting five more Challenge Certificates. After coming to the States, his many wins here included a Working Group fourth at the 1939 Westminster show and Best of Breed at the 1939 PWCCA Specialty show.

Fitzdown Paul, a Red Dragon son, sired a number of winners for the Andelys Kennels, his best-known being out of a Dragon granddaughter, Eng. Am. Ch. Fire Bird of Cogges of Andely.

Fresh from a glamorous show career in England, where she had the distinc-

Eng. Am. Ch. Fitzdown Paul of Andely (Eng. Ch. Rozavel Red Dragon ex Pantyblaidd Wonder), whelped in 1934.

tion of being the first Pembroke to hold a Junior Warrant from the Kennel Club, Eng. Am. Ch. Rozavel Traveller's Joy joined the growing number of English imports at Andelys late in 1938. This nearly solid flame red daughter of Eng. Ch. Rozavel Scarlet Emperor was Best of Breed at the 1940 Westminister show, completing her American title later that year.

Perhaps the most valuable of the imports at Andelys, in terms of her contribution, was Eng. Am. Ch. Fire Bird of Cogges. She was another Scarlet Emperor daughter and also a half sister to the earlier import Ch. Scarbo of Cogges. It is not surprising that Fire Bird proved to be a good producer, as she came from a line noted for its ability to breed on. Eng. Ch. Tiffany of Cogges, dam of both Fire Bird and Scarbo, was from the famous litter that included Aus. Ch. Titania of Sealy and Eng. Ch. Teresa of Sealy.

Successful in the show ring as well, Fire Bird completed her English championship in only four months. A highlight of Fire Bird's American show career occurred in 1940 when Derek Rayne placed her Best of Breed over a record entry at the Eastern Dog Club show. The remarkable entry of forty-four Pembrokes, making up forty-nine entries, at that Boston show was a record that was to hold for a number of years to come. The large entry was an obvious tribute to Mr. Rayne as the judge and a good measure of the heights to which interest in the breed had risen.

Pembroke Welsh Corgi registrations at the American Kennel Club indicated, as did show entries, that the breed had become securely established in this country in a phenomenally short time. By the end of 1934, the first year the Welsh Corgi was eligible for registration with the American Kennel Club, a total of 9 Corgis were registered, and the Welsh Corgi ranked in seventy-sixth place

Eng. Am. Ch. Fire Bird of Cogges of Andely (Eng. Ch. Rozavel Scarlet Emperor ex Eng. Ch. Tiffany of Cogges), whelped in 1937.

among all breeds registered. Within four years, with 135 Pembroke Welsh Corgis registered in 1938, the breed moved up to forty-fifth place.

Except for the brief time when there was a sudden rise in Corgi popularity following the television presentation in 1963 of the Walt Disney film featuring a Corgi, *Little Dog Lost*, registrations have maintained a ranking for the Pembroke close to that set in 1938. The registration of approximately 6,700 Pembroke Welsh Corgis during 1993, giving the breed a ranking of thirty-eighth place, indicates the popularity of the Pembroke has clearly kept pace with the expanding dog scene in America, without the breed becoming so popular as to fall victim to commercialism.

4

The Postwar Comeback

WHEN THE TRAGEDIES of World War II silenced Corgi activity around the world, many Pembroke kennels were disbanded, some never to resume activity again. Fortunately, the strong foundation of Pembroke bloodlines established prior to the war was carried on by those able to maintain their kennels on a limited scale.

INFLUENTIAL SIRES OF THE PERIOD

Red Dragon breeding survived the difficult times in good strength, with two of his most successful sons, Eng. Ch. Rozavel Scarlet Emperor and Int. Ch. Rozavel Lucky Strike, proving to be at the head of all prominent bloodlines in America today.

Eng. Ch. Rozavel Scarlet Emperor, particularly, suited many of the bitches of his day. Not only was he a Red Dragon son, but also he was out of a Bowhit Pepper daughter, Rozavel Pollyanna, who was heavily bred on Pepper's sire, Caleb. Whelped in 1935, Scarlet Emperor was just coming into his prime when war broke out. Because of this unfortunate timing, the dog was never used to his fullest potential. Despite his limited use, Scarlet Emperor's impact on the breed through his famous daughters is immeasurable.

As a youngster, Scarlet Emperor sired the winning bitches, Int. Ch. Rozavel Traveller's Joy and Int. Ch. Fire Bird of Cogges, imported by the Andelys Kennels. Three other well-known Emperor daughters remained in England, and it is they who must be given considerable credit for the tremendous quality found in the postwar English bloodlines.

Larkwhistle Golden Vanity, following in the wake of her half-sister, Traveller's Joy, was one of the breed's earliest Junior Warrant winners. With one CC and a Reserve CC to her credit before the war began, Golden Vanity returned to the show ring when championship shows were resumed to gain a second CC at the age of ten years, but was unlucky never to win the third. All of Miss E. J. Boyt's Larkwhistle dogs descended from Golden Vanity, as did the famous postwar dogs Int. Ch. Formakin Orangeman and Int. Ch. Broom of Ballybentra.

Bronwen of Lees, another of Scarlet Emperor's noted daughters, transmitted the line's ability to breed on to her grandson, Ch. Teekay's Felcourt Supremacy, a particularly valuable postwar sire. Known as Old Bob to his many friends, Ch. Teekay's Felcourt Supremacy was originally registered as Berach Bach. The Kennel Club permitted names to be changed in those days, so when Mr. Gwyn Jones obtained the dog, he became Felcourt Supremacy. With another change of ownership, this time to Anne Biddlecombe, the Teekay was added.

Supremacy was a popular stud for, though a smallish dog himself, he passed on substance and bone to his progeny. These important qualities were lacking in much of the postwar stock. The show ring successes of his offspring earned for Supremacy the Welsh Corgi League's Formakin Stud Dog Cup for four years in succession, 1947 through 1950.

Though Supremacy was primarily noted for his six champion daughters, he figured strongly in many American pedigrees through his grandson, Eng. Ch. Knowland Clipper. Many of our present bloodlines are steeped in Supremacy breeding due to the widely used combination of Knowland Clipper lines and those of the world-famous Int. Ch. Lees Symphony. The Symphony grandams, Eng. Ch. Lees Coronet and Chorus Girl of Cowfold, were both Supremacy daughters.

Scarlet Emperor breeding was consolidated to perfection in Eng. Ch. Lees Coronet, who was said to be the best of the Supremacy daughters. In turn, Coronet's grandam, Faireyhaze Empress, was the most famous of the Scarlet Emperor daughters.

Miss Anne Biddlecombe, whose Teekay dogs emerged from the war years as a dominant force in the breed, received Faireyhaze Empress from her breeders, the Misses Peat and Harle, when the war broke out. Undoubtedly, Empress would have been another champion added to Scarlet Emperor' record if not for the war. She had proven her quality by winning a strong class at the Kensington championship show while still quite a young puppy. Though Faireyhaze Empress never won a Challenge Certificate, she twice won the Welsh Corgi League's Coronet Brood Bitch Cup, both in 1947 and 1948, and she would have won it in 1946 as well, had the Cup been offered that year. To date, the Coronet Brood Bitch Challenge Cup has not been won three times by the same bitch.

Truly a great brood bitch and the start of the strongest bitch line the breed has ever known, Empress was mated back to her grandsire, Ch. Rozavel Red

Eng. Ch. Teekay's Felcourt Supremacy (Hill Billy of Lees ex Floss), leading stud dog in England 1947–1950. *Fall*

Eng. Ch. Lees Coronet, winner of nine Challenge Certificates and said to have had the greatest value of any Supremacy daughter. *Marjorie Baker*

Dragon, to produce Eng. Ch. Teekay Foxfire; Teekay Vivien, dam of the lovely Ch. Lees Coronet; and the two useful stud dogs Teekay Marquess and Teekay Pendragon. Empress was then mated to Ch. Teekay's Felcourt Supremacy for another remarkable litter. This union gave the breed the two notable bitches, Ch. Teekay Diadem and Ch. Teekay Tiara, each the winner of seven Challenge Certificates. Tiara was the first Pembroke Welsh Corgi to win, in 1947, a Non-Sporting Group at an English Championship show.

Though not possessing the glittering record of her half-sisters, Sally Jane of Dursley, again a Scarlet Emperor daughter, was the dam of an important dog in America, Ch. Hollyheath Pilot of Waseeka. Imported by Mrs. Power in 1951, Pilot had a decided influence on the breed in America. Several Pilot daughters became the foundation of lines successfully carried on today. Pilot's most celebrated descendant was his grandson, Ch. Willets Red Jacket, ROM, who held the record as the top winning Pembroke Welsh Corgi in the United States for many years.

As Ch. Rozavel Scarlet Emperor was enjoying his retirement years in the company of Mr. and Mrs. Charles Lister-Kaye and their Lisaye Corgis, Int. Ch. Rozavel Lucky Strike was making his presence felt through his glamorous offspring. A number of these subsequently made their way to the United States and Canada.

POSTWAR IMPORTS

Lucky Strike, one of Ch. Rozavel Red Dragon's last surviving sons, was whelped in 1943 out of Rozavel Land Girl, a Red Dragon granddaughter. Mated to a bitch with the unassuming name of Snooks, a Red Dragon–Supremacy granddaughter, Lucky Strike sired the noted postwar American champions Rozavel Lucky Fellow of Merriedip, Rozavel Uncle Sam of Waseeka and Rozavel Miss Bobby Sox, CD.

Of these three renowned litter mates, who with their offspring quite dominated the Pembroke show ring during the late 1940s and into the fifties, Uncle Sam was the most successful winner and producer. Uncle Sam covered himself with glory on the 1949 Florida show circuit. By taking top honors at the Tampa Bay Kennel Club show, he became the first Pembroke Welsh Corgi to win a Best in Show in the United States. Following his Florida winning spree, which included three Group firsts in succession, Uncle Sam placed second in a strong Working Group at the 1949 Westminister Kennel Club show.

The sire of a number of homebred champions for Waseeka Kennels, Uncle Sam bred on primarily through Ch. Waseeka's Coaltown, the Alexandre Orlowskis' Ch. Esmeralda of Furnace Brook and Ch. Cote de Neige Samson, one of the early Cote de Neige stud dogs. The most recent Pembrokes tracing back in any depth to Uncle Sam are those of Rover Run breeding in this country and of the Mackson line in Canada. Both kennels are no longer active in Corgis.

Ch. Rozavel Uncle Sam of Waseeka, ROM, the first Pembroke
Welsh Corgi to win a Best in Show in the United States. This
historic milestone occurred in 1949.   *Brown*

Due to maternal duties upon arrival, Ch. Rozavel Miss Bobby Sox, CD,
was the last of the famous trio to complete her championship. Miss Bobby Sox
was purchased as a foundation bitch by Mrs. Katherine Bartlett (later Mrs. J.
Donald Duncan), and she was imported in whelp to Rozavel Thumbs Up.

In her second litter, by Stanley Logan's Int. Ch. Upperton Corncob, a
grandson of Int. Ch. Formakin Orangeman and Eng. Ch. Teekay's Felcourt
Supremacy, Rozavel Miss Bobby Sox produced the popular winner and showman
Ch. Kaydon's Happy Talk. Happy Talk, whose brilliant career began at six and
a half months with a Best of Breed win at the 1950 Westminster Kennel Club
show, became the first American-bred Pembroke to win a Best in Show.

Ch. Rozavel Lucky Fellow of Merriedip did not have the same impact on
the breed as did Uncle Sam and Miss Bobby Sox. Even so, Lucky Fellow, or
Tubby, as he was known to his friends, won Best of Breed at the 1950 PWCCA
Specialty Show under breeder-judge Mrs. William Long, giving the Merriedip
Kennels their third such win. In keeping with family tradition, Rozavel Lucky
Fellow sired the striking, deep red Best in Show winner Ch. Toelmag's Tommy
Lad. Tommy Lad was owned by Dr. Herbert Talmadge.

It is interesting to note that Dr. Talmadge's daughter, Mrs. Thelma von
Thaden, still carries on the family interest in Corgis in Mexico, where she is
now living. Mrs. von Thaden was a well-known judge of Corgis and many other
breeds. She has owned an American and Mexican champion and Best in Show
winner in Mexico.

Eng. Am. Ch. Rozavel Rainbow, the first Pembroke Welsh Corgi to win Best in Show at an all-breed English Championship show.

The Lucky Strike offspring in America were not alone in capturing Best in Show honors. Ch. Rozavel Rainbow, a lovely Lucky Strike daughter, made breed history in England at the City of Birmingham show in September 1950, when she became the first Pembroke Welsh Corgi to win Best in Show at an all-breed English Championship show.

Purchased for what is said to have been a record four-figure price, Rainbow was subsequently imported by Mrs. Andrew Porter's Tred Avon Kennels in Maryland. Rainbow won Best of Breed at the 1952 PWCCA Specialty held in conjunction with the prestigious Westchester Kennel Club show and went on to win the Working Group at that event. Although Rainbow had other Group wins, she was never able to add an American Best in Show win to her laurels. Neither was she a producer, an unfortunate loss for her owners and for the breed.

The imports sired by Int. Ch. Rozavel Lucky Strike marked the end of an era in Pembroke history in America. It was a time when the immortal Ch. Rozavel Red Dragon was well to the fore in the pedigrees of our current winners. Kennels in this country were turning back to England to import offspring of the latest winners, dogs in whose pedigrees Red Dragon was the foundation but also the past.

POSTWAR KENNELS

During the postwar years a number of new kennels began in the breed, many of which continued on to form the backbone of today's fancy. In England the popularity of the Pembroke Welsh Corgi continued to climb with unbelievable momentum, reaching its peak with 8,933 registrations during 1960. New kennels were established at such a rate, it is impossible to single out a few for recognition here.

In America dogs from Merriedip, Waseeka and Andelys Kennels remained out front in Corgi competition after the war ended.

At the first postwar PWCCA Specialty, held with the Greenwich Kennel Club show in 1946, at which Thelma Gray was the judge, Mrs. Fallass's Ch. Peppercorn Formakin Fascination of Andely was Best of Breed. This bitch, eight years old at the time, had also been the Winners Bitch at the 1941 PWCCA Specialty before war called a halt to most dog show activities. And Ch. Tormentor of Andelys's Best of Breed win at the 1947 PWCCA Specialty gave Andelys Kennels its fourth PWCCA Specialty Best of Breed win, a record later equaled only by Cote de Neige Kennels.

The Pembroke entries at the Westminster Kennel Club show reflected the strength of the leading kennels of the late 1940s. The Andelys dogs dominated the Pembroke entry at the 1947 Westminster. Out of a total entry of eighteen Pembrokes, eleven were owned by Mrs. Fallass. In addition, two other entries were bred at the Andelys Kennels. The following year Mrs. Margery Renner judged an entry of twenty-nine Pembrokes at the Garden, eleven of which were owned by Waseeka Kennels, and two more entries were Waseeka bred.

Although Ch. Peppercorn Formakin Fascination was the only entry from the Andelys Kennels in competition at the 1948 Westminster show, five famous Andelys champions were entered for Exhibition Only. What a memorable sight it must have been, with Ch. Spring Robin of Andely, Ch. Robin Hood of Andely, Ch. Tormentor of Andeley, Ch. Firelight of Andely and Int. Ch. Fire Bird of Cogges on display for the two days of Westminster.

By 1949 the Andelys Kennels had bowed out of Corgi activities. For reasons of poor health, Mrs. Fallass decided the kennels had to be cut back. Consequently, only the Smooth Fox Terriers were retained. Ch. Robin Hood of Andely and Ch. Tormentor of Andely were exported to England, where, following quarantine, they joined Rozavel Kennels, making available to England some of the bloodlines lost during the war.

By the mid-1940s Mrs. Marjorie Butcher's Cote de Neige Pembrokes were beginning to make frequent appearances at the shows. Their wins were just an indication of the strength that was yet to come from Cote de Neige. Before Mrs. Butcher turned her attention entirely to the Corgis, many of the best-known, top winning Great Pyrenees in this country carried the Cote de Neige prefix. Descriptive of the Great Pyrenees, the name Cote de Neige when translated from the French means ''snow drift.''

The first Pembroke to join the Great Pyrenees at Cote de Neige was Far Away Tawny Goch, obtained before the war from Jean and Marjorie Walker's Far Away Kennels. Later, Mrs. Butcher purchased Far Away Goch of Cote de Neige, who became the first champion Pembroke at Cote de Neige, a kennel that was to breed 140 Pembroke champions in the years that followed.

In their early days, Cote de Neige Kennels and Far Away Kennels were

Percy Roberts judging the first PWCCA Sweepstakes in 1953. On the left is Mrs. Marjorie Butcher with Cote de Neige Happy Time, Best in Sweepstakes. At the right is Mrs. J. Donald Duncan with her homebred Kaydon's Anthony.   *Shafer*

located in the Berkshires of Massachusetts. After a move to Connecticut in the late forties, Cote de Neige Kennels permanently relocated to Bedford, New York, in 1953. Far removed from practically all civilization, Faraway (now one word) Kennels became happily situated on San Juan Island, Washington. Pembrokes harking back to the Faraway prefix are still much in evidence on the West Coast.

In 1947 Mrs. Irene Green's Greencorg Kennels, established during the war years, rose to sudden prominence with the arrival of the noted English winner Int. Ch. Formakin Orangeman.

Whelped in 1944, Formakin Orangeman was the first Pembroke Welsh Corgi to make up his championship when shows were resumed in England after the war. He gained his title at the first three Championship shows held in 1946. Following what was perhaps his greatest win, Best in Show at the Irish Kennel Club Championship show in Dublin, "Paddy" came to America in search of new victories. Though he won a Best in Show in Sydney, Nova Scotia, a Reserve Best in Show in Halifax and ten Group firsts in the States, he was never quite lucky enough to capture top honors in this country.

It was unfortunate that Orangeman, an exceptionally sound, rich red sable dog, did not prove to be a particularly useful stud. His only descendant of real note was a grandson, Int. Ch. Upperton Corncob, sire of Ch. Kaydon's Happy Talk.

The 1954 PWCCA Specialty with Ch. Kaydon's Happy Talk (right), BOB, and Ch. Kaydon Aimhi's Kate, BOS. Judge: Derek Rayne. Happy Talk's show record included ninety-one Group placings, including twenty-two Group firsts and five Bests in Show.   *Shafer*

Mrs. Donald Duncan's Kaydon Kennels, officially established with the importation of Ch. Rozavel Miss Bobby Sox, CD, made a tremendous impact upon the breed during its brief period of activity. Three Best in Show winners from this kennel, Ch. Kaydon's Happy Talk, Ch. Craythorne's Domino and Eng. Am. Can. Ch. Lees Symphony, ROMX, stood at the top of Corgi competition up and down the Eastern seaboard until the kennel was closed following Kay Duncan's tragic death during Hurricane Hazel in October 1954.

Through Mrs. Duncan's tireless efforts on behalf of the breed, not only as a breeder and exhibitor but as secretary of the Pembroke Welsh Corgi Club of America and breed columnist for *Pure-Bred Dogs—American Kennel Gazette* as well, the Pembroke Welsh Corgi made new inroads into the southern and western regions of the country. A number of the Pembroke kennels established in this country during the early 1950s were founded with Kaydon-bred stock. And the phenomenal influence on the breed by the Kaydon import, Ch. Lees Symphony, has rarely been challenged by any modern-day Pembroke.

Eng. Am. Can. Ch. Lees Symphony, ROMX

Teekay's Felcourt Autocrat
Lisaye Lees Laurence
Lees Laurel
Lees Laureate
Eng. Ch. Teekay's Felcourt Supremacy
Eng. Ch. Lees Coronet
Teekay Vivien
ENG. AM. CAN. CH. LEES SYMPHONY, ROMX
Teekay Pendragon
Corker of Cowfold
Larkwhistle Valerie
Cantata of Cowfold
Eng. Ch. Teekay's Felcourt Supremacy
Chorus Girl of Cowfold
Teekay Tansy

5

Breeding On

TODAY'S PROMINENT BLOODLINES stem from three out-standing sources—Int. Ch. Lees Symphony, ROMX; Eng. Ch. Knowland Clipper; and the combination of Stormerbanks-Ambrose and Stormerbanks-Supersonic breeding.

As would be expected, many of our best dogs represent various combinations of these important lines, but, where possible, the top-producing dogs and noted winners presented here are grouped together to illustrate the family type and quality that has consistently bred on.

THE SYMPHONY SAGA

Bred by Miss Pat Curties, Lees Symphony was whelped April 10, 1951. A Junior Warrant winner at eight months of age, Symphony completed his English championship prior to his first birthday.

In 1952 Symphony was imported to the States by Mrs. J. Donald Duncan. Apparently he reacted poorly to the change and was a difficult dog to show here. As Miss Curties was to comment later, Symphony did not look to be the same dog in this country as he did at home, for he had become feisty in temperament and hard in eye. Slower to gain his American title than would be expected of a dog fresh from a fine show career in England, Symphony won his finishing points late in the spring of 1953. Later, a Canadian championship was added as well. Campaigned from 1953 to 1957, Symphony won three Bests in Show and thirteen Group firsts out of a total of forty Group placings.

At ten years of age, Symphony was sent back to England to spend his retirement years in the company of his many friends at Lees. Happy to be home, Symphony once again became the gentle, sweet-natured dog he was known to have been as a youngster.

It is as a sire that Symphony will long be remembered, and oddly enough, his greatest impact on the breed came from dogs he sired during the brief time he was at stud in England before leaving for America.

Mated to a Knowland Clipper daughter, Maracas Helarian Gale, Symphony sired the two famous littermates, Eng. Ch. Maracas Masterpiece and Eng. Ch. Kaytop Maracas Mist. Eng. Ch. Kaytop Maracas Mist distinguished herself by winning Best Bitch in Show, All Breeds, at Crufts in 1955, and she remains the only Corgi to have such a high placing at that giant of all shows.

The sensational Eng. Ch. Kaytop Marshall, himself the winner of the Gold Trophy for Best in the Working Group at Crufts in 1972, is a direct descendant of Eng. Ch. Kaytop Maracas Mist, the foundation bitch of Mrs. Leila Moore's Kaytop Kennels.

A valuable sire as well as a striking showman, Marshall is found in the pedigrees of countless winners during the seventies and eighties. His winning progeny in England earned for him the Int. Ch. Lees Symphony Memorial Trophy as runner-up to the Formakin Stud Dog Cup winner in 1970 and 1971. Two of his best-known daughters, Eng. Ch. Stormerbanks Mame and Eng. Ch. Stormerbanks Martha appeared in the Welsh Corgi League's listing of leading brood bitches every year from 1971 to 1976. In 1975 a Martha son, Eng. Ch. Stormerbanks Vainglory, was England's leading sire and winner of the Formakin Stud Dog Cup. Carrying on the family tradition, Eng. Ch. Lynfarne Pacesetter, a Vainglory son, won the Formakin Cup in 1977 and 1979.

Eng. Ch. Maracas Masterpiece. Breeder-owner: Mrs. M. T. S. Thornycroft. Masterpiece was the leading stud dog in England from 1956 through 1960. *Fall*

Eng. Ch. Kaytop Marshall, whelped May 8, 1967. Breeder-owner: Mrs. L. K. Moore. Marshall is the only Pembroke of either sex to win a CC at Crufts for four years in a row, which he did in 1969 through 1972, when he was retired from the ring.   *Sivert Nilsson*

Eng. Ch. Maracas Masterpiece, one of Symphony's most successful sons, was a legendary sire in his own right. Hesitant in temperament, a condition blamed on illness early in puppyhood, Masterpiece was not everybody's cup of tea. Nonetheless, he sired many outstanding offspring, whose temperaments were beyond reproach. While it is impossible to give credit here to all of the many well-known Masterpiece progeny who have been important to the breed, note must be made of three sons particularly outstanding for their contribution to the breed in America—Eng. Ch. Crowleythorn Snowman, Am. Can. Bda. Ch. Maracas Monarch of Cleden, ROMX, and Am. Ch. Gladiator of Rode, UD, Can. CDX.

The sire of twenty-seven champions, Ch. Maracas Monarch of Cleden, ROMX, for many years ranked high on the PWCCA listing of the all-time top-ten producing sires in the United States.

Ch. Gladiator of Rode, UD, Can. CDX, is found in the pedigrees of a number of West Coast Pembrokes. Mated to a Symphony daughter, he sired the stylish tricolor, Ch. Rover Run Minstrel Man. Owned for a time by Derek Rayne before going back to his breeder, Carol Simonds, Minstrel Man won seven Group firsts and the 1961 PWCCA Specialty. "Speedie" bred on through his famous son, the captivating Ch. Cote de Neige Derek, a multiple Best in Show and Specialty winner.

Ch. Cote de Neige Derek with his breeder-owner, Marjorie Butcher. Derek was the top winning Pembroke in the United States in 1964, 1965 and 1966. *Ritter*

Of the three Masterpiece sons, Eng. Ch. Crowleythorn Snowman had the greatest influence on the breed, mainly through his sons, Ch. Halmor Hi-Fi, ROM, and Eng. Irish and Am. Ch. Crowleythorn Ladomoorlands, ROM, in this country, and in England through his daughter, Evancoyd True Love. True Love is the dam of the celebrated Eng. Ch. Evancoyd Personality Girl, and of England's leading stud dog in 1972 and 1974, Evancoyd Contender.

Am. Can. Ch. Bear Acres Mister Snowshoes, UD, ROM, whelped March 17, 1972. Breeder: Mrs. Stanley Bear; owner: Mrs. Frank Hayward. Fifth top Working Dog in 1975 and 1976 and top winning Pembroke from 1974 through 1976. He was Group first at Westminster in 1976 and the first BIS winning champion UD Pembroke Welsh Corgi. *Callea*

40

America's top winning Welsh Corgi from 1974 through 1976, Am. Can. Ch. Bear Acres Mister Snowshoes, UD, ROM, represents a highly successful combination of Hi-Fi and Ladomoorlands breeding. Carried down from his sire, Ch. Bear Acres Two for the Road, ROM, the line's ability to breed on successfully through "Mister" has been demonstrated by his two Best in Show winning sons, Ch. Vangard Mr. Ski Bum, ROMX, and Am. Can. Ch. Suzyque's Southern Snowbear, ROMX. Snowbear broke breed records when he became the youngest American Pembroke champion by finishing his title at the age of six months and twenty-three days.

Although never receiving the loud acclaim that came to Masterpiece, another Symphony son, South African Ch. Drumbeat of Wyldingtree of Wey, contributed immeasurable quality to the breed. An excellent showman of superb type, Drumbeat was purchased as the foundation dog for the Kenneth Butlers' highly successful Wey Kennels in England. Drumbeat passed on his lovely head quality, refined yet masculine, to his offspring and was in part responsible for the typical "Wey" head, which was praised the world over.

Drumbeat's son, Int. Ch. Gayelord of Wey, was a most useful dog in that he did well by bitches of Masterpiece breeding and was also a suitable outcross for bitches of a number of different lines. Likewise, Gayelord's grandson, Pennywise of Wey, has proven himself in much the same manner.

In addition to siring the first Pembroke Welsh Corgi to win a Best in Show in the Midwest, Ruth Cooper's Ch. Craythorne's Fleetfoot of Wey, Drumbeat sired a dog who was to head a remarkable line of winners in America, Ch. Stormerbanks Big Drum, CDX. Big Drum was purchased by the Robert Haights as a family pet. Once he embarked on a show career, Big Drum easily completed his championship, shown by Bill Haight, then a junior handler.

Big Drum combined the foundation breeding of two of England's most famous kennels, Wey and Stormerbanks, through Drumbeat and Eng. Ch. Stormerbanks Dairymaid, one of the breed's finest brood bitches. With excellent quality

South African Ch. Drumbeat of Wyldingtree of Wey.   *Fall*

41

Pennywise of Wey. Breeders on both sides of the Atlantic still turn to lines that go back to Pennywise to bring in good head and expression.   *Fall*

behind him, it is no wonder we find Big Drum in the pedigrees of a number of our best American-bred Pembrokes of this era.

Big Drum's famous son, Ch. Cote de Neige Sundew, ROMX, was greatly admired by Corgi fanciers everywhere, with many believing he more closely represented the Standard for the breed than any Pembroke dog yet to appear in this country. Purchased at the start of his career from Cote de Neige Kennels by Mrs. William B. Long, Sundew piled up an enviable show record with seven Bests in Show. His greatest victory, and one that provided a tremendous thrill for the nation's Corgi lovers, was his Best American-Bred in Show win at the 1960 Westminster Kennel Club show.

Sundew's array of top wins might well have been greater still had it not been for the fact that he was upstaged by his dashing young son, Ch. Willets Red Jacket, ROM. Red Jacket, or Barney as he was known, had not started as a promising show puppy. He was a gangly, clumsy youngster and had gone off to a pet home. Not only did the fable of the ugly duckling turning into a beautiful swan come true for Barney, but when problems arose in his new home, he was returned to Stephen Shaw, his handler and lifelong friend. In Mrs. William Long's ownership, Red Jacket sailed through to his championship and became a leading Working Group and Best in Show contender throughout his entire career. To date he remains fifth on the all-time top Best in Show–winning Pembroke Welsh Corgi list, with eighteen such awards to his credit.

In the Midwest a strong line of winning Pembrokes was established by Mrs. Barbara Hedberg at her Cormanby Kennels by linebreeding on both Ch. Drumbeat of Wyldingtree of Wey and Eng. Ch. Stormerbanks Dairymaid, through Cormanby's foundation bitch, Stormerbanks Saucebox. The mating of a Big Drum daughter to a son of Ch. Craythorne's Fleetfoot of Wey produced Ch. Cormanby Cavalier, ROMX. A Cavalier son, Ch. Cormanby Cadenza was a noted midwestern winner whose record included multiple Specialty, Group and Best in Show wins.

Stormerbanks Big Drum (left) pictured winning Best of Opposite Sex under Pat Curties (Lees Kennels, England), with Mrs. McCammon's Ch. Crawleycrow Coracle of Aimhi, ROM, winning BOB at the 1955 PWCCA Specialty show. *Brown*

The illustrious son of Big Drum, Ch. Cote de Neige Sundew, ROMX, was Best American-bred in Show at the 1960 Westminster show under George Hartman. Sundew's record included seven BIS and fifty-four Group placings, of which twenty-three were Group firsts. *Shafer*

Ch. Willets Red Jacket, whelped July 13, 1958. Breeder: Dr. Matthew Ratchford; owner: Mrs. William B. Long. Sired by Sundew, he won eighteen BIS under sixteen different judges. He also topped fifty-five Groups from a total of 107 Group placings.

Tauskey

Of the American-bred dogs sired by Ch. Lees Symphony, ROMX, Ch. Kaydon's Anthony and Am. Mex. Ch. Penrick Most Happy Fella stand out as the most noteworthy. Owned by Mrs. Carol Simonds, Ch. Kaydon's Anthony was campaigned in California during the mid 1950s, and many times was the only Corgi entered at the show. Anthony, a Best in Show winner himself, has bred on through his Best in Show–winning son, Can. Am. Ch. Macksons Golden Sceptre and Sceptre's litter sister, Can., Am. Ch. Macksons Coronet, both owned by Pamela Mack.

Another of Anthony's offspring, Rover Run Romance, became the foundation bitch of the Larklain Kennels. Her breeding has been perpetuated through Busy B's, Katydid, Larchmont and other lines.

Mr. and Mrs. J. Liecty had considerable success with closely bred Symphony stock. Ch. Penrick Princess, a double Symphony granddaughter, mated back to Symphony produced Symphony's second Best in Show–winning son, Am. Mex. Ch. Penrick Most Happy Fella, and a Group-winning daughter, Am. Mex. Ch. Penrick Belle A'Ringing. Ch. Penrick Flewellyn, CDX, ROM, a litter sister of Princess, was mated back to Symphony and gave the Liectys yet another Group winner, Ch. Penrick Sonny.

While the Symphony offspring were making their mark in America, the pendulum of breed type was in motion, shifting toward a preference for heavier-boned, lower-to-ground Pembrokes than had been sought in years past. Masterpiece breeding put with other lines to Eng. Ch. Knowland Clipper provided what breeders were seeking.

THE KNOWLAND CLIPPER INFLUENCE

Mrs. D. E. Foster's homebred, Eng. Ch. Knowland Clipper, was the breed's youngest champion in England. He completed his title at the age of

Ch. Cormanby Cadenza, whelped March 9, 1966. Breeder: Barbara Hedberg; owners: Michael Sauve and Barbara Hedberg. The winner of the Lakeshore PWCC Specialties from 1970 through 1972, Cadenza garnered four Group firsts and twenty-three Group placings. *Tauskey*

fourteen and a half months in 1950. Clipper was judged Best Puppy at Crufts in 1950, and in March of that year he went Best Dog all breeds on the first day of the Manchester championship show. By the time he was eighteen months old he had amassed a total of six CCs, four Reserve CCs and 89 Junior Warrant points. Clipper's total record of eighteen CCs placed him in the listing of Great Britain's top ten Pembroke CC winners for many years.

Runner-up for the League's Formakin Stud Dog Cup in 1951, Clipper won the Cup as the leading stud dog in England from 1952 through 1955. His place at the top of the stud dog list was taken over in 1957 by his grandson, Ch. Maracas Masterpiece, a position Masterpiece was to maintain through 1960.

Although Knowland Clipper appears in the pedigrees of many American-bred Pembrokes, few of his sons and daughters came to this country; of those who did, only a daughter, Ch. Crawleycrow Coracle of Aimhi, ROM, has bred on to any significant extent. Coracle, imported and owned by Mary McCammon, produced a number of outstanding bitches carrying the Aimhi's prefix. Of these Coracle daughters, Ch. Kaydon Aimhi's Kate had the greatest influence and is behind the foundation stock of several prominent kennels of the sixties and seventies, Penrick, Eversridge, Benfro and Erhstag, to name a few.

Much of the Knowland Clipper breeding in this country was brought in by offspring of Eng. Irish Ch. Zephyr of Brome, a Clipper son. Zephyr, bred and owned by Mrs. Rose Johnson, was a Junior Warrant winner at eight months and a champion at twelve months, thus taking over his sire's position as the breed's youngest champion in England. Zephyr's total wins included twenty-seven CCs and a Best in Show at an all-breed Championship show.

In a very short time Philip and Louise Cleland established a successful and readily identifiable line of Cleden Corgis by using a carefully selected nucleus of imported linebred Masterpiece-Zephyr-Clipper stock. Their two foundation stud dogs, Am. Can. Bda. Ch. Maracas Monarch of Cleden, ROMX (a Masterpiece son out of a Zephyr daughter), and Am. Bda. Ch. Maracas Gale Force of

Eng. Ch. Knowland Clipper.   *Fall*

Cleden, ROM (a Zephyr son out of a Clipper daughter), proved tremendously strong as sires in this country.

Although Gale Force, with fourteen champion offspring, had to relinquish his placing on the ten top producing sires listing to current dogs, two of his offspring out of Ch. Cote de Neige Garland, ROM—namely Ch. Cote de Neige Christmas Candy, ROMX, and Ch. Cote de Neige Christmas Rush, ROM—proved to be top producers as well.

A Christmas Candy grandson, the famous Ch. Cote de Neige Pennysaver, ROMX, and a Pennysaver son, Ch. Cote de Neige Instant Replay, ROMX, each had eighteen champion get. Out of a Christmas Rush daughter, Instant Replay is from a repeat of the breeding that produced the Best in Show winner, Ch. Cote de Neige Chance of Fox Run, ROMX.

Elaine Swinney Erganbright, the breeder of almost two hundred Pembroke champions bearing the Larklain prefix, made what appears to be the most concentrated use of Zephyr lines of any breeder in this country. Her imported stud dogs included Ch. Viceroy of Brome, a Zephyr son; Ch. Red Envoy of Brome CD, ROMX, sired by Red Major of Brome—a Zephyr brother, and out of a Zephyr daughter; and Ch. Enterprise of Brome, again sired by Red Major and out of a Viceroy daughter.

As the sire of fifty-one champions, Red Envoy has the honored position of second on the all-time top sires listing. Not only has Red Envoy sired a tremendous number of champions, his record of siring four Best in Show winners has not, to date, been equaled. Of his four Best in Show sons, Ch. Larklain's Firebright, ROM, was the best-known winner with a total of two Bests in Show, thirty Working Groups, seventy Group placements and 175 Bests of Breed.

Eng. Irish Ch. Zephyr of Brome (Eng. Ch. Knowland Clipper ex Katrina of Brome), a ranking British top ten CC winner.   *Fall*

Am. Bda. Ch. Maracas Gale Force of Cleden, ROM, whelped November 19, 1955. Breeder: Mrs. M. T. S. Thornycroft; owner: Louise Cleland. A winner of twenty-three Group placements, he was Best of Breed at the 1958 PWCCA Specialty show. A double Knowland Clipper grandson, Gale Force sired fourteen champions.   *Brown*

Ch. Cote de Neige Christmas Candy, ROMX, an all-time top ten sire with twenty-two champions to his credit. Christmas Candy is the sire of Ch. Cote de Neige Penny Wise, which gives Penny lines to Knowland Clipper through Candy as well as through her dam, Gold Coin.   *Tauskey*

47

Ch. Cote de Neige Pennysaver, ROMX (Ch. Stokeplain Fair Chance of Cote de Neige, ROM, ex Ch. Cote de Neige Penny Wise), whelped December 13, 1964. The top winning Pembroke Welsh Corgi in 1966 and 1967, Pennysaver had a total record of five BIS wins, twenty-two firsts out of seventy-three Group placings and 118 BOBs. He also won two PWCCA Specialties and is shown winning BIS at the KC of Philadelphia under judge Albert E. Van Court. *Gilbert*

A number of today's active breeders owned as their first Corgi a Larklain-bred dog or bitch. As a result, lines to Zephyr and Clipper became widely dispersed around the country as the foundation stock for many of the new kennels formed during the late 1950s and early 1960s.

THE AMBROSE-SUPERSONIC COMBINATION

Quite apart from the Clipper-Masterpiece-Zephyr breeding, which was being carried out the world over, was the emergence of a powerful line in England. Miss Patsy Hewan's Stormerbanks line first made its presence felt late in the 1930s. For fifty years Stormerbanks dogs were to rank among the top winners and producers of the day until the kennel was closed in 1986 after Miss Hewan's death. The success of the line is evidenced by the annual listings of England's top producing sires and dams, in which at least one dog or bitch carrying the Stormerbanks prefix could be found every year for almost thirty

Ch. Red Envoy of Brome, CD, ROMX. Breeder: Mrs. Rose Johnson; owner: Elaine Swinney Erganbright. Runner-up for all-time top sire in the United States, with fifty-one champion offspring, of which four were Best in Show winners.

years. In all, seventeen English champions were produced, plus countless others in America and around the Corgi world.

The ability to breed on was undoubtedly transmitted to the Stormerbanks Pembrokes in part by the noted postwar winner and sire, Eng. Irish Ch. Broom of Ballybentra through his son, Churchleigh Ballybentra Cowboy. Broom appears in many pedigrees through his sons, Eng. Ch. Lisaye Disturbance and Eng. Ch. Crawleycrow's Bannow Master Broom, and through his famous grandson, Eng. Ch. Zephyr of Brome. Many of the Wey and Hildenmanor dogs trace back to Master Broom, which explains the compatibility often found between these lines and those of Stormerbanks breeding.

Churchleigh Ballybentra Cowboy sired Eng. Ch. Stormerbanks Cowbelle, the first of a long line of champions at Stormerbanks, and also Eng. Ch. Stormerbanks Dairymaid. Dairymaid mated to Stormerbanks Parmel Audacity, a dog Miss Hewan brought in after Cowboy's untimely death, produced Stormerbanks Ambrose and Stormerbanks Amanda. Bred to Eng. Ch. Sonec of Rode, one of England's leading stud dogs throughout the 1950s, Amanda produced Stormerbanks Supersonic. In the Dairymaid son, Ambrose, and grandson, Supersonic, Miss Hewan had a nucleus from which careful line breeding would produce generations of famous Stormerbanks winners.

In a personal letter, Miss Hewan modestly writes of the Ambrose-Supersonic combination:

Int. Ch. Broom of Ballybentra, great-grandsire of Eng. Irish Ch. Zephyr of Brome and grandsire of the first champion at Stormerbanks, Eng. Ch. Stormerbanks Cowbelle, and of Eng. Ch. Stormerbanks Dairymaid. Broom was worked regularly as a cattle dog while in his native Ireland. He was the first Irish-bred dog to become an English champion and was runner-up for the Formakin Stud Dog Cup in 1948 and 1949.   *Fall*

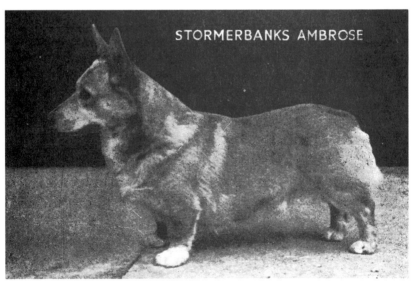

Stormerbanks Ambrose.   *Fall*

Stormerbanks Supersonic.   *F.W. Simms*

I think it was just one of those lucky bits of line breeding that seemed to work out exceptionally well, and the influence has carried on over the years. I suppose you could say that the combination produced what people call the Stormerbanks type, and I think each of the dogs had an equal influence on the offspring. One of the main good things from the breeding of these two was that they never produced (and would actually correct) all the serious faults like fluffies, bluies, mismarks, sharks etc. I don't think either of them ever sired one, which didn't make such an impression on me at the time.

Of the Ambrose-Supersonic breeding imported into the United States, Ch. Stormerbanks Tristram of Cote de Neige, ROMX, stands out as the most important producer. Whelped in June 1956, Tris was sired by Stormerbanks Supersabre, a Supersonic son. His dam, Tresarden Trinket, was an Ambrose daughter who already had proven herself as the dam of one of the breed's prettiest bitches, Eng. Ch. Stormerbanks Superfine. Superfine, sired by Supersonic, bred on through her son, Eng. Ch. Stormerbanks Indigo, the sire of Eng. Ch. Stormerbanks Invader.

Stormerbanks Tristram was imported in January 1957 by Marjorie Butcher. With a Group first and frequent Group placings en route, Tris completed his championship undefeated in the classes at eleven months of age. With a total of forty championship offspring to his credit, Tris ranks as the fifth top producing sire of all time in the United States.

Of the many Tris offspring who have bred on well for their owners, Am. Can. Ch. Welcanis Adulation heads the list. She was renowned not only for her record as a producer but for her successes in the show ring as well. Her daughter, Am. Can. Ch. Welcanis Duplication, was an important brood bitch at the Leetwood Kennels owned by Mr. and Mrs. Elwin Leet. Another Adulation daughter, Am. Can. Ch. Welcanis Constellation Faraway, ROM, is prominent in many pedigrees through Faraway and Schaferhaus breeding.

Am. Can. Ch. Stormerbanks Tristram of Cote de Neige, ROMX,
was the leading sire in 1960, 1961, 1962, 1964 and 1965 (tied
with Envoy in 1962 and 1964). He sired forty champions and is
in the pedigree of many others. *Tauskey*

Perhaps one of the best-known dogs to represent Ambrose-Supersonic
breeding outside the Stormerbanks Kennels is Lees Jackpot, owned by Miss Pat
Curties. Whelped in September 1956, Jackpot was sired by Ambrose out of a
Supersonic daughter, Stormerbanks Supersweet. Unlucky to never make up his
championship, Jackpot exhibited his worth as a sire instead. His name appears
on the listings of England's leading stud dogs every year from 1959 through
1965.

Jackpot breeding is found more frequently in American pedigrees through
his son, Eng. Ch. Lees Sunsalve, than directly by himself. Sunsalve, a grandson

Can. Am. Bda. Ch. Welcanis Adulation (Ch. Stormerbanks Tris-
tram of Cote de Neige, ROMX, ex Ch. Corgana Fascination).
Breeder-owners: Dr. and Mrs. G. Wilkins. She was the top winning
Corgi in Canada in 1964, 1965 and 1967 and BOB at the Golden
Gate PWCF Specialty show in 1963. *January*

Lees Jackpot.   *C.M. Cooke*

of Int. Ch. Gayelord of Wey, brings the familiar breeding of Ch. Drumbeat of Wyldingtree of Wey into the pedigrees of a number of our winning dogs. A top winner bred and owned by Mr. and Mrs. Dennis Van Velzer, Ch. Wicklow's Whizzer, ROM, was a linebred Sunsalve grandson.

Am. Can. Ch. Llanfair Night Owl, ROMX, was one of this country's most successful Specialty winners and popular stud dogs. Night Owl, or Hooter as he was affectionately known, was bred by Henrik and Irene Sorley, and was co-owned by Irene Sorley, Fred Omer and Don Christie. Ambrose-Supersonic breeding is found mainly through Jackpot in Night Owl's pedigree, as the Winrod breeding also goes back to Jackpot.

Another popular English stud whose name appears frequently in American pedigrees is Eng. Ch. Lees Wennam Eagle. Wennam Eagle was brought into Miss Curties's Lees Kennels to serve as an outcross for Jackpot and Sunsalve daughters. Through Eng. Ch. Kentwood Cogges Woodpecker on both sides of his pedigree, Wennam Eagle combined heavy Masterpiece breeding with Supersonic breeding. Additional Ambrose-Supersonic lines are found behind Wennam Eagle's grandam, Eng. Ch. Winrod Rhapsody, a Jackpot granddaughter. Not only did Wennam Eagle prove to be a successful outcross for bitches of Jackpot and Sunsalve breeding, but his son, Ch. Lees Craythorne's Golden Plover, ROM, was a valuable sire for various outcross lines in the United States.

A combination of Winrod breeding with Masterpiece lines, similar to what is behind Wennam Eagle, was perpetuated by the Pimlotts' Ch. Halmor's Winrod Spencer, ROM, grandsire of Ch. Llanfair Night Owl, ROMX.

In turn, a Spencer son and a well-known West Coast stud dog, Ch. Larchmont's Golden Triumph, CD, ROMX, combined the Masterpiece-Supersonic lines of the Winrod stock with his dam's Masterpiece-Clipper breeding and a line to Ch. Stormerbanks Tristram of Cote de Neige, ROMX, the sire of Larklains Token, ROM. "Britt's" pedigree, probably as well as any, represents a complete integration of Symphony, Clipper and Ambrose-Supersonic lines.

Eng. Ch. Lees Sunsalve (Lees Jackpot ex Lees Firefly), whelped August 24, 1960.   *Sally Anne Thompson*

Ch. Wicklow's Whizzer, ROM (Am. Can. Ch. Lees Briardale Midnight, ROMX, ex Ch. Fox Run's All Bets Down), whelped August 3, 1971. A Specialty and BIS winner, Whizzer was the top Pembroke Welsh Corgi for 1974. Breeder-owners: Mr. and Mrs. Dennis Van Velzer.

Eng. Ch. Lees Wennam Eagle (Eng. Ch. Winrod Peregrine ex Wennam Snowbunting). Breeder: Mrs. M. New; owner: Miss P.L. Curties. Runner-up for the Formakin Stud Dog Cup in 1967, Wennam Eagle was ranked one of England's leading stud dogs from 1966 through 1969. *Sally Anne Thompson*

THE SIXTIES AND EARLY SEVENTIES

In contrast to the depth of quality seen in English Pembrokes, a number of our American Pembrokes from the mid-1950s through the 1960s were sadly lacking in overall quality. Coarse, heavy-headed dogs with overly long muzzles, small eyes and hard expressions were seen with alarming frequency. Unfortunately, newcomers to the breed during that time, be they future breeders or judges, had no way of knowing the Corgis they saw did not represent the ideal in Pembroke type.

Perhaps the wider exposure to different dogs from a variety of geographical areas, made possible by the increasing number of annual Specialty shows, has

Ch. Stormerbanks Winrod Fergus, ROMX, imported in 1968 and owned by Marjorie Butcher. Fergus has lines to Ambrose and Supersonic through both his sire, Eng. Ch. Foxyface, and his dam, Eng. Ch. Winrod Rhapsody. Fergus is the sire of twenty-three American champions and one English champion.

Am. Can. Ch. Llanfair Night Owl, ROMX, holds the breed record with Bests of Breed at one Canadian and six American Specialty shows. He also won BOS at one American and one Canadian Specialty. He was owner-handled to all his wins and sired forty-eight champions.

Eng. Ch. Winrod Peregrine
Eng. Ch. Lees Wennam Eagle
Wennam Snowbunting
Am. Can. Ch. Lees Mynah, CD, TD, ROM
Lees Jackpot
Lees Brunette
Lees Sonatina
AM. CAN. CH. LLANFAIR NIGHT OWL, ROMX
Eng. Ch. Winrod Rob Roy
Ch. Halmor's Winrod Spencer, ROM
Winrod Belinda
Llanfair Bee Balm, CD, TD
Ch. Cyclone of Cowfold
Cappykorns Carousel, CDX
Lees Gaiety Girl

Ch. Larchmont's Golden Triumph, CD, ROMX (Ch. Halmor's Winrod Spencer, ROM, ex Ch. Kem's Candy), whelped December 6, 1965. Breeders: Bob and Esther Britain; owner: Mrs. Pat Jensen. He sired fifteen champions, including the 1970–1971 top winning Pembroke Corgi in the United States, Ch. Nebriowa Miss Bobbisox.

                Eng. Ch. Kentwood Cogges Woodpecker
          Eng. Ch. Winrod Rob Roy
          Winrod Vanessa
    Ch. Halmor's Winrod Spencer, ROM
                Eng. Ch. Maracas Masterpiece
          Winrod Belinda
                Stormerbanks Emma of Corig
CH. LARCHMONT'S GOLDEN TRIUMPH, CD, ROMX
                Ch. Cleden's Portrait of Force
          Ch. Larklain Toddy
                Larklains Token, ROM
    Ch. Kem's Candy
                Ch. Enterprise of Brome
          Larklain Coquette
                Ch. Larklain's Cinderella

provided most of today's breeders with a better understanding of what constitutes desired Pembroke type and quality. Breeders across the country have made good use of English imports to upgrade the level of quality within their own lines. While many of the names that appeared in pedigrees of American-bred Corgis during this period would seem to represent new bloodlines, they all trace back in some degree to one or more of the early greats, Symphony, Masterpiece and Clipper.

6

Tracking Today's Trends

AS TIME PASSES, generation upon generation is added, and dogs prominent in the postwar days are pushed further back in the pedigrees. Outstanding new lines emerge, and they in turn become the backbone of the future. The years from 1975 to 1990 was a period of tremendous importance for the Pembroke Welsh Corgi in England, and consequently for the many countries that have always relied upon England for quality breeding stock. During these years of peace and prosperity, many small kennels produced superb animals, records of all kinds were broken, and new names became byword to every student of the breed.

CROWN PRINCE AND SUCH FUN

Eng. Ch. Hildenmanor Crown Prince, bred and owned by Mrs. Dickie Albin, was one of England's leading stud dogs during the late 1960s and into the 1970s. Shown extensively for only one year, in 1967 he gained eight Challenge Certificates and was England's Corgi of the Year. He carries Ambrose-Supersonic breeding through his grandsire, Eng. Ch. Lees Sunsalve, and also has a line back to Masterpiece. The attractive head quality for which the Hildenmanor dogs are known can be traced back to Laddie of Veryan, the dog from whom all the Hildenmanor Pembrokes descend.

Eng. Ch. Hildenmanor Crown Prince (Hildenmanor Bonilad ex Hildenmanor Gold Crown) (1965–1977). Breeder-owner: Mrs. Dickie Albin. He was the sire of six British champions and is in the pedigrees of many top dogs around the world with quality that bred on.

Crown Prince is found in the pedigrees of some of our best known dogs of the seventies and eighties—Ch. Bekonpenn Count Doronicum, CD, ROMX; Ch. Cappykorns Bach, ROMX; Am. Can. Ch. Velour of Rowell, ROM; and Ch. Hildenmanor Master Spy, ROMX, come first to mind.

Both Doronicum and Bach combined Crown Prince breeding with that of the famous and extremely successful English stud dog Eng. Ch. Caswell Duskie Knight, who, as the sire of twelve British champions, exerted a strong influence at home and to a lesser extent abroad. Duskie Knight, himself a combination of several important earlier lines, brings in the additional lovely type and head quality for which his grandsire, Pennywise of Wey, is noted. One of Elaine Erganbright's top producers, Ch. Larklain's Redd Dandy, ROMX, sire of forty-three champions, was by a Duskie Knight son out of Doronicum's daughter.

More typical of Crown Prince stock, Ch. Velour of Rowell, ROM, a Crown Prince grandson, bred to his beloved kennelmate, Ch. Glynea Red Rose, headed a dynasty of look-alike Corgis with the Snowdonia prefix of Janet Robinson, who resides in South Carolina. In upstate New York, Ch. Hildenmanor Master Spy, ROMX, is behind numerous winners from Maitland and Blandie Ijams' Roughhouse Kennels. Margie Miller of the Millerhof Kennels in Alabama did well with a grandson, Ch. Master Major of Millerhof, ROM, whose dam was imported in whelp. Master Major was a triple Best in Show winner.

Ch. Cappykorns Bach, ROMX, whelped October 8, 1973. Breeder: Dorothy Lacy; owners: Ken and Patricia Pettipiece. Bach was BOB at the 1977 Golden Gate Specialty under Margaret Cole. One of the outstanding sires of the late 1970s, producing thirty champions, he is pictured as WD at the 1975 Cascade Specialty under Mrs. Dickie Albin.   *Smith*

Mrs. Anne Bowes of Massachusetts has had considerable success combining these lines. A bitch, Ch. Heronsway Free At Last, "Tootsie," has had multiple Specialty wins and one Best in Show. "Tyler," the versatile Ch. Heronsway Free Style, UDT, HT, ROMX, VC, owned and trained by Tibby Chase, also has bred on. Many Corgi kennels in the United States and other countries have utilized Crown Prince-Hildenmanor bloodlines.

Of major significance in the late 1970s was the appearance of Mrs. Maureen Johnston's Eng. Ch. Penmoel Such Fun of Rivona, bred by Miss J. Evans. He was by a fine tri dog, Eng. Ch. Penmoel Minstrel, a Duskie Knight grandson, out of a Crown Prince granddaughter. Although he won a respectable total of twelve CCs, one earned at eleven years of age, it was as a sire that he excelled. He first appeared on the list of leading stud dogs in 1978 and remained there for eleven years. Among Such Fun's eleven English champion offspring is the spectacular bitch, Eng. Ch. Belroyd Lovebird. Owned, bred and handled by Idris Jones and Allan Taylor, Lovebird amassed thirty Challenge Certificates, was named Pembroke Welsh Corgi of the Year in 1983 and 1984 and is the top Best

Eng. Ch. Caswell Duskie Knight, winner of the Welsh Corgi League's Formakin Stud Dog Cup for six successive years, runner-up in 1972 and again winner of the cup in 1973. He sired twelve English champions and at least six overseas champions, and his show record included thirty-eight CCs and twenty-one Reserve CCs. He was Pembroke Welsh Corgi of the Year in 1965 and 1970.   *Diane Pearce*

in Show Pembroke in Great Britain, having been awarded that honor on four occasions.

Another Such Fun champion of special note was Eng. Ch. Revelmere Cock-A-Hoop, bred by Mrs. Doris Mason. After siring several English and American champions and starting a line of lovely Revelmere bitches, Cock-A-Hoop was exported to New Zealand. Other Such Fun progeny was eagerly sought, and the strength of his line extends internationally, especially through his grandchildren. Ch. Irisan Bengimum Boy of Rivona, CD, ROMX, a Such Fun grandson, was particularly useful to his owner, Anne Bowes, and is the sire of her Ch. Heronsway Free At Last.

STORMERBANKS-LYNFARNE

From the mid-seventies to the mid-eighties Patsy Hewan continued with her successful Stormerbanks line. Putting her Kaytop Marshall daughter, Eng. Ch. Stormerbanks Martha to her own grandson, Eng. Ch. Lynfarne Pacesetter (all Stormerbanks breeding), Patsy produced one of her most outstanding bitches, Eng. Ch. Stormerbanks Patience. In turn, Patience bred to Pacesetter's son, Eng. Am. Ch. Lynfarne Poldark, ROMX (bred and owned at that time by Louise

Ch. Larklains Redd Dandy, ROMX (Convista Envoy of Brome, a Duskie Knight son, ex Ch. Larklains Bronze Duchess, a Doronicum daughter). Whelped June 22, 1975, he finished his championship at nine and a half months of age. With forty-three champions to his credit, he ranks high on the list of top producing sires in the United States. Breeder-owner: Elaine Swinney Erganbright.

Clarke), resulted in Ch. Stormerbanks Poetry, ROM, who won high honors at many American specialties and was still going strong as a veteran. Poetry and Poldark both were imported by Peggy Kessler of the prominent Wakefield Kennels in Virginia. After Patsy's death, several other Stormerbanks dogs joined those already at Wakefield.

A family group that bred on for Patsy was the "Stormerbanks Bears." Before he left for America, Ch. Stormerbanks Paddy Bear, owned by Celia Wells of Connecticut, sired the good producer, Stormerbanks Bertram Bear, who fathered Patsy's last champion, Eng. Ch. Stormerbanks Bearable.

Once in America, Poldark created great impact as a stud, with thirty-four champions to his credit. A tricolor son, Ch. Lamin Ross Poldark, had a long and impressive show career.

However his most important son, out of Ch. Virginia of Fox Covert, ROM, was the outstanding producer Ch. Martindale Butter Brickle, ROMX, bred by Mrs. Joan Jensen and owned by Mrs. Jan Edwards (Penways) and Mrs. Joan Gibson Reid (Jade Tree). Not only did "Ricky" have a fine show record himself, but he sired winner after winner, forty-eight champions in the United States, and stamped his identity on many lines throughout the United States and Canada. Mrs. Camilla Thorne had good luck breeding her Ch. Mar-Wil's Cayenne Pepper,

Ch. Bekonpenn Count Doronicum, CD, ROMX, whelped October 12, 1971. Breeder: L. F. Needham; owner: Elaine Swinney Erganbright. A Crown Prince–Duskie Knight grandson, Count Doronicum was also a successful sire.

Hildenmanor Bonilad

Eng. Ch. Hildenmanor Crown Prince

Hildenmanor Gold Crown

Carabana Foxash Milord

Eng. Ch. Caswell Duskie Knight

Foxash Bright Star

Foxash Winrod Juliet

CH. BEKONPENN COUNT DORONICUM, CD, ROMX

Caswell Marcus

Eng. Ch. Caswell Duskie Knight

Mynthurst Duskie Princess

Anemone of Bekonpenn

Eng. Ch. Stormerbanks Invader

Candytuft of Bekonpenn

Stormerbanks Fuchsia of Bekonpenn

Eng. Ch. Penmoel Such Fun of Rivona (1976–1989). Breeder: Miss J. Evans; owner: Mrs. Maureen Johnston. His influence as a sire extends to many countries through his children and grandchildren.

Ashbarton Laughing Cavalier
Ashbarton Merry Monarch
Penmoel Bon Ton
Eng. Ch. Penmoel Minstrel
Eng. Ch. Caswell Duskie Knight
Penmoel Sound of Music
Ashbarton Fantasia
ENG. CH. PENMOEL SUCH FUN OF RIVONA
Penmoel Ferguson
Trewlign Eastertime of Penmoel
Trewlign Easter Bonnet
Penmoel Time for Fun
Eng. Ch. Hildenmanor Crown Prince
Penmoel Gay Princess
Ashbarton Fantasia

Ch. Heronsway Free At Last (Ch. Irisan Bengimum Boy of Rivona, CD, ROMX, ex Ch. Heronsway Free Spirit) combines Crown Prince and Pacesetter through her dam with Such Fun from her sire. "Tootsie" started her career in 1985 as Best in Sweepstakes at both the Mayflower Classic and the PWCCA National Specialty. With many other Specialty honors as well, she was Best of Breed at Lakeshore in 1988, and won one all-breed Best in Show. Breeder-owner: Mrs. Anne Bowes. *Moments by Jane*

ROMX, to both Butter Brickle and his father, Poldark, as did Dawn and Judy Vargas of the Linvar Kennels in California. Dogs with wonderful candy names were in the ribbons everywhere.

The cream of the crop and a perennial favorite is the exquisite Ch. Trewyl Lyric of Pennington, ROM, bred by Margie Paton and Sue K. Vahaly and owned by Shirley Brooks. Among Rosie's many specialty wins were Best of Breed at the 1985 PWCCA National Specialty and Best of Opposite Sex the following year, twice Best of Breed at the Mayflower Corgi Classic, and two all-breed Bests in Show following major Corgi events. Meanwhile, she whelped three litters, from which six earned American championships, four were top winners at specialties and two earned multiple Specialty BOBs.

Close behind is a second Butter Brickle daughter bred by Sue Vahaly, Ch. Pennington Gloriand, winner of many major awards at specialties and twice Best of Breed at the Lakeshore Pembroke Welsh Corgi Club Specialty. She in turn is the dam of Ch. Pennington Glory Hallelujah, again with an impressive Specialty record, who continues the tradition via her son, Pennington Parable, who was Winners Dog at the 1992 National.

An all-around dog, Ch. Heronsway Free Style, UDT, HT, ROMX, VC, was whelped July 29, 1983 (Ch. Happiharbor Tom of Heronsway ex Ch. Heronsway Free Spirit). "Tyler" has had numerous top awards at Specialties, including Best of Breed at North Texas in 1985 and BOS at the PWCCA National in 1989. As a sire he has proven to be extremely dominant, placing his identifiable stamp on many winning progeny. He is owned by Tibby Chase and was bred by Anne Bowes.   *Vahaly*

A particularly successful combination was Butter Brickle bred to Ch. Walborah's Xie Xie of Renefield, ROM (by Ch. Tymawr Roamer, ROMX, a Pacesetter son, out of Ch. Beaujolais of Revelmere, ROMX). Carol Asteris and Linda Canfield repeated the breeding, and the famous "Quite" litter contained five who finished their championships and went on to produce more champions. The star of this bunch was Ch. Renefield Bunny Quite Funny. Dubbed "the energizer bunny" because she kept going and going, at just under seven years old she went BOS at the 1992 PWCCA National and BOB at the Lakeshore Specialty for the second time. Her daughter, Ch. Renefield Fancy Pants, carries on her winning ways.

BLANDS

To return to England, another name that began to appear with considerable frequency in the seventies was Blands, Mrs. Peggy Gamble's kennel prefix. The Blands line has been built astutely on a foundation of Zephyr lines heavily crossed

67

Ch. Irisan Bengimum Boy of Rivona, CD, ROMX.

Moments by Jane

Eng. Ch. Lynfarne Pacesetter, whelped July 1, 1973. England's top Pembroke sire in 1977 and 1979. *C.M. Cooke & Son*

Eng. Am. Ch. Lynfarne Poldark, ROMX (Eng. Ch. Lynfarne Pacesetter ex Lynfarne Querida), although bred selectively, became one of America's top ten sires, with thirty-four champion offspring who went on to produce generations of top winners. *Brant Gamma*

Ch. Stormerbanks Poetry, ROM, Poldark's daughter, owned and imported by Peggy Kessler, was Winners Bitch at the PWCCA National Specialty in 1979. *B. Kernan*

Ch. Martindale Butter Brickle, ROMX (1980–1987), sire of forty-eight champions, with 35 percent of that number going Winners or better at Specialties. Breeders: Joan and Ray Jensen; co-owners: Jan Edwards and Joan Gibson Reid. *Vahaly*

Eng. Ch. Stormerbanks Vainglory
Eng. Ch. Lynfarne Pacesetter
Stormerbanks Katie
Eng. Am. Ch. Lynfarne Poldark, ROMX
Lynfarne Jubilation
Lynfarne Querida
Lynfarne Operetta
CH. MARTINDALE BUTTER BRICKLE, ROMX
Eng. Ch. Orangeade of Olantigh
Ch. Olantigh Victory
Eng. Ch. Olantigh Christmas Carol
Ch. Virginia of Fox Covert, ROM
Eng. Ch. Evancoyd Audacious
Stormerbanks Alberta
Eng. Ch. Stormerbanks Mame

Ch. Pennington Ramblin' Lad, ROM, by Ch. Apollinaris Artful Lad, an import with an impressive English pedigree, and out of Ch. Trewhyl Lyric of Pennington, a Butter Brickle daughter. Whelped November 21, 1984. Breeder: Sue K. Vahaly; owner: Rhoann H. Carlin. "Rambler" had a successful show career starting with Best Puppy at the 1985 PWCCA Specialty. He went on to win two Specialty Bests of Breed and one BOS. Several of his get have continued his success in the show ring. *Vahaly*

with Masterpiece breeding. The foundation bitch at Blands Kennels, Dawn of Brome, was a Zephyr daughter and out of a Clipper daughter. Dawn bred to Eng. Ch. Sonec of Rode, a dog found in the foundation breeding at Stormerbanks as well, produced Blands Satinette. Linebreeding Dawn and Satinette together with a popular stud dog in the north of England, Thornbelle Cointreau of Trewake (inbred on Masterpiece), gave Mrs. Gamble the well-known English sires, Blands Telstar, Eng. Ch. Blands Ambassador, Eng. Ch. Blands Impresario and Eng. Ch. Kathla's Dusky Sparkler of Blands. As so many breeders have done, Mrs. Gamble turned to Pennywise of Wey breeding to successfully strengthen head quality and expression in her Blands line. Sparkler, in 1976, was the first dog from the north of England to become Top Stud dog, and he remained on the list for years.

The top winning Corgi in England for 1976 and 1978, Eng. Ch. Blands Solomon of Bardrigg, by Sparkler, represented concentrated line breeding on Pennywise of Wey through his two sons, Blands Telstar and Eng. NZ Ch.

Ch. Renefield Bunny Quite Funny (Ch. Martindale Butter Brickle, ROMX, ex Ch. Walborah Xie Xie of Renefield, ROM).

Eng. Ch. Blands Solomon of Bardrigg (Eng. Ch. Kathla's Dusky Sparkler of Blands ex Blands Belinda), whelped October 28, 1974. Breeder: Mrs. P. Gamble; owners: Mr. and Mrs. W. D. Noall. Solomon won the Leslie Perrins Memorial Trophy in 1976 and 1978.   *Diane Pearce*

Eng. Ch. Kathla's Dusky Sparkler of Blands, whelped November 4, 1971. Breeders: Mr. and Mrs. E. Lacey; owner: Peggy Gamble. One of England's leading stud dogs, Sparkler won the League's Formakin Stud dog Cup in 1976 and 1978. *Diane Pearce*

Int. Ch. Corgwyn Shillelah
Eng. Ch. Jomaro Midnight Special
Jomaro Winrod Juno
Eng. Ch. Jomaro Midnight Sun
Eng. Ch. Blands Ambassador
Jomaro Blands Candida
Blands Caroline
ENG. CH. KATHLA'S DUSKY SPARKLER OF BLANDS
Pennywise of Wey
Blands Telstar
Corgwyn Lucky Lady of Blands
Dusky Rosaday of Kathla
Blands Duskie Knight
Kathla's Roxi of Edlands
Kathla's Super Star

Corgwyn Shillelah. Solomon held the record of forty-one CCs in 1980. Breeders from the south of England soon turned to Yorkshire and Peggy Gamble's strong stud force.

That was just the beginning. Put to Eng. Ch. Olantigh Christmas Carol, a Telstar daughter, Sparkler, known to his friends as Toby, sired another super tri male, Eng. Ch. Olantigh Black Diamond. This handsome fellow in due time topped his half-brother's record by winning the all-time high of 42 Challenge Certificates for his breeder, Mrs. Wynn Lepper. He was the winner of the Leslie Perrins trophy in 1981 and 1982. Eng. Ch. Olantigh Christmas Gift, Carol's littermate, became the sire of Eng. Ch. Apollinaris Angel Clare, Corgi of the Year for 1979 and 1980. Christmas Gift's son, Ch. Foxash Dawn Piper of Rowell, ROMX, was used widely in America.

For twelve years Mrs. Gamble had been looking for a way to improve her bitch line, as her kennel was dominated by males. Blands Marmoset, a red bitch by Impresario, was just what she wanted. After she won her Junior Warrant, she never went in the ring again, as Peggy was anxious to breed her. And what a gem she turned out to be. From her first litter by Eng. Aust. Ch. Kydor Cossack, she produced two champions. From an all-dog litter by Solomon, Eng. Ch. Blands Sonny Boy was retained. Her fourth litter, again by Solomon, yielded the lovely Eng. Ch. Blands Sweet Someday. Dear little Marmoset certainly proved her worth as the first of only three bitches ever to have produced four English champions.

Another bitch bred to Solomon was Eng. Ch. Evancoyd Miss Daring, by the strong sire Eng. Ch. Fitzdown Badger out of Eng. Ch. Dream Girl of Evancoyd. Miss Daring was the second dam of four champions, two by Solomon, for Mrs. Beryl Thompson, her breeder and owner. One of these was Eng. Ch. Evancoyd Mr. Wonderful, the sire of seven champions and many times on the Top Stud list. Mr. Wonderful made quite a splash in the show ring. As a youngster he had won three CCs by the time he was ten months old, another a month later, but he had to win one after he was a year old before he could be granted his championship.

Sonny Boy soon joined Sparkler at the head of the Top Stud list. Sweet Someday was bred to Black Diamond. From a promising litter of seven puppies, all but two were lost to parvovirus, but one, Eng. Ch. Blands Status Symbol, continued the tradition by being Top Stud in 1984 at only three years of age. By combining Marmoset daughters with Toby, Sonny Boy daughters with Status Symbol and other versions of linebreeding, Blands produced numerous champions, mostly tris, and became a colossal force in the breed both in England and overseas.

Americans soon realized the quality and potential of the Blands stock. In the mid seventies for about a decade, several excellent Pembrokes were imported either directly from Mrs. Gamble or from one of the other northern breeders working primarily with the Blands line. Mrs. Walton and Mrs. Hill, affectionately known to all as "The Twinnies," of the Anzil prefix, were closely involved,

Eng. Ch. Olantigh Black Diamond, a Sparkler son ex Eng. Ch. Olantigh Christmas Carol, holds the record of forty-two Challenge Certificates. He was the top Pembroke Welsh Corgi in Britain in 1981 and 1982 for his breeder-owner Mrs. Wyn Lepper.   *Diane Pearce*

Eng. Ch. Olantigh Christmas Gift.   *Diane Pearce*

Eng. Ch. Blands Sonny Boy (Eng. Aus. Ch. Kydor Cossak ex Blands Marmoset). Breeder-owner: Peggy Gamble. *Diane Pearce*

Eng. Ch. Evancoyd Mr. Wonderful (Eng. Ch. Blands Solomon of Bardrigg ex Eng. Ch. Evancoyd Miss Daring). Breeder-owner: Beryl J. Thompson. *Fall*

and sent Ch. Anzil Honey Dew of Blands to Mrs. Jan Edwards in California. Dewey, bred to Butter Brickle, produced three champion daughters. Two have figured extensively in the Penways-Jade Tree line and are behind the successful stud Ch. Penways Town and Country.

In 1979 Jan brought in an Anzil bitch, by Sparkler, in whelp to Eng. Ch. Blands Sonny Boy. In the resulting litter was Ch. Penways Silversmith, the sire of Thomas (Tim) Mathiesen's Ch. Nebriowa The Blacksmith, CDX, ROMX, sire of twenty-nine champions.

Tim and his partner Larry Cunha purchased Ch. Anzil Elegant Lady, ROMX, who has the identical breeding as Silversmith, and was Best of Breed at the 1981 Southern California Specialty.

Ch. Nebriowa Coco Chanel, by The Blacksmith, had an outstanding show career, with three all-breed Bests in Show and Best of Breed at the 1987 PWCCA National. When Chanel was put to Ch. Martindale Drummer Boy, with two lines back to Blands Telstar through Eng. Chs. Olantigh Christmas Gift and Carol, she whelped Ch. Nebriowa Christian Dior, ROMX, sire of thirty-three champions to date, and Am. Can. Ch. Nebriowa Jordache of Fox Meadow, ROMX.

The East Coast of the United States also piped into the Blands line. The first to arrive in 1975 was Am. Can. Ch. Spartan of Blands of Werwow, ROM,

Ch. Anzil Honey Dew of Blands (Am. Can. Ch. Spartan of Blands of Werwow ex Anzil Amber Garter). *Portraits by Allan*

Ch. Penways Town and Country (Ch. Jade Tree Levi of Penway ex Ch. Penways Dew It Again). "TC" is Honey Dew's grandson, linebred on Butter Brickle, with a line back to Eng. Ch. Belroyd Nut Cracker through his sire. When bred to Ch. Jade Tree Just Desserts, they produced such notables as Ch. Jade Tree Penways Remington, Ch. Jade Tree Penways Raconteur and Ch. Jade Tree Penways The Trollop, all top winners at Specialties across the country.

a Sparkler son. When Margaret Thomas of the Festiniog Kennels in Massachusetts bred her Sparkler daughter, Am. Can. Ch. Werwow Katrena, to Spartan, she came up with Ch. Festiniog's Toby Two, ROM. Toby Two, in turn, sired the well-known, prepotent stud, Ch. Festiniog's Moonraker, ROMX, whose influence extends today through his look-alike sons Ch. Festiniog's Linebacker, HT, and Ch. Festiniog's Touchdown, UD, PT, VC, and Touchdown's son, Ch. Arbor Festiniog Rickover, CDX, PT. And so the Blands force continues. Interestingly enough, while there have been many lovely red dogs as well, a significant portion of the red-headed tricolors seen today can be found to have direct lines to Yorkshire.

BELROYD-PEMLAND-BLANDS

Back again in England during the late 1970s, another kennel rose to prominence. Although Idris Jones's and Allan Taylor's Belroyd Pembrokes had been winning well for years with dogs combining Hildenmanor, Stormerbanks and other top bloodlines, one of their bitches, Belroyd Gaybird, made a fortuitous

Ch. Nebriowa Christian Dior, whelped January 15, 1985. Breeders-owners: Thomas Mathiesen and Larry Cunha. Best of Breed at the Southern California Specialty in 1986, top Pembroke sire in 1989 and 1990, and national top sire in the Herding Group for 1990, he sired thirty-three champions.

Eng. Ch. Olantigh Christmas Gift

Am. Can. Ch. Foxash Dawn Piper of Rowell, ROMX

Foxash Daybreak

Ch. Martindale Drummer Boy

Ch. Olantigh Victory

Ch. Virginia of Fox Covert, ROM

Stormerbanks Alberta

CH. NEBRIOWA CHRISTIAN DIOR, ROMX

Ch. Penways Silversmith

Ch. Nebriowa The Blacksmith, CDX, ROMX

Cappykorns Crescent

Ch. Nebriowa Coco Chanel

Ch. Vangard Madison Avenue

Ch. Vangard Ambra

Ch. Schaferhaus Danielle, ROM

Am. Can. Ch. Nebriowa Jordache of Fox Meadow, ROMX, Dior's littermate, sire of three Best in Show winners. Owner: Sally Stewart Bishop. *Carl Lindemaier*

trip north to visit Eng. Ch. Blands Sonny Boy in March of 1979. The resulting litter produced Eng. Ch. Belroyd Jacana, a beautiful Corgi who not only won eighteen Challenge Certificates, but went on to be the third bitch to produce four English champions.

At the same time, Mary and Stuart Magness were developing their Pemland Kennel, skillfully combining Hildenmanor and Stormerbanks lines. Enter Pemland Royal Command. Although he was successfully shown as a puppy, he was retired from the ring because of a bad experience on a bench. However, he has had a vast impact on the Pembroke Welsh Corgi in England and overseas. To date he has sired eleven English champions, won major nationwide awards, and has been runner-up for Top Pembroke Welsh Corgi Stud of the Year three times to his son; and thereby hangs the connection.

The union of Pemland Royal Command and Eng. Ch. Belroyd Jacana produced Eng. Ch. Belroyd Nut Cracker. Whelped November 28, 1983, Nut Cracker and his litter sister, Nestling, finished their championships in 1985. By 1986 he placed second on England's list of Top Studs. From 1987 to 1991 Nut Cracker topped the list, followed by either his sire or his son, Eng. Ch. Blands Limited Edition of Belroyd. In 1991, eight out of twelve leading studs in England were sired by one of these three dogs. To date Nut Cracker has produced thirteen English champions, tying Red Dragon's record set four decades earlier. Perhaps there are more to come.

Am. Can. Ch. Festiniog's Moonraker, HC, ROMX (Ch. Festiniog's Toby Two ex Fenlea Special Moonshine), whelped July 5, 1978. Breeder: Margaret Thomas; owners: Margaret Burnett and Rosemary Carvallo. Moonraker was Best in Sweepstakes at the PWCCA Specialty in 1979 and went Best of Breed at the same show in 1980, followed by Selection of Merit there in 1981 and 1982. *Ashbey*

Nut Cracker has been a phenomenal sire, and has had sensational success in the ring. In 1991 alone he won the Working Group at the Crufts Centenary show, was top Working Group stud dog and won the finals of the nationwide Petfoods Veteran Stakes. Overall he has earned thirty-one CCs. His other honors are too numerous to mention.

One other dog deserves attention here, as he is a Royal Command grandson. Eng. Ch. Pemland Magnus, sired by Eng. Ch. Lees Mastermind (by Such Fun), has been used widely, with several of his get appearing in this country, primarily through Pemland and Revelmere breeding.

As Nut Cracker was from an outcross breeding, he was an obvious choice for Peggy Gambles's closely linebred bitches, tying in through his dam, Jacana. Taking four different bitches to him, there soon were three new Blands champions plus other CC winners. They continue the dynasty.

So popular was the combination of Pemland, Blands and Belroyd dogs during the eighties and early nineties, a major portion of the Corgis being shown

81

Ch. Festiniog's Linebacker, PT, a Moonraker son.

Petrulis

Ch. Arbor Festiniog Rickover, CDX, PT, linebred on Moonraker. These two Corgis illustrate the strong family resemblance of Festiniog dogs due to Moonraker's prepotence.

Chuck Tatham

Eng. Ch. Belroyd Nut Cracker, whelped in 1983, was a top winner in England and a tremendously influential sire both at home and abroad. Breeders-owners: Allan Taylor and Idris Jones.   *Fall*

               Eng. Ch. Hildenmanor Crown Prince
          Cordach Mastercopy of Hildenmanor
               Faine of Bulcorig
     Pemland Royal Command
               Eng. Ch. Stormerbanks Vainglory
          Pemland Court Dancer
               Pemland Dancing Princess
ENG. CH. BELROYD NUT CRACKER
               Eng. Ch. Blands Solomon of Bardrigg
          Eng. Ch. Blands Sonny Boy
               Blands Marmoset
     Eng. Ch. Belroyd Jacana
               Carabana Foxash Offenbach
          Belroyd Gaybird
               Belroyd Blackbird

Eng. Ch. Pemland Magnus (Eng. Ch. Lees Mastermind, a Such Fun son, ex a Royal Command daughter), whelped in 1982, a top sire in England and a strong force behind several American lines. Owned and bred by Stuart and Mary Magness. *Fall*

                    Eng. Ch. Penmoel Minstrel
            Eng. Ch. Penmoel Such Fun of Rivona
                Penmoel Time for Fun
      Eng. Ch. Lees Mastermind
                    Aus. Ch. Scottholme Red Ember of Lees
            Lees Radiant
                Lees Fireworks
ENG. CH. PEMLAND MAGNUS
                    Cordach Mastercopy of Hildenmanor
            Pemland Royal Command
                Pemland Court Dancer
      Pemland Royal Romance
                  Pemland Magnetic
            Hildenmanor Frederika
                Hildenmanor Set the Pace

Pemland Royal Command (Cordach Mastercopy of Hildenmanor, a Crown Prince son, ex Pemland Court Dancer, by Eng. Ch. Stormerbanks Vainglory), who sired eleven English champions. Breeders-owners: Stuart and Mary Magness. *Fall*

in England during this period were closely related. However, several kennels stayed apart from the tide. Although he was sired by Eng. Ch. Olantigh Christmas Gift, a good example is Eng. Ch. Fitzdown Dorian of Deavitte. "Derry" is owned by Mr. Simon Parsons, the noted Corgi historian, and bred by Miss Jessie Fitzwilliams, whose first champion was made up in the 1930s. To date Dorian has sired seven champions, most notably Miss Sarah Taylor's Eng. Ch. Bymil Black Nymph and her littermate, Eng. Ch. Bymil Gold Sylph. The exceptional Black Nymph won the Leslie Perrins trophy for three years in a row, earned thirty-one CCs and an all-breed Best in Show. Gold Sylph was Reserve Group at Crufts in 1986 and Top Brood Bitch in 1989, and is the dam of three champions.

Several American breeders who already were working with Hildenmanor bloodlines imported Pemland Corgis from the Magnesses to try for a similar type and quality here. Ch. Pemland Maestro, ROM, a Magnus son out of a Royal Command daughter, owned by Gene Schwartz and Sharon Hichens, was one. Put to Roughouse Standing Ovation, ROM, a Hildenmanor-Stormerbanks combination, "Bobby" sired a winning litter for Mr. and Mrs. Ijams and Sue Vahaly. In it was Ch. Roughouse Pennington Daryl. This glamorous dog was handled to perfection by Michael Scott. Together they won the PWCCA National Specialty in 1990, Best in Show at the prestigious Kennel Club of Philadelphia event that same year, and many other major awards. Daryl and Rosie (Ch. Trewyl Lyric of Pennington, ROM) passed on their excellence to their daughters Chs. Pennington Portrait and Pastel.

Eng. Ch. Fitzdown Dorian of Deavitte (Eng. Ch. Olantigh Christmas Gift ex Eng. Ch. Fitzdown Starbelle).   *Fall*

Further south, Shirley Brooks imported the Magnus son, Ch. Revelmere Bring Me Joy, ROMX. ''Tully'' goes back on his dam's side to Such Fun and Pacesetter, and therefore was useful for bitches stemming from these lines. His get include two Best in Show winners.

A Magnus son active in Colorado and bred by Miss Sally Rich-Lenthall was Ch. Magnum of Vennwoods, ROMX, who carried through his dam an additional line to Such Fun. Magnum was yet another dog imported by Elaine Erganbright to enhance her Larklain Kennels. It is a great pity he lived only six and a half years, as he was an outstanding producer both for Elaine and to outside bitches. Ch. Nebriowa Front and Center and Ch. Nebriowa Vangard Center Line, by Magnum and out of Ch. Nebriowa Stitch in Time, ROM, have done well for Tim Mathiesen and Robert Simpson on the West Coast.

Needless to say, a dog as influential as Eng. Ch. Belroyd Nut Cracker could not be ignored by breeders in the United States. Many of his get arrived upon these shores. Dr. and Mrs. Harold Small campaigned their Nut Cracker son, Am. Can. Ch. Blaizewood Hooray Henry, CDX, in the Northeast. Mrs. Shirley Hickman's Karenhurst Kennel in England has been the source of several of Nut Cracker's line. Mrs. Lynn Brooks of the Busy B's Kennels in Wisconsin, who has imported several Karenhurst dogs, brought in Ch. Karenhurst Nut-crunch, who had already sired champions in several countries. His son, Ch.

Ch. Roughouse Pennington Daryl (Ch. Pemland Maestro, ROM, ex Roughouse Standing Ovation, ROM) is pictured winning the PWCCA National Specialty in 1990 under judge Simon Parsons. Daryl is shown with his handler, Michael Scott, and Jean Scott and co-owner Blandina Ijams. *Callea*

Dylan of Karenhurst, owned by Joan Scott and Blandie Ijams, arrived in 1989, and won well at various specialties, including Best of Breed at the Canadian National in May 1991. He has lived up to expectations as a sire as well.

Another Nut Cracker son, Ch. Cinnonie Cavalier, is the sire of Ch. Triumph's Turning Heads, BOB at the 1989 PWCCA National Specialty, and grandsire of Ch. Howbout Welsh Wonder Boy, BOB at the National in 1991 and 1992.

The strength of English Pembroke Welsh Corgi bloodlines has and always will cross the Atlantic. Many breeders throughout North America continue to work with lines closely linked to Britain. There is, however, one monumental family that is at this point All-American.

YUL B'S FRIENDS AND RELATIONS

It all began in the hands of Dr. Charles C. Kruger through Am. Can. Ch. Leonine Leprechaun, ROMX, a son of Int. Ch. Corgwyn Shillelah, and the

Ch. Pennington Pastel, a Daryl daughter ex Ch. Trewhyl Lyric of Pennington, whelped December 9, 1987, has had several major wins to date, including Best in Sweepstakes at the 1988 PWCCA National and twice Best of Breed at the Mayflower Corgi Classic. She is shown winning the PWCA/Quebec Specialty with her co-owner and breeder, Sue Vahaly. The judge is Doris Mason (Revelmere). *Vahaly*

foundation stud dog at Schaferhaus Kennels. Leprechaun had been bred in England by Mrs. June Froggatt. Dr. Kruger spotted ''Peter'' at a dog show and purchased him. He was the only Corgi that Chuck Kruger, a German Shepherd Dog breeder and veterinarian, felt he had seen with the desired topline and exemplary hindquarters. Peter was bred first to Am. Can. Ch. Welcanis Constellation Faraway and produced, among other champions, Ch. Faraway The Magic Kan-D-Kid, CD, ROMX, a top winner in 1974.

Leprechaun was a somewhat leggy dog. Ch. Rryde Symphony, an Australian bitch with a deep-bodied build, suited him well. From that mating came the tri bitch Ch. Schaferhaus Danielle, ROM, winner of seven all-breed Bests in Show, two Specialties and many other honors. She stopped all ringside chatter as she floated around the ring with her breath-taking, fluid movement. What is

A Magnus son, Ch. Revelmere Bring Me Joy, ROMX, has two lines back to Such Fun. Whelped in 1985. Breeder: Doris Mason; owner: Shirley M. Brooks.

more, when bred to her grandson, Ch. Vangard Mr. Ski Bum, ROMX, himself a winner of ten Bests in Show, Danielle bore Am. Bda. Can. Mex. Int. FCI Ch. Vangard Jenelle. Jenelle's record includes twenty-one all-breed BISs (seventeen in one year) and Top Herding Dog in the nation that year.

Another Leprechaun daughter out of his granddaughter, Schaferhaus Honey N'Cream, ROM, was Ch. Clayfield Paisley, ROMX, one of the all-time Top Dams.

Three years earlier Leprechaun had been bred to Honey N'Cream to produce Am. Can. Ch. Schaferhaus Aeroglend Tupnc, ROM. At this point Dr. Kruger decided he would try an outcross mating after all the close line breeding he had been doing to set the topline and rear angulation from Peter. He selected Ch. Cappykorns Bach, ROMX, for Tupnc with spectacular results. From the first litter came Yul B, Yasmin, Yoni and Yum Yum. A repeat breeding produced Turncoat, Trifle, Tristram and Touche. In all, ten of the twelve puppies were either American and/or Canadian champions; and they bred on.

The great Am. Can. Ch. Schaferhaus Yul B of Quanda, ROMX, 1975–1986, owned and bred by Schaferhaus Kennels and Sandy and Marilyn Clarke, had a splendid record in the show ring that included twelve Bests in Show in the United States, more in Canada, many Specialty high honors, and

Ch. Magnum of Vennwoods, ROMX, by Magnus, doubles up on both Such Fun and Royal Command in the third generation of his pedigree.

Best of Breed at the PWCCA National 1978. But it is as a sire that Yul will be long remembered. He stands by far the All-time Top Producing Sire in the United States with seventy champion get.

Although he produced champions from bitches of a number of different lines, because he was an outcross himself, his greatest success was with closely linebred Schaferhaus and related bitches. And tight breeding it was! Yul daughters bred to Yul, Yul bred to his sister Trifle, nieces, cousins—it became a concentrated gene pool.

Many breeders in the Northwest and Midwest purchased Yul relatives, which became foundations of their lines. For example, Am. Can. Ch. Schaferhaus Quanda Trifle, co-owned with Helen (''Scootie'') Sherlock and Pat Parsons, produced for their Caralon Kennels Am. Can. Ch. Caralon's Q-T Sequoya, ROMX. His sire was Can. Ch. Donna's Pride of Willoan, a dog who excelled in good shoulder placement and front extension. Punkin, as Sequoya was called, was a great ball-chasing character. He proved to be prepotent for his strong movement, sturdy body and big white collar. Tragically he was lost at the age of four and a half. In his short life he sired twenty-six champions, many of whom have received top awards at Specialties over the years and have been good producers themselves.

Am. Can. Ch. Leonine Leprechaun, ROMX, whelped November 21, 1965. Breeder: Mrs. J. Froggatt; owners: Charles Kruger, D.V.M., and Robert Simpson. "Peter," a Group winner, ranks high on the listing for top producing sires in this country, with twenty-two champion get, including several multiple Best in Show winners. *Robert*

One such Sequoya daughter, out of the English bitch Anzil Bit O'Luck, was Am. Can. Ch. Caralon's Q-S Hot Wheels, ROM, who lived with her co-owner Judy Nolde. Wheels was bred to Yul B twice. The first litter gave Caralon three champions, and the second, in 1985, produced Am. Can. Ch. Horoko Caralon Dickens, ROMX, who to date has had multiple Bests in Show in Canada and the United States along with Specialty Bests of Breed and Selections of Merit. So far Dickens has twenty-seven champions to his credit.

Another Sequoya offspring, owned and bred by Larry Adams and David Guempel, was Ch. Gaylord's Bobbindobber, ROMX, who continued the looks and achievement. Bobbindobber was Best of Breed at the 1985 Potomac Specialty. A Sequoya grandson with another line to Donna's Pride of Willoan is Ch. Blujor Dickens Desert Fox, owned by Neena Van Camp.

Many other breeders have profited by strong family ties to the Schaferhaus legend. Sandy Becker's Beckridge Kennels has long been affiliated with Chuck Kruger and has a Sequoya son, Ch. Beckridge Boy George.

Judy Zimmerman Hart's Sua Mah Kennels started with Ch. Faraway The Magic Kan-D-Kid, ROMX. Marge Bennett's Ch. Vangard The Last Chance, ROMX, when bred to Yul, whelped Am. Can. Ch. Dellmoor Jelly Bean and others by doubling up on Leprechaun. Am. Can. Ch. Jareaux's Willie Waddle, HC, with twenty-five all-breed Bests in Show for his owner Sally Stewart Bishop,

Am. Can. Ch. Schaferhaus Yul B of Quanda, ROMX, whelped December 10, 1975. Breeders: G. A. and M. Clarke and Schaferhaus Kennels; owners: Schaferhaus Kennels and G. A. Clarke. Yul has twelve American Bests in Show to his credit, plus five more in Canada. He was BOB at the PWCCA and Cascade Specialties and was BOS at two other Specialties. He is the all-time top producing Pembroke Welsh Corgi sire in the United States, with an impressive number of seventy champion offspring.

Eng. Ch. Lees Orpheus
Carabana Foxash Offenbach
Foxash Bright Star
Ch. Cappykorns Bach, ROMX
How's That of Ormareon
Ch. Ormareon Grace and Favour
Raymardene Marchioness of Ormareon
AM. CAN. CH. SCHAFERHAUS YUL B OF QUANDA, ROMX
Int. Ch. Corgwyn Shillelah
Am. Can. Ch. Leonine Leprechaun, ROMX
Leonine Golden Maid
Ch. Schaferhaus Aeroglend Tupnc, ROM
Leonine Call Boy
Schaferhaus Honey N' Cream, ROM
Ch. Faraway The Magic Flame

Am. Can. Ch. Caralon's Q-T Sequoya (Can. Ch. Donna's Pride of Willoan ex Am. Can. Ch. Schaferhaus Quanda Trifle, Yul's sister) is shown with co-owner Patricia A. Parsons, D.D.S.
Booth

is the product of Yul bred to his sister Yasmin's daughter by a Leprechaun son. Floyd and Norine Houpt have founded the Pemlea Kennels with Ch. Schaferhaus Relindo's Pele by Leprechaun out of a Leprechaun daughter. Currently, Lonnie and Janice Lipoglav of the M-Candol Kennels have been going strong with Corgis by Dickens out of the fine brood, Ch. Adastar's Good Golly Ms Dolly, ROM.

Am. Can. Ch. Caralon's Q-T Hot Wheels, ROM, a Sequoya daughter, was an outstanding mover well into her Veterans years.   *Nugent*

It would be impossible to mention all who have used, benefited from and continue to breed into this major family.

The pattern of success was very clear. Inbred and linebred matings to Leprechaun, Yul and Sequoya interwove these prepotent dogs. So strong was the genetic influence they possessed, outcross matings would maintain the quality and type typical of the line. It became a vast network all across America of Corgis whose parentage was very apparent just by looking at them. Now, in the 1990s these bloodlines have been integrated and diffused with many other top-producing lines arising from different origins. They continue to breed on.

Today's breeders are much more aware of, and concerned with, sound movement in the Pembroke Welsh Corgi than at any other point in the history of the breed. Not realizing that it was not only desirable but also entirely possible for the Corgi to have the free, seemingly effortless movement associated with larger breeds, many breeders overlooked the stilted, mincing, or shuffling movement that was all too common in the breed. Now, with the quality of stock at

94

Am. Can. Ch. Horoko Caralon Dickens, ROMX (Yul B ex Hot Wheels), whelped November 26, 1985. Among other wins, he was BOB at the North Texas Specialty in 1988.

hand, coupled with generally increased understanding of correct movement as it relates to proper body structure, breeders today are in a position to establish lines from which true Corgi type, character and soundness will breed on for generations to come.

Eng. Ch. Stormerbanks Dairymaid, whelped April 21, 1948. Breeder: H. Whitworth; owner: P. Hewan. A granddaughter of both Int. Ch. Broom of Ballybentra and Eng. Ch. Teekay's Felcourt Supremacy, she was the dam of Ch. Stormerbanks Big Drum, CDX, Stormerbanks Ambrose and Stormerbanks Amanda (Stormerbanks Supersonic's dam). The son-grandson combination was successful for Miss Hewan.

```
                    Crawleycrow Banjo
            Int. Ch. Broom of Ballybentra
                    Teekay Bramble
        Churchleigh Ballybentra Cowboy
                    Eng. Ch. Bowhit Prince
            Teekay Mistress Quickly
                    Teekay Quicksilver
ENG. CH. STORMERBANKS DAIRYMAID
                    Hill Billy of Lees
            Eng. Ch. Teekay's Felcourt Supremacy
                    Floss
        Sandra of the Butts
                    Int. Ch. Rozavel Lucky Strike
            Foxy of Helpric
                    Red Vixen
```

7

Outstanding Pembroke Bitches

$\mathbf{A}$S WITH most breeds, male Pembroke Welsh Corgis reap the lion's share of show ring glory. The bitches pay the penalty for changing coats between seasons and for taking time off for maternity duties. They do not have the size or the heavy, glamorous coats of many of the breed's flashy males that make for top wins. Thus the bitches may appear less impressive to some eyes. Yet, the outstanding bitches in the breed, rather than most of the top winning males, are the ones who have gained the universal approval of Pembroke connoisseurs. Bitches such as Personality Girl, Fergwyn Frith, Red Rose, and Trewhyl Lyric of Pennington come as close to being "everybody's cup of tea" as any animal ever could.

Space does not permit coverage for every bitch that has made an important contribution to the breed. Some of the breed's best-known bitches that have obtained impressive show records and/or have proven to be important producers have been selected for presentation here.

Ch. Crawleycrow Coracle of Aimhi, ROM (Eng. Ch. Knowland Clipper ex Crawleycrow Cloverhoney), whelped August 27, 1950. This noted import finished with Group placements after three litters, all by Ch. Hollyheath Pilot of Waseeka. She was the dam of Ch. Kaydon Aimhi's Kate and was BOB at the 1955 Specialty under Miss Curties. Breeder: Mrs. Christopher Firbank; owner: Mrs. M. D. McCammon. *Shafer*

Ch. Cote de Neige Posy (Less Lancelot ex Brendon Myrtle of Cote de Neige), whelped October 8, 1950, was heavily linebred on Eng. Ch. Teekay's Felcourt Supremacy. Breeder-owner: Marjorie Butcher. Posy was the granddam of Ch. Cote de Neige Sundew, ROMX, and many other Cote de Neige champions, most notably through her daughters Petal and Garland. Posy achieved further renown as the "official greeter" at Cote de Neige Kennels. *Shafer*

Ch. Cote de Neige Penny Wise, whelped September 10, 1958. Breeder-owner: Marjorie Butcher. Dam of Best in Show winners Ch. Cote de Neige Derek and Ch. Cote de Neige Pennysaver, ROMX. Through Penny Wise and her sons descended numerous Cote de Neige champions.

Eng. Irish Ch. Zephyr of Brome
Am. Bda. Ch. Maracas Gale Force of Cleden, ROM
Maracas Helarian Gale
Ch. Cote de Neige Christmas Candy, ROMX
Ch. Cote de Neige Shadow
Ch. Cote de Neige Garland, ROM
Ch. Cote de Neige Posy
CH. COTE DE NEIGE PENNY WISE
Stormerbanks Supersabre
Ch. Stormerbanks Tristram of Cote de Neige, ROMX
Tresarden Trinket
Cote de Neige Gold Coin
Eng. Am. Can. Ch. Lees Symphony, ROMX
Ch. Kaydon's Eversridge Penny, ROM
Ch. Kaydon Aimhi's Kate

Ch. Busy B's Cherry Bark Key, ROMX, whelped January 25, 1967. Breeder-owner: Lynn Brooks. All-time top producing dam, with twenty champion offspring to her credit. Out of five litters she whelped between the ages of two and seven, there were thirty living puppies. Five puppies from one litter alone finished their titles. Others have earned advanced Obedience degrees. Her record as a pro will be difficult to surpass.

```
                    Eng. Ch. Maracas Masterpiece
          Ch. Coster of Cowfold
                    Cherryripe of Cowfold
     Ch. Larklain's Prince Charming
                    Ch. Red Envoy of Brome, CD, ROMX
          Ch. Larklain's Cinderella
                    Ch. Larklain Babeta, ROM
CH. BUSY B'S CHERRY BARK KEY, ROMX
                    Ch. Hi Ho Ranger, CD
          Corwyne Arwr of Bi Lu
                    Ch. Larklain's Illusion
     Busy B's Really Moxie, CD
                    Cormanby Cabin Boy
          Gold Star's Blondie
                    Vagabond's Gold Star
```

Eng. Ch. Evancoyd Personality Girl, whelped February 18, 1967. Breeder-owner: Beryl J. Thompson. Winner of the greatest number of bitch Challenge Certificates in the history of the breed. By the time she was retired in 1974, Personality Girl had won forty CCs. She was Pembroke Welsh Corgi of the Year in 1968, 1969 and 1973. Her son Am. Ch. Evancoyd Something Special sired Eng. Ch. Evancoyd Audacious, Pembroke Welsh Corgi of the Year in 1972.

<pre>
                    Pennywise of Wey
            Caswell Marcus
                    Eng. Ch. Caswell My Fair Lady
        Eng. Ch. Caswell Duskie Knight
                    Mynthurst Artful Dodger
            Mynthurst Duskie Princess
                    Eng. Ch. Mynthurst Carousel of Cellerhof
ENG. CH. EVANCOYD PERSONALITY GIRL
                    Eng. Ch. Maracas Masterpiece
            Eng. Ch. Crowleythorn Showman
                    Crowleythorn Snowdrift
        Evancoyd True Love
                    Evancoyd Brokencote Benedictine
            Eng. Ch. Evancoyd Cover Girl
                    Evancoyd Romance
</pre>

Am. Can. Ch. Glynea Red Rose, whelped June 16, 1969. Breeder: D. Charles Lewis; owner: Janet Robinson. The lovely "Rosie" had notable success at Specialties. Her PWCCA Specialty wins include BOB in 1972 and 1974 plus BOS in 1975 and 1977 (from the Veterans Bitch class), BOS at Lakeshore in 1977 and Potomac in 1978. Consistent winner of the Brood Bitch class with her three champion offspring by her beloved kennel mate Ch. Velour of Rowell, ROM. Her record in all-breed competition certainly would have been far greater had she been an outgoing show girl.   *Ashbey*

<pre>
                    Eng. Ch. Stormerbanks Indigo
           Eng. Ch. Stormerbanks Invader
                    Stormerbanks Flashback
        Imperial of Pendcrest
                    Pennywise of Wey
           Isolda of Pendcrest
                    Stormerbanks Ice Magic of Pendcrest
CH. GLYNEA RED ROSE
                    Stormerbanks Boniface
           Hildenmanor Bonilad
                    Hildenmanor Mermaid
        Belroyd Skylark
                    Corporal of Cowfold
           Belroyd Orange Blossom
                    Belroyd Kittiwake
</pre>

Am. Bda. Can. Mex. Int. FCI Ch. Vangard Jenelle, whelped April 19, 1977. Breeders-owners: Robert Simpson and Margaret C. Shepard. Later owned and campaigned by Dr. and Mrs. Patrick Baymiller. With her handler and good friend, Ray McGinnis, Jenelle won Best in Show at twenty-one all-breed events plus several Specialty wins. She is the runner-up all-time top winning Pembroke bitch in America.

Ludwig

```
                    Ch. Bear Acres Two for the Road, ROM
             Ch. Bear Acres Mister Snowshoes, UD, ROM
                    Ch. Cote de Neige Sweet Message
      Ch. Vangar Mister Ski Bum, ROMX
                    Ch. Stokeplain Fair Chance of Cote de Neige, ROM
             Ch. Vangards Danzon in the Dark
                    Ch. Schaferhaus Danielle, ROM
AM. BDA. CAN. MEX. INT. FCI CH. VANGARD JENELLE
                    Int. Ch. Corgwyn Shillelah
             Am. Can. Ch. Leonine Leprechaun, ROMX
                    Leonine Golden Maid
      Ch. Schaferhaus Danielle, ROM
                    Lodestar of Elsdyle
             Am. Aust. Can. Ch. Rryde Symphony, ROM
                    Rryde Lyrebird
```

Ch. Schaferhaus Danielle, whelped October 10, 1971. Breeders: C. C. Kruger and Louise Vantrease; owner: Margaret C. Shepard. Dam of top winner Ch. Vangard Jenelle. Known for her superlative movement, she lived with her handler and former co-owner, Robert Simpson.

Ch. Pegasus Lori of Pennington had a glowing Specialty record and was BOB at Lakeshore in 1978 and at the PWCCA National in 1981. Whelped October 19, 1976, she is by Can. Am. Ch. Revelmere Cordoba, ROM, ex Pegasus Lady Heather. Breeders: Mr. and Mrs. D. R. Timmins; owners: John and Sue Vahaly. *Vahaly*

Eng. Ch. Wey Blackmint (Wey Magic ex Caramel of Wey), on the right, with her son Eng. Ch. Wey Spearmint (by Eng. Ch. Sonny Boy). She was whelped September 6, 1975. Breeder-owner: Mrs. K. Butler. Blackmint quickly amassed twenty-three CCs, a BOS to BIS at an all-breed Championship show, several Working Groups and Reserve Working Groups. Pembroke of the Year and top Working Dog in England in 1977, she had a litter after winning BOB at Crufts in 1978. *Sally Anne Thompson*

Eng. Ch. Belroyd Jacana (Eng. Ch. Blands Sonny Boy ex Belroyd Gaybird), whelped May 9, 1979. Breeders-owners: Allan Taylor and Idris Jones. Winner of eighteen CCs and one Working Group, Jacana was the dam of four British champions, including Eng. Ch. Belroyd Nut Cracker. *Fall*

Eng. Ch. Bymil Black Nymph (Eng. Ch. Fitzdown Dorin of Deavitte ex Bymil Sherry Spinner), whelped December 29, 1983. She was owned and bred by Sarah Taylor. With thirty-one CCs, a Best in Show, a Reserve Best in Show and a number of Group wins, she was Pembroke Welsh Corgi of the Year from 1985 to 1987 and top winning bitch in 1988 and 1989. *Fall*

Eng. Ch. Belroyd Lovebird, whelped June 16, 1981. Breeders-owners: Allan Taylor and Idris Jones. Twice England's Pembroke Welsh Corgi of the Year, and winner of 30 CCs and twelve Working Groups, Lovebird has won the greatest number of all-breed Bests in Show for the breed in England. She was Top Bitch all breeds in 1983 and top Working Dog in 1984.

Fall

Ashbarton Merry Monarch
Eng. Ch. Penmoel Minstrel
Penmoel Sound of Music
Eng. Ch. Penmoel Such Fun of Rivona
Trewlign Eastertime of Penmoel
Penmoel Time for Fun
Penmoel Gay Princess
ENG. CH. BELROYD LOVEBIRD
Eng. Ch. Evancoyd Audacious
Stormerbanks Achilles
Eng. Ch. Stomerbanks Mame
Eng. Ch. Belroyd Firebird
Hildenmanor Red Duster
Hildenmanor Amber of Belroyd
Cordach Royal Jewel

Ch. Trewhyl Lyric of Pennington, ROM, whelped February 7, 1982. Breeders: Margie Patton and Sue K. Vahaly; owner: Shirley Brooks. "Rosie" has received the admiration of Corgi fanciers across the country with her classic type and excellent movement. She has won numerous major awards at Specialty shows topped by Best of Breed at the 1985 PWCCA National Specialty plus two all-breed Bests in Show. She was the dam of six American champions, two of which have had multiple Specialty Bests. *Vahaly*

                          Eng. Ch. Lynfarne Pacesetter
                Eng. Am. Ch. Lynfarne Poldark, ROMX
                Lynfarne Querida
        Ch. Martindale Butter Brickle, ROMX
                Ch. Olantigh Victory
            Ch. Virginia of Fox Covert, ROM
                Stormerbanks Alberta
CH. TREWHYL LYRIC OF PENNINGTON, ROM
                Eng. Ch. Lees Wennam Eagle
            Am. Can. Ch. Lees Mynah, CD, TD, ROM
                Lees Brunette
        Pennington The Little Vixen
                Ch. Cappykorns Bach, ROMX
            Ch. Pennington Chelsea Morning
                Ch. Blujor Pennington Maple Leaf

Ch. Renefield Rockhopper (Ch. Pennington Ramblin' Lad, ROM, ex Renefield Reverie) comes from a long line of major winners. Shown but thirty-two times in all-breed competition, "Geraldine" has four Bests in Show, thirteen Group firsts and six other Group placements. She has won three Specialties and gone BOS at three others, including the 1988 PWCCA National. Whelped January 4, 1986, she was bred and owned by Carol Asteris and Linda Canfield.

Ch. Nebriowa Coco Chanel (Ch. Nebriowa The Blacksmith, ROMX, ex Ch. Vangard Ambra) was bred and owned by Thomas Mathiesen and Larry Cunha. Winner of over forty Groups and eight all-breed Bests in Show. In 1987 Coco was Best of Breed at the PWCCA National Specialty and the Cascade Specialty. Coco's two champion sons between them have sired over fifty American champions. *Missy*

Am. Can. Ch. Fox Meadows Obsession, whelped November 24, 1988. Breeders-owners: Sally Stewart Bishop and John C. Wilcox. As of March 1993, "Weezie," with her handler, John Wilcox, has achieved the admirable distinction of all-time top winning Pembroke Welsh Corgi in the history of the breed, with forty-five all-breed Bests in Show. Specialty honors have been bestowed on her as well from Best in Sweepstakes as a puppy to Best of Breed in 1992. She was #1 Pembroke Welsh Corgi from 1989 through 1992. It will be quite a while before another dog comes along to challenge the record of this ultimate show girl.   *Carol*

              Am. Can. Ch. Foxash Dawn Piper of Rowell
        Ch. Martindale Drummer Boy
           Ch. Virginia of Fox Covert, ROM
    Am. Can. Ch. Nebriowa Jordache of Fox Meadow, ROMX
           Ch. Nebriowa The Blacksmith, CDX, ROMX
        Ch. Nebriowa Coco Chanel
           Ch. Vangard Ambra
AM. CAN. CH. FOX MEADOWS OBSESSION
           Ch. Cappykorns Bach, ROMX
        Am. Can. Ch. Schaferhaus Yul B of Quanda, ROMX
           Am. Can. Ch. Schaferhaus Aeroglend Tupnc, ROM
    Am. Can. Ch. Jareaux's Kayla
           Am. Can. Ch. Schaferhaus Freddy Fox
        Schaferhaus Maggie Mae
           Am. Can. Ch. Schaferhaus Yasmin of Quanda

Can. Am. Ch. Tiverton Talk of Th'Town (Can. Am. Ch. Cleden's Gale Storm ex Can. Ch. Colwyn's Copper Coin). *DNH*

Can. Am. Bda. Ch. Macksons The Young Pretender, ROM, owned and bred by Pamela Mack, shown with handler Peter Green after winning the 1968 PWCCA Specialty under Eileen Pimlott. He sired nineteen champions in Canada and the United States. *Gilbert*

Can. Am. Ch. Convista Sunsabre of Lees with Helen Timmins. *H.R. Cauldwell*

8

The Pembroke Welsh Corgi in Other Countries

ONCE PEMBROKE CORGIS began to be seen away from their Welsh farmlands, they soon attracted the attention of dog-minded folk from many parts of the globe. The little Welshmen traveled to new owners, breeders and exhibitors throughout the world, and thus became the foundation stock for major centers of Corgidom in Canada, Australia, New Zealand, South Africa and continental Europe.

No one volume could attempt to include the many details of individual dogs, contributing bloodlines and development of type necessary for a thorough, worldwide study of the Pembroke Welsh Corgi. Only the most outstanding dogs and their influence on the breed in each country can be given recognition in this chapter. Special emphasis is given to the first three countries, as the large number of Corgis found there and the splendid level of breed quality warrants it.

CANADA

It is not surprising that Miss Thelma Evans (later Mrs. Gray) of Rozavel Kennels was involved in exporting the first Pembroke Corgis to both Canada and Australia in the 1930s. Her ad in the League Handbook in 1957 states: *Exports a Specialty*. Rozavel Foxface and Rozavel Pimpernel were imported by Mr. Ralph H. M. Gardener to Sundance, Alberta, in February 1932, and were mated to produce the first Canadian litter. Two more Rozavel dogs joined Mr. Gardener's Tamarac Kennel. In 1937 fourteen additional Corgis with the Tamarac prefix were imported. From this nucleus in 1935 Mr. Gardener bred the first Canadian Pembroke champion, Ch. Tamarac Red Duke (Rozavel Red Admiral ex Rozavel Foxface). Mr. Gardener was such an avid exhibitor that he traveled in a truck on a single-lane gravel road through the Rockies with five Corgis and seven children to attend a show in British Columbia.

In 1947 Sheilah Parry (later Mrs. Sheilah Roberts) founded her Bhilwara Kennels, again with stock out of Rozavel bitches. Mrs. Roberts imported Can. Ch. Lees Moonlight of Brow (Lees Cracker ex Erica's Bertha) in 1949. This dog had a grand show career, topped by the first Best in Show in Western Canada at the Pacific Exhibition show in 1952 under Derek Rayne. A Companion Dog degree in Obedience also became part of his title.

In Eastern Canada the Upperton Kennels of Reginald Foster and Cam Baxter were founded in 1946. Can. Am. Ch. Upperton Corncob was noteworthy and sired Am. Ch. Kaydon's Happy Talk for Mrs. Duncan in New York.

Another prominent exhibitor in Ontario in the 1940s was Cmdr. Peter Hopkinson of the Uxmore prefix. His import Can. Am. Ch. Daleviz Red Ink was the first Corgi bitch in North America to win a Best in Show. The year was 1951.

In the mid 1950s Mrs. Pamela B. Mack of Quebec began showing Corgis under her Macksons prefix. Many of her dogs had splendid show careers not only in Canada but also in the United States. Of particular note are Can. Am. Ch. Macksons Golden Sceptre, Can. Am. Ch. Macksons Coronet and Can. Am. Ch. Macksons The Young Pretender. The latter did a great deal of stud work in both countries, won the PWCCA Specialty in 1968, was top winning Corgi in Canada in 1968 and 1969 as well as top Working dog in 1967 and 1968. He sired over twenty-five champions.

Several other Canadian Corgis along the way are noteworthy. Can. Am. Bda. Ch. Welcanis Adulation, bred and owned by Dr. and Mrs. George Wilkins, was the top winning Corgi in 1964, 1965 and 1967. This outstanding bitch had a number of Specialty wins as well as eight Bests in Show, including one in Bermuda.

Can. Am. Ch. Tiverton Talk of Th'Town, owned by John and Rod Heartz, had a record number of fourteen Bests in Show. She was Top Corgi in 1971 and 1973, and winner of the 1973 Purina Invitational Show of Shows for the title of Canada's Best Show Dog of the Year—1973.

Can. Am. Bda. Ch. Convista Sunsabre of Lees, owned by Mr. and Mrs. D. R. Timmins, gained three titles in ten months, was the top winning Corgi in 1974 and had multiple Best in Show wins as well as a Specialty win. Sunsabre has proven to be a successful sire of champions.

In the late 1970s Rosalie Harvie of Polruan Kennels in Ontario imported the impressive bitch Can. Ch. Stormerbanks Timer, a Pacesetter granddaughter. At three 1979 Canadian Specialities she was either Best of Breed or Best of

Opposite Sex, and she placed well at several American Specialties too. She bred on through her winning son Can. Ch. Polruan Lucifer and great producing daughter, Polruan Lovely Moment, who is behind many champions in both countries.

Another of Rosalie's imports, Am. Can. Ch. Pendogett Pimpernel of Kilvewood, by Eng. Ch. Stormerbanks Bearable, holds the record in Canada for winning four Specialties 1987–1989. He finished his American title with five-point majors. "Barney" and his sister, Can. Ch. Pendogett Pussy Willow, have produced several generations of top winning Canadian dogs.

Established in 1961, William and Joan Kennedy's Willoan Kennels has been prominent for years. Can. Ch. Donna's Pride of Willoan was an influential stud, with twenty-five champions to his credit. One import, Can. Ch. Blands Saga, by Sparkler, produced well for them in the mid 1970s. In 1978 they were fortunate to purchase Am. Can. Ch. Blands Lucky Lad from Peggy Gamble. Lad is again by Eng. Ch. Kathla's Dusky Sparkler of Blands out of Eng. Ch. Blands Lisabelle. Not only did he excel in the show ring by winning Specialties in both countries, he also has been the sire of Specialty winners. His daughter, Am. Can. Ch. Willoan's Lucky Lady, won the PWCCA Specialty in 1982 and Veterans Bitch in 1993, and will be remembered for her outstanding, flowing movement. Both dogs completed their American titles with three Specialty wins.

Lad's son, Am. Can. Ch. Stonecroft's Simply Sinful, owned and bred by Kristen L. Francis, was out of a bitch by Sparkler's littermate, and therefore heavy Blands breeding. "Max" was the number one Pembroke in Canada for

Can. Ch. Stormerbanks Timer.   *Diane Pearce*

113

Can. Am. Ch. Pendogett Pimpernel of Kilvewood, imported by Roslie Harvie.

Can. Am. Ch. Blands Lucky Lad, shown going Best of Breed at the 1981 Potomac Specialty. Judge: Margaret Downing.

Kristen Francis's Can. Am. Ch. Stonecroft's Simply Sinful.

Lad's daughter Can. Am. Ch. Willoan's Lucky Lady, shown going Best of Breed at the 1982 PWCCA National under judge Paddy Date (Rowell). *Diane Pearce*

1984, 1985 and 1986, won five Bests in Show, one Specialty, and Top Herding Dog the year the Working Group was divided to make the new Herding Group.

AUSTRALIA

Although not Rozavel dogs nor even the first Corgis to arrive, the foundation of the breed in Australia was sent to Mrs. V. Nish and her son Ian of Victoria in 1934 via Mrs. Gray. Mrs. Nish adopted the kennel prefix Benfro and started off with Titania of Sealy, who became an Australian champion. She had been imported in whelp to Eng. Ch. Rozavel Red Dragon. Titania was one of the three famous ''of Sealy'' litter sisters sired by Eng. Ch. Trier of Sealy out of Tea Rose of Sealy. Ch. Tiffany and Ch. Teresa did much in England, while Titania virtually founded the breed in Australia.

The first Corgis to come to New South Wales, Aus. Ch. Rozavel Ranger and Ch. Rozavel Pipkin, were originally imported by Mrs. Nish. Benfro Anwyl can be traced back to Pipkin and was mated to Benfro Bronelydan to produce the very promising early sire Benfro Gelert. Two well-known breeders who bought puppies from Mrs. Nish in the early days were Mrs. C. Smith, originally of Werribee, and Mrs. A. E. Bridgford of Taumac fame.

One of the first dogs bred in New South Wales was Mrs. J. M. Campbell's Aus. Ch. Picton Bronelydan, sired by Benfro Gelert. Picton Bronelydan went to the Taumac Kennels in Victoria, where he sired, among others, the sensational bitch Ch. Rrac Seren, a challenge winner at three successive New South Wales Corgi Club shows and the Sydney Royal.

During the war, English importations ceased and the breed became somewhat static. Ch. Bowhit Purser was the first to arrive once the flow resumed. Mrs. Darlington of the Radnor Kennel soon brought out Ch. Scarlett Pimpernel and Ch. Red Pavon of Elsdyle, both sired by Eng. Ch. Red Pennon of Elsdyle. Mated to a third import, the influential stud Rozavel Prime Minister, Red Pavon produced Ch. Radnor David, who did much for the breed in the late 1950s.

A great winner and four states champion, Mrs. Stevens's Aus. Ch. Scotby Sergeant Major, was a great-grandson of Red Dragon and was used at stud in Victoria, New South Wales and Queensland.

In the late 1950s Mrs. Beryl Cornwell of Aurglyn Kennels was influential to the breed in the Sydney area. Her import, Brockencote Best Man, an Eng. Ch. Maracas Masterpiece son, was a top sire and the foundation of a good line when combined with bitches descending from Knowland Clipper. Ch. Aurglyn Clipper, sired by Knowland Clipper, also figured into this line.

Perhaps the most famous Aurglyn bitch from an outstanding litter sired by Maracas Masterpiece was Ch. Aurglyn Damask Rose, owned by Mrs. Gordon McKay of Carbeth Kennels. ''Teena'' won fifty-four Challenge Certificates, including four at Royal shows, and was the dam of several champions who continued to breed on, particularly in combination with Mrs. McKay's Ch. Wiseguy of Wey.

Aus. Ch. Rrac Seren. Breeder: C. Carr; owner: Miss B. Wilhelm.

Aus. Ch. Aurglyn Damask Rose.

Aus. Ch. Fergwyn Frith (Aus. Ch. Crowleythorn Maccason ex Braxentra Quite Contrary of Camcounty).

A most successful Pembroke was Aus. Ch. Chetwyn Merthytidvill. His sparkling show record was climaxed by a Best Exhibit in Show at the 1961 Sydney Royal Easter show under American judge Percy Roberts. As a product of such greats as Aus. Ch. Lymepark Orange Fire of Gedney, Aus. Ch. Lymepark Rideacre Rose, Aus. Ch. Scarlett Pimpernel, Aus. Ch. Red Pavon of Elsdyle and Aus. Ch. Radnor David, Merthytidvill was proof that quality begets quality. Superb conditioning and handling also contributed to his stardom.

Australian Pembroke Welsh Corgis in the 1960s and early 1970s flourished. Several outstanding English imports from world-famous kennels added strength to the quality of the growing native population. Dogs descending from Masterpiece, and later Marshall, arrived. The kennels of Stormerbanks, Wey, Lees, Braxentra, Crowleythorn, Falaise, Wyeford, Hildenmanor—all impressive English prefixes—were the source of top winning and producing stock. An outstanding example, the bitch Braxentra Quite Contrary of Camcounty, bred to Aus. Ch. Crowleytorn Maccason, produced three Best in Show–winning sisters for Mrs. Barbara Ludowici. One of the three, Aus. Ch. Fergwyn Frith, won eighty-two CCs, eleven Bests in Show and eighteen Runner Up Bests in Show. Frith was considered one of the breed's most beautiful bitches.

Mrs. Ludowici has written to suggest that to the late 1970s three or four English sires dominated the breeding in Australia. Stormerbanks Boniface and Invader, Pennywise of Wey and Lees Sunsalve appeared in the pedigrees of all the prominent imports. For example, two English bitches by Eng. Ch. Hildenmanor Crown Prince, Ch. Wyeford May Princess and Braxtentra Quite Contrary of Camcounty, were Brood Bitch of the Year; and Crown Prince combines both the Boniface and Sunsalve lines.

During the years 1978 to 1992, importation of excellent dogs from the cream of the English crop continued. When combined with influential Australian lines, some super stars emerged.

Jean Johnson's Jodiwyn breeding in New South Wales, together with her two top stud dogs, Aus. Ch. Jodiwyn Beau Geste and Aus. Ch. Dawco Midnight Sparkle, have had an enormous impact on the breed. Beau Geste, by an Aus. Ch. Crocket of Wey son out of an Aus. Ch. Stormerbanks Bonaparte daughter, sired thirty champions and was a multiple Best in Show winner. He features in the pedigrees of many of the current top Corgis.

Aus. Ch. Dawco Midnight Sparkle, bred by David Dawes, is by a Beau Geste son out of Blands Glory Be. ''Sparkie'' was Corgi of the Year in 1981 and 1982, won twenty-four Bests in Show, and sired more than twenty-seven champions. When he was bred to Aus. Ch. Jodiwyn Harlequin Girl, they produced the top winning Aus. Ch. Dawco Dusty Sandman, owned by Athol and Betty Searston of the Athwin prefix, whose phenomenal career included twenty-seven Bests in Show, the 1984 Contest of Champions, Best at the prestigious Spring Fair Show in 1986 and Corgi of the Year 1983–1986.

A second Midnight Sparkle son, bred by Mrs. Johnson and owned by the Searstons, also is a top winner and producer. Aus. Ch. Jodiwyn Midnight Magic won the first Australian National Specialty in 1985, a feat two of his daughters

Aus. Ch. Jodiwyn Beau Geste, owned and bred by Mrs. J. Johnson, pictured at eleven years of age.

Aus. Ch. Dawco Midnight Sparkle, a Beau Geste son, also owned by Mrs. Johnson, bred by David Dawes.

Aus. Ch. Dawco Dusty Sandman, a Sparkle son. *Michael M. Trafford*

Aus. Ch. Jodiwyn Midnight Magic, another Sparkle son.

120

repeated at the third National in 1988 and the fifth National in 1991. He has sired twenty-eight champions to date, many of them Best in Show winners. He is the sire of Am. Ch. Athwin Magic Flute, who has done a great deal of winning in the United States.

Bob and Joan Hutton's Bojojamile line has had a string of successes. Her Aus. Ch. Jodiwyn Letisha Belle was bred to Eng. Aus. Ch. Wyeford Black Tweed. One of the daughters was then put to Aus. Ch. Rudgecombe Hayne of Rivona (a son of Eng. Ch. Penmoel Such Fun of Rivona), whom the Huttons imported in 1981. The litter included the excellent brood, Aus. Ch. Springridge Rebecca. Hayne went on to win three Specialties and sire many champions, and his grandchildren and great-grandchildren continue to win at top levels of competition.

Rebecca was mated to Aus. Ch. Jodiwyn Midnight Magic, and in her first litter produced Aus. Ch. Bojojamile Becyleigh, who won seven Specialties, three all-breed shows, the third Australian National, and Best in Group at the Sydney Royal. A repeat breeding worked just as well. Aus. Ch. Bojojamile Beckncall gained four Specialty wins and the fifth Australian National. Beckncall, and a bitch from a third mating were bred back to Hayne and his son to produce more champions. Both Becyleigh and Beckncall were bred to Aus. Ch. Dearways Herdsman (by Aus. Ch. Lees Trailblazer) with additional big winners including Aus. Ch. Bojojamile Brendaleigh. Mrs. Hutton attributes her success to the combination of Such Fun and Jodiwyn bloodlines.

The Dygae Kennels of Diane Baillie in Victoria were established in 1962 from stock bred by Rrac Kennels. Breeding on, using selected early Lees imports, she established a dominant Australian-based bitch line, strengthened by breeding to outcross sires. Di never has brought in an English dog herself, but has been free to use the "cream" of others' importations to integrate with her original lines. From Aus. Ch. Bowmore Mark Time, whose dam was Aus. Ch. Braxentra Mary Quaint, there were three Dygae champions, among them Aus. Ch. Dygae Prince Charming, sire of the fabulous Aus. Ch. Dygae Gypsy Princess.

Gypsy Princess was a top showgirl, winning the WCC of Victoria Annual Specialty four times plus an all-breed Best in Show. She was renowned for her floating movement. And as a brood bitch she was equally outstanding. She was the dam of eight champions, all Best in Show winners. From her mating to Aus. Ch. Dawco Midnight Sparkle came three giants. Aus. Ch. Dygae Super Spark was a multiple Best in Show winner, including the Melbourne Royal in 1987. Aus. NZ Ch. Dygae Super Tramp and Aus. Ch. Dygae Gold Spark each won CCs at the Australian Nationals and other top awards. Through her sons Super Tramp and Aus. Ch. Dygae Dire Straits (by Aus. NZ Ch. Belroyd Ocean Flyer) Gypsy Princess has bred on throughout Australia, New Zealand, South Africa and the United States. Her linebred grandson, Aus. Ch. Dygae Wildside, continues her influence.

Throughout the years Di Baillie's breeding program has had a close liaison with the Windyle prefix of Ray Barwick and with Vicki Scott's Scottholme

Aus. Ch. Rudgecombe Hayne of Rivona, imported by Mr. and Mrs. R. Hutton.

Aus. Ch. Bojojamile Becyleigh (Aus. Ch. Jodiwyn Midnight Magic ex Aus. Ch. Springridge Rebecca) owned and bred by the Huttons. *Michael M. Trafford*

A repeat breeding of Becyleigh produced Aus. Ch. Bojojamile Beckncall.

Michael M. Trafford

The top showgirl, Aus. Ch. Dygae Gypsy Princess, owned and bred by Diane Baillie.

Baillie

Kennels in New South Wales. Mr. Barwick has handled most of the Dygae dogs for Mrs. Baillie. Mrs. Scott's long established line stems from early imports of Lees (Pat Curties) Corgis. Later imports were from Doris Mason's Revelmere stock. Two outstanding litter sisters of the late seventies were Aus. Ch. Scottholme Roxi Glow and Aus. Ch. Scottholme Amber Glow, owned by Ray Barwick.

In 1984 Vicki Scott brought in Aus. Ch. Lees Mindreader (by Such Fun out of Lees Radiant) whose litter mate sired Eng. Ch. Pemland Magnus. Another of her imports was Aus. Ch. Belroyd Queens Heron (Pemland Royal Command ex Belroyd Kiwi, Jacana's litter mate). These two studs became influential sires in Australia.

Barbara Ludowici in New South Wales has continued her Fergwyn line with basically Stormerbanks and later Lynfarne breeding. Aust Ch. Stormerbanks Paragon and Stormerbanks Dream Girl of Lynfarne imported in whelp to Lynfarne Turmoil have bred on nicely.

Peter and Helen Thompson of Dearways fame returned from the United States via England in 1983 with five Corgis bred in the United States plus Lees Trailblazer, then a puppy. Since then Trailblazer has sired nine champions, four out of bitches by Am. Ch. Snowdonia's Black Knight. The American-bred Aus. Ch. Dearways Midnight Lace, "Flag," has had a particularly good influence as a brood bitch, and she won Best Veteran in Show five times in 1991.

Aus. NZ Ch. Dygae Super Tramp.

Baillie

Aus. Ch. Dygae Wildside. *Twigg*

Aus. Ch. Dearways Herdsman, bred by Helen Thompson; owner: Joan Watson.

In 1986, Aus. Ch. Karenhurst Nutbrown (by Nut Cracker) joined the group. His line has combined well, as in England, with bitches descending from Such Fun. Aus. Ch. Spellbound Debonair is another import. Perhaps the best known Dearways dog is Aus. Ch. Dearways Herdsman, Stud Dog of the Year in 1991, who has sired twelve champions so far and is a multiple Best in Show winner. He is owned by Joan Watson in Tasmania.

Of special interest is the use of frozen semen from several top winning California dogs thanks to the efforts of Tim Mathiesen and Ray Barwick. Four people in Victoria, Glenda Cook (Westglen), Ray Barwick, Di Baillie and Di Drayton (Dusidan) were able to import a quantity from Ch. Greenforest Ranger and Ch. Nebriowa Christian Dior, ROMX. Margaret Wilby (Kamiri) has used semen from Ch. Nebriowa Front and Center. Although some semen did not take, several promising puppies sired across the sea resulted. With the obstacles of distance and expensive, lengthy quarantine to import a dog, frozen semen seems a viable alternative to advance the breed.

To quote Di Baillie, "Hence in Australia, the stamp of English type and glamour, legacy of continuing select importations, is integrated with the style of a very workmanlike Corgi—and this soundness has become a feature of the breed in Australia."

NEW ZEALAND

In New Zealand imports also played the major role in the development of the breed. Ringbourne Owain, bred by Miss B. A. Talmondt, was the first to arrive on the South Island in 1939. Not much is known about prewar New Zealand Corgis, but in the early 1950s the flow from England brought several prominent studs. Mrs. E. M. Adamson imported a tricolor son of Int. Ch. Formakin Orangeman, Ch. Scarab from Shiel, who in turn sired several New Zealand champions for her West Country Kennels. Many Australian dogs were added to the New Zealand population. For example, Aus. Ch. Stormerbanks Bonaparte, an English import, was brought to New Zealand from Australia by Mrs. S. C. Skurr of the Oakbridge prefix.

By the mid-1950s Mr. and Mrs. M. S. Russell began receiving dogs from the Rozavel Kennel to add to their earlier imports. NZ Ch. Snowman of Wey came to Miss E. L. J. Davis's Kings Ride Kennel in the late fifties. He was followed by other notables, including the outstanding bitch, NZ Ch. Costons Consequence of Wey. NZ Ch. Corgwyn Shillelah was New Zealand's top stud dog in 1967 and 1968.

The Tintagel Kennels of breeders Mr. and Mrs. Stewart Lusk were well known in the 1960s, putting to use such imports as NZ Ch. Crusader of Cowfold. Their Ch. Tintagel Mister Tody was Corgi of the Year in 1963, 1964 and 1965. Mated to imported NZ Ch. Dronlow's Sarah Thompson, he sired Aus. NZ Ch. Tintagel Salvation Yeo, winner of at least twelve Bests in Show and Corgi of the Year in 1969.

Messrs. B. M. Giles and L. Ellis of Leea-Von fame have been active and brought out from England Int. Ch. Sealord of Wey, featured in many pedigrees. And Mr. and Mrs. Bruce Hyde of Stormwey Kennels were the proud owners of NZ Ch. Crocket of Wey, a top winner and influential stud in the 1970s.

During the 1980s, the Stormwey dogs rose to great heights. From Doris Mason came Eng. Ch. Revelmere Cock-A-Hoop, a Such Fun son. He did extremely well in New Zealand and was Top Stud Dog in 1985. One of his get, Grand Ch. Stormwey Justa Beauty, won numerous Bests in Show, the first New Zealand Champion of Champions contest, and was Top Working Dog in the South Island for two years. Several other Revelmere dogs were sent to the Hydes. NZ Ch. Stormwey Royal Romance is the product of Nut Cracker and NZ Ch. Revelmere Cock-A-Too. Another superstar, and the only other Grand Champion in New Zealand is Stormwey Supa Chance. He was sired by NZ Aus. Ch. Dygae Super Tramp out of NZ Ch. Stormwey Alicia. Included in his impressive show record are four Bests of Breed at the SIWCL Specialty shows. In 1992 he was exported to Mr. Robert Simpson's Vangard Kennels in Washington, where he quickly gained his American championship.

A thriving kennel in Christchurch is the Merthyr Corgis owned and bred by Lesley and Allan Chalmers. NZ Ch. Merthyr Midnight Rebel, a Kydor Cossack granddaughter, won the Group at the 1986 NZ Kennel Club's Centennial National Dog Show plus other honors. The kennel imported NZ Ch. Bulcorig Zola of Cordach in whelp to Nut Cracker with much success. Her son, Merthyr Desmond Tutu was named Top Stud Dog in 1988. Other important English dogs

Grand Champion in New Zealand and American champion Stormwey Supa Chance, bred by the Bruce Hydes and imported to the United States by Robert Simpson and Jill White.

Vajdik

to arrive were Eng. Ch. Belroyd Puffin (Blands Status Symbol ex Belroyd Jacana), Eng. Ch. Bulcorig Zenita (Crown Prince/Such Fun bloodlines), and NZ Ch. Cordach Chieftan (Royal Command ex Eng. Ch. Cordach Lucinda). With this lineup, no wonder Merthyr has excelled both in the ring and the whelping box.

First place at the Anwyl Kennels of Dr. Bruce and Robin Robertson of Wellington must go to NZ Aus. Ch. Anwyl Snow Dragon, CD, CDX. "James" (1972–1987) was a special dog even at birth. His sire, Eng. Aus. Ch. Wyeford Black Tweed was to go over to Australia, where he became an important stud. His dam, NZ Ch. Anwyl Enchantress, by Eng. NZ Ch. Corgwyn Shillelah, was a Best in Show winner and four times New Zealand's Leading Brood Bitch. During his twelve years in competition, James topped five Specialties, took Best of Breed at the New Zealand National Dog Show in 1978, and won over forty Challenge Certificates in two countries. He gained his CD in a matter of weeks, and his CDX three months later. James sired twenty-three champions and for eleven years was either New Zealand's Leading Sire or Runner-Up. A daughter, Aus. Ch. Anwyl Starry Night, was Leading Brood Bitch for a record five years. Mrs. Robertson writes, "He had all those things I hold to be so very important in a Corgi—substance, perfect temperament and bone within standard size, as well as balance and quality that compliment a clearly defined breed type." Besides, he had great charm.

The second star in the Anwyl galaxy is "Luke," formally known as NZ Ch. Belroyd Ocean Flyer. He was selected in Wales by the Robertsons when just a young puppy from a litter by Eng. Ch. Blands Status Symbol out of Am. Ch. Belroyd Meadowlark. He started his show career with four Best Puppy wins and became a multi-Best in Show winner. He won the first nationwide Supreme Dog Contest in 1989 in which only champions were entered. He shone at stud as well. He has been New Zealand's Leading stud from 1987 to 1991, and has fourteen champion progeny to date. From each of his first four litters came a BIS winner, and they have produced champions. One, NZ Ch. Anwyl Flight of Fancy, has been Leading Brood twice.

Luke's daughter, NZ Ch. Anwyl Tickle My Fancy, by a Welsh Corgi League Jubilee "souvenir," NZ Ch. Belroyd Stormbird, had extended the list of achievements for this outstanding kennel. She was Pembroke of the Year in 1990, and has earned twenty Challenge Certificates, four BIS with two of them at Specialties. And there are more Anwyls waiting on the horizon.

While imported English dogs feature heavily in the pedigrees of many of the top dogs, there is no doubt that the quality of the breed in Australia and New Zealand runs very high.

SOUTH AFRICA, ZIMBABWE

Taking a large leap, we find South Africa is the next center of Corgi activity. Many fine English dogs have been exported to this country and have

"James"—Aus. NZ Ch. Anwyl Snow Dragon, CDX.

formed the basis of its winning stock today. Once again, the name Rozavel crops up in the earlier imports, notably Rozavel Supersinger and Rozavel Yours Sincerely of Southwell.

Mrs. Gray was not the only one to send dogs to Africa. South African Ch. Morzine Mosaic of Wey, by Eng. Ch. Knowland Clipper, was dominant in the

129

Aus. NZ Ch. Belroyd Ocean Flyer, bred by Allan Taylor and Idris Jones. Owners: Dr. and Mrs. Robertson. *Cabal*

NZ Ch. Anwyl Tickle My Fancy, an Ocean Flyer daughter.

1950s. Such famous English prefixes as Wennam, Wey, Lees, Stormerbanks and Falaise can be found in the names of South African champions.

Int. Ch. Daleviz Copperfield of Ballyvoreen, at first in Kenya, was bought by Mr. and Mrs. C. G. A. Bowring, who established a strong line of Hillhead Corgis. Some of these dogs are behind the South African winners from the Oldlands Kennels of the American breeder, Mrs. Gordon-Creed, when she lived there. Other active kennels are Norsongula, operated by Mrs. S. Palmer; Roodedraai of Mrs. Y. Du Preez; and Stuartfield of Mr. K. W. King.

Over the years the Corgi population in Africa has dispersed and increased. Now there are active groups in the Transvaal, Zimbabwe and the Republic of South Africa, to name a few. Shirley Bloomfield's Kimfield Kennels appears to be producing winning, African-bred stock. Her Ch. Kimfield Pebbles is the double grandsire of Ch. Darlyn Crackerjack of Bondjueve, Supreme Corgi of 1989. The Darlyn Kennels of Mrs. M. R. Van Smaalen also is exhibiting typey stock. Two of the Waycliff dogs of Christine Beeby have been shown to the top at the Welsh Corgi Club of the Transvaal Championship show. Others have brought in quality animals. Mrs. Van Zyl (Pengib) imported a pretty Australian bitch, Westglen Wicked Ways, from Glenda Cook. Ch. Revelmere Phantom of Bonanza, by a Royal Command son, Eng. Ch. Forestop Royal Salute, out of a Magnus daughter, was named Zimbabwe Corgi of the Year in 1989, for his owner, Miss J. I. Way.

As before, most of the aforementioned Corgis have been English imports or first- or second-generation descendants from imported stock. However, the listing has been pieced together without a genuine, first-hand knowledge of the Pembroke Welsh Corgi in faraway Africa.

HOLLAND

By the time Corgis from England became established on the shores of nearby Holland, many breeders other than the pioneer Mrs. Gray were exporting quality animals, as it was after the war. The two Pembrokes at the Delft Championship show in 1950 were Radnor Robin Goodfellow, a son of Eng. Ch. Red Pennon of Elsdyle, and Larkwhistle Mirella, daughter of Eng. Ch. Teekay's Felcourt Supremacy. Both finished their Dutch titles. The first litter in Holland was out of Daleviz Kay imported in whelp to Eng. Ch. Woodvale Woodpigeon. The first litter bred on Dutch soil was sired by Mrs. J. M. van Ommen Kloeke's Ch. Radnor Robin Goodfellow and whelped on the last day of 1951.

Four years later Felcourt Choirboy, the son of Eng. Ch. Knowland Clipper out of a Rozavel Lucky Strike daughter, topped an entry of twenty-one Pembrokes in Rotterdam. Later, as a champion, he continued to contribute to the progress of the breed, siring such notables as Dutch Ch. Cadnoaidd Cadno.

Another dog used extensively at stud was Ch. Shucks of Bablake, an Eng. Ch. Zephyr of Brome son. He went on to sire Int. Ch. Flame's Gwendolyn van

'T Hooyvelt. Mrs. C. M. de Weerd-Schippers's Int. Ch. Lees Berry did well. A top winner in the 1970s, Dutch and Int. Ch. Beau of Humdinger, owned and bred by Merv. A. v.d. Burg-Buitendarp, was a combination of Helarian and Wey bloodlines.

The Sheerin prefix of Mrs. Lans v.d. Meer continues to be a force in Holland, as she has been breeding Pembrokes for many generations. Floatin', the kennel of H. M. van Voorthuysen-Dykhuis, has used the import Dutch Belg. Int. Ch. Lees Another Arrow to success. As before, English dogs continue to be imported.

Currently the future of the breed in Holland is in jeopardy due to legislation that prohibits linebreeding and inbreeding (however it is defined), and makes it illegal to either exhibit or own a dog of any breed with a docked tail.

SWEDEN

An early Swedish Corgi in the 1930s was Bucklers Megan, sired by Crymmch President, and mated to imported Rozavel Tuck and for a later litter to Wolfox Walker. In 1945 an Eng. Ch. Teekay's Felcourt Supremacy son, Teekay Mannikin, was imported. He never gained his title but sired three Swedish champions to Megan daughters. Nonetheless, Corgis were rare until 1953–54, when twelve arrived from leading English kennels.

The first really top sire was Int. Nordic Ch. Crawleycrow Prank (Int. Ch. Crawleycrow Bannow Master Broom ex Crawleycrow Perky), owned by Per-Erik Wallin. Prank lived to the age of seventeen and did much to benefit the breed. He sired the first Corgi to win a Best in Show at an all-breed event, not an International show, Int. Nordic Ch. Benedicts Belinda.

The top winning Pembroke of all time in Sweden is Int. Nordic Ch. Ryttarens Narcissos (Butterybar of Braxentra ex Ch. Gerona's Killarney Rose), again owned by Per-Erik Wallin. He was the Corgi Club's Corgi of the Year in 1972, 1973, 1974 and 1976, and sire of the top Corgi, Swed. Finn. Norw. Ch. Red Sheila, in 1977. Narcissos was the first Corgi to win Best in Show at an International show, which he did twice, once in Sweden and then in Finland. He has won the Corgi Club show twice as well. He continued to influence the breed well into the 1980s.

An outstanding bitch and top-producing dam, Int. Nordic Ch. Moonrocks Binette, is a direct descendant of Bucklers Megan. Binette's sire, Ch. Ryttarens Iller, was sired by Eng. Ch. Zephyr of Brome, and her bloodlines in combination with Narcissos have come up with constant winners.

The superstar of the 1980s unquestionably was Int. Swed. Nord. Finnish Ch. Olantigh Wayfarer, who was Swedish Corgi of the Year for seven years straight. He was bred by Mrs. Wynn Lepper in England and owned by Hans Dagerteg and Ove Germundsson. Mr. Dagerteg's newest dog, Swed. Ch. Karenhurst Chikor (a Nut Cracker grandson), has won the honor for the last three years.

Int. Nordic Ch. Crawleycrow Prank.

Int. Nordic Ch. Ryttarens Narcissos. *Lasse Rudberg*

133

Int. Nordic Ch. Olantigh Wayfarer.

NORWAY

Corgis were slower to penetrate Norway to the west, not arriving until about 1950 from England for Mrs. E. Galtung. She and Mrs. Anspach were the only breeders until 1967. This year marked the arrival of Mr. Knut S. Wilberg's Nord. Swed. Ch. Yorken Gallant Knight (Blands Duskie Knight ex Yorken Ramona of Kathla). His impressive wins include the Norwegian Kennel Klub's highest award for the top winning dog of any breed at the Kennel Klub's Championship shows in 1968. At a time when there were only seven championship shows a year, he earned three Bests in Show and five Group firsts. As a sire he produced twelve champions and many other CC winners.

The first Corgi in Norway to become an International Champion was Nordic Ch. Siggen's Dusky Queen (Wennam Sea King ex Norw. Swed. Ch. Yorken Dusky Mandy of Kathla), owned by Mrs. L. Wilberg. As a top dam, six of her ten puppies became champions. Her most famous daughter is Mr. L. H. Wilberg's Int. Nordic Ch. Siggen's Treasure, top winning Corgi in 1974 and 1975.

Treasure, herself, was the dam of two winners of Corgi of the Year in 1976 and in 1977, sired by different studs.

Siggens dogs continued to be named Corgi of the Year by the Norwegian Welsh Corgi Klubb for more than a decade. Of particular note are Int. Nord. Ch. Siggens Hi-Fi, Dog of the Year all breeds in 1983, and his dam, Nor. Ch. Siggens Anke, whose sire, Int. Nord. Swed. Fin. Ch. Meljac Brandy Snap, was imported from England. Hi-Fi went to England for a time and there won two CCs and four reserve CCs. Int. Nord. Ch. Blands Gamblin' Man, owned by the Wilbergs, was Corgi of the Year in 1986, and his son, Nord. Swed. Ch. Siggen Vanco, won the honor three years in a row. In fact, so powerful is the Siggens Kennels that in fourteen years, one of their dogs or get from one of their dogs was Norwegian Corgi of the year eleven times.

The other main kennel in Norway is that of Mrs. Grete Hedne, Borgatun. Two of her dogs, Nord. Ch. Borgatun's Urchin and Nord. Swed. Ch. Borgatun's Kristel, have been named Corgi of the Year.

On January 1, 1989, a docking ban was instated in Sweden and Norway. Several long-tailed champions have been made up already. It is reported that the general pet-owning public is happy enough to have their dogs with something longer to wag. However, serious breeders have banded together to try to recoup the natural bobtail so prevalent in the early days of the breed in Wales. To that end Mrs. Hedne imported Nord. Ch. Jofren Nabob, a bobtail, from Mrs. Hopwood in England. He goes back on his dam's side to Am. Ch. Stormerbanks Paddy Bear, who has sired an occasional bobtail in the United States, although he was not a bobtail himself. Nabob is the sire of Borgatun's Urchin, a bobtail. Mr. Wilberg reports that within a few years of careful breeding, about 65 percent of all the puppies born in Norway now carry the bobtail gene and are free from defects. In 1992 both the Corgi of the Year, Nord. Swed. Ch. Siggen's Conny, and Best of Opposite Sex, Nord. Ch. Siggen's Ernst Ludvig, were bobtails. Conny was one of the top ten dogs all breeds, proving that quality can be kept while breeding for bobtails.

Norw. Swed. Ch. Yorken Gallant Knight.   *Brenna*

Int. Nordic Ch. Siggens Hi-Fi.

Int. Nordic Ch. Siggens Vanco.

Per Unden

136

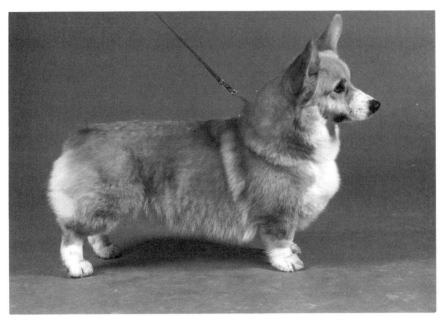

Nordic Swed. Ch. Siggen's Conny, a natural bobtail.

FINLAND

The Finnish Corgi Club was founded in 1971, with the first dogs being imported in the 1960s. Since that time the club has grown to about 800 members, with 400 Pembrokes registered in 1992. An early standout was Int. Nord. Ch. Vincos Apus, twice Corgi of the Year, who was all English breeding except for his dam. Another top winner was Int. Nord. Ch. Hildenmanor Annline Copy imported by Anneli Sutela in 1979. Not only was he twice Corgi of the Year, some of his twelve champion get have repeated this honor and bred on as well. One of his litters in Denmark, out of Danviking's Dagmar, produced three champions, including Int. Dan. Fin. Ch. Remu, Corgi of the Year 1990–1992, for Tuula-Maija Tammelin (Tuulantei Kennels).

Mrs. Raija Laakso's Natural Kennels has been another force in Finland. Her bitch, Int. Nord. Ch. Natural av Nino-Heide, was Pembroke of the Year in 1978, and bred to Int. Nord. Ch. Ryttarens Narcissos, produced the record-breaking sire, Int. Nord. Ch. Natural Partisan. He fathered champions for Mrs. M. L. Kouvola (Finnheeler) and Mrs. Helmi Hartonen (Zo-Fo), two other leading breeders in this country.

Within the Scandinavian region the Pembroke Welsh Corgi is thriving in the 1990s.

Int. Nordic Ch. Hildenmanor Annline Copy, imported to Finland by Anneli Sutela.

OTHER COUNTRIES

Other countries have had excellent Corgis of which to be proud, as the breed has found its way into Belgium, France, Italy, Switzerland, Austria, Germany, Poland, and Czechoslovakia, among others. Corgis also reside in India, Zambia, Kenya and East Africa. South America and Mexico claim Corgi greats as well. In Ireland, Corgis have been quality bred, exhibited and comingled with English dogs since the early days.

For the most part, the Pembroke Welsh Corgi has become established in the various countries with stock imported from England. Mexico is a notable exception, for its Corgi population, while admittedly small, consists mainly of dogs coming from the United States. American Pembrokes owned and exhibited by Dr. Herbert Talmadge became the first Mexican champions of the breed, when Dr. Talmadge took his Ch. Toelmag's Tommy Lad and Toelmag Telmie on a Mexican show circuit in 1958.

9

The Pembroke Welsh Corgi—a Working Dog

THE CORGI'S REPUTATION as a working dog was established clearly from the start. The Welsh farmer found he had a superb cattle dog, ratter, guardian and clever companion all in one. The Corgi's characteristic intelligence, determination and agility served him well as he performed a variety of tasks around the homestead.

THE CORGI AS A FARM DOG

It is the Corgi's ability as a herder that we look first. Many are the amazing tales of this little dog's effectiveness with cattle. Many are the skeptics won over to hearty respect for his abilities.

Most Pembroke Welsh Corgis seem to be born with a special sense about working with other animals. Miss Eve Forsyth-Forrest, in her charming book, *Welsh Corgis* (edited by S. M. Lampson, A. S. Barnes & Co., New York), says:

> Corgis who like working with cattle and ponies have a great gift of getting the confidence of other animals. They are quick to realize where one wants or does not want the herd or an individual beast, and their way of collection or removal is by the nose-and-heel method. When herding they single out the leader and appear to have a little conversation on the desirability of obeying instructions. Usually the horse or cow puts its head down and follows, and any insurrections in the rank and

Ch. Shonleh Song and Dance Man moves in on a straggler. *Callea*

file calls forth more persuasive conversation, a great deal of threats and an occasional nip at the heels.

Under more demanding circumstances it is the Corgi's low, agile build, ever-alert mind and indefatigable spirit that are called to the fore. According to John Holmes, famous in the field of working breeds, in his article "All in the

Day's Work," *1955 Welsh Corgi League Handbook*, the Corgi's small size is an advantage in several ways: "First of all, by keeping up close to the heels the cattle kick over him, and so long as he keeps his head down, he does not seem to have to duck at all."

Too, the Corgi's lowness puts him in the correct position to grab the tender part of the heels rather than the more dangerous hind tendon higher up the leg. And finally:

> Their small size also makes them more difficult to see, which means that the cattle have something, they know not quite what, which they can only hear and feel tearing around their heels, here, there and everywhere. As a result they have much more respect for the Corgi than for the enemy they can see.

Exaggerated lowness and heaviness can be a disadvantage, though, as all-important agility is lost, and the stamina to last the full day in the field is diminished. Holmes says, ". . . The real working-type Corgi had speed quite out of proportion to his size and build."

Above all, Mr. Holmes stresses an agile mind is essential, for ". . . if the cattle dog does not keep his wits about him every minute and every second, he is liable to collect a hoof in the ribs or on the side of the head." Yet a good working dog must know how to sneak in a moment of relaxation and rest.

He goes on to state, "Combined with agility of mind must be levelheadedness, otherwise the dog is sure to get over-excited and land in trouble."

With mind and body in order, the Corgi adds an extra portion of courage and determination. Once again we quote Mr. Holmes, with his description of a Corgi escorting a drove of wily, somewhat frightened steers or heifers down a country road to market:

> For that sort of work one needs a dog with what is known as "plenty of force" to keep the cattle moving . . . There is nothing "wide run" or "stylish" in the Corgi's work. He stays right in amongst their heels, and in deep mud such as forcing through gateways, he sometimes seems to be lost altogether. Another point is that he does not stick to one beast and let all the others scatter. He tears round from heel to heel, biting and barking, never relaxing for a second, thereby preventing the cattle from collecting their wits until they are where they are wanted—through the gate, past the traffic or whatever it happens to be. Of course, if one turns its head and charges, he does not "heel" that, he "moves" it.

Here in the United States today the Corgi is not likely to be called upon to offer his skills as a drover. There are, nonetheless, a few farmers or ranchers who still work or have recently worked their dogs actively with cattle. Miss Virginia Farr and Miss Vivien Jeffery of the V2 Ranch in Templeton, California, turned to raising purebred Hereford cattle after a career as flyers in World War II's "Bombers to England delivery program." They acquired two Corgi puppies as working dogs in 1959. Many of the prize-winning dogs shown under their Pen-y-Bont prefix added their special version of help around the ranch.

Mrs. Lynn Brooks and her husband raised Black Angus beef cattle on their

Busy B's Ranch in Wisconsin. Three to six Corgis at a time were used as a team to work the cattle, which as a breed are known to be highly excitable animals. She describes their style of working in the March 1974 *Pembroke Welsh Corgi Newsletter*:

> If we want a particular animal or animals put somewhere, the dogs when sent will usually rush the cow or cows to get them moving. Then they circle at a run and with what seems like wild, uncontrolled foolishness drive the cow where it's supposed to go. Often one or the other of the dogs will lead the cattle, cavorting and teasing, which entices the lead cow to chase it. Often cows with calves or the bulls will get in a fence corner or against a building and turn to face the dogs, lower its head and refuse to move. This is about the only time the Corgis do bite and then they will occasionally draw blood.
>
> As for ducking flat, I have yet to see one do it. Animals do not kick that high and they are fairly accurate in hitting what they kick at. I'm sure a dog that practiced this method would be in a constant state of injury. Our dogs depend on their quickness and agility to keep out of flying hooves' way. They dash and dart around, always on the move and always barking. They are absolutely fearless, taking on the biggest bull, if asked.

Mrs. Brooks reports a few drawbacks she has experienced with her dogs, however. Heavy coats lovely in the show ring become a hazard in the mud. Not all dogs are endowed with an equal herding instinct, a trait which usually can be determined by three months of age, and join the others only to heckle. And a few get carried away with their zeal, going so far as to take delight in stuffing too many cows in one barn.

Corgis do not limit their herding activities to large hoofed creatures. Although reportedly less reliable with skittish sheep, several farm Corgis in various parts of the world have coped admirably. Today, with the AKC herding program, sheep rather than cattle are the animals selected for training and trials.

Mrs. Brooks bought her first Corgi from a breeder who used them to herd pigs, not cattle. This skill is not uncommon; as John Holmes wrote, ". . . they are said to be the only dogs for which a pig has any respect at all." They have even been known to herd llamas.

Often a young Corgi will turn his attention first to herding poultry of various sorts. Ducks, geese, turkeys and chickens all have been sorted out and moved here and there in perfect safety. Sometimes a dog will be a boon in fetching eggs as well.

The versatile Corgi has other useful tricks in his bag. Right from the start he has earned praise as an indomitable ratter. The Welsh farmers could count upon him to control vermin with a short pounce, lethal nip and rapid shake. Some barns today are equally blessed; and even a suburban backyard offers opportunity to a proficient moler. Farm stock and well-bred show dogs alike have shared this occupation with great success. Back in the 1950s Miss E. Boyt's prize-winning Larkwhistle Golden Vanity and her dam proved themselves handy one afternoon by dispatching fifty-six rats flushed out by the threshing.

Even more impressive is the feat described in a letter from Mrs. Thelma Gray appearing in the April 1952 *Pure-Bred Dogs—American Kennel Gazette*. It tells of Eng. Ch. Rozavel Golden Corn:

> It will amuse you to know that since we started to farm, Golden Corn has become a super farm dog. She fetches all the cows daily as if she had done it all her life, and is so crazy to do so we can't keep her in; she scales a five and six foot wall to get out when she knows milking time is near. When we were threshing out a few ricks of corn she killed over 200 rats and mice, and was so worn out at the end of the day that she quite literally couldn't stand, but by 8 A.M. next morning was chewing at her kennel door to get out and be on the job again. Nothing remarkable in this, of course, excepting that for a bitch that has lived in a kennel and show life until eight years of age, to take to farming in such a big way, is a tribute to the inborn abilities of the breed and a sock in the jaw for the people who say that show dogs have no brains. She is still one of the leading Chs. with her eight Challenge Certificates.

THE CORGI AS A GUARD DOG

Another plus for a Corgi earning his keep is as a guardian of the home. Provided with a rural life, he uses his extremely keen sense of hearing and his vigilance to protect not only his owner but also the livestock on the farm. He repels thieves and prowlers of both the two-and four-legged kind. Even in an urban environment a low growl or the tone of his bark clearly indicates something is amiss. Foolhardy is the marauder who does not heed this warning. A letter from a Mrs. Branson, of Ravenna, Ohio, published in the January 1954 *Gazette*, reports the effectiveness of Dugoed Queen:

> It was about an hour after the family had retired, when Queen awakened them with her restless short, sharp barking—she would not be hushed. A series of burglaries had nervous citizens bolting and barring their doors securely at night. With this in mind, my brother-in-law decided to investigate. Queen became extremely agitated as he came down, ran to the door scratching furiously; convinced that something was seriously amiss, he first called the police and then flicked the switch to the yard lights, opened the door, and away went Queen.
>
> Within a moment or so, he heard loud angry shouts, deep furious growls of anger from Queen. Stepping outside, the sight that greeted him was almost unbelievable. One prowler, so frightened by the little Corgi, had run blind, and unthinking into a tree, and was lying unconscious beneath it, the second was firmly held by the pants leg—an infuriated Queen determined never to let go.
>
> The police arrived, and the prowlers were taken off to jail. Now the citizens of this small Wisconsin town sleep at peace these nights always with a thought of the brave little Corgi that had accomplished so much.

In line with his role as a guardian, the watchful Corgi sits beneath the baby carriage, minds the toddlers, turns tears to smiles, and even separates sibling squabbles. It is no chore, of course, to tidy up the spills and rejects from the children's plates.

Sinbad of Wey, TDX, UD, CDX, with his owner, Kenneth Butler, after a successful day in the field.

The list of small services, taught or self-assumed, that Corgis all over the world perform is lengthy. Whether or not these efforts can be classified as work is questionable, for Corgis obviously derive much pleasure in their execution. Bringing in the paper, fetching the slippers, even supplying "the boss" with filched tomatoes from the neighbor's yard—there is room for endless and amusing variation from the Corgi's fertile mind.

THE CORGI AS A GUN DOG

As a jack-of-all-trades many a Corgi steps over into the realm of the Sporting breeds. Major Branson, in the 1959 *Gazette* column, recommends:

> For the sportsman who is looking for a dog that is useful, as well as ornamental, the very talented Corgi is a happy solution. He is a natural hunter of game and birds found throughout the United States. His keen ear, remarkable sense of smell, interest in the game and strong aptitude for obedience all combine to make the Pembroke an outstanding partridge and pheasant hunter. These characteristics have made Ch. Tobbe Petworth one of the outstanding pheasant hunting dogs in recent years. His ability to trail, locate and recover is unexcelled in the field.

Others have found the Corgi to be a suitable hunting companion. Mr. Kenneth Butler's Sinbad of Wey was well known in hunting circles. Brigadier

Brown's Falaise Fanfare, as described in Miss Forsyth-Forrest's book noted earlier, was trained and at nine months of age took in his first day of hunting, soon found the fallen birds without direction, had a gentle mouth, retrieved equally well from the water, and gained the respect of other hunters in spite of his unorthodox appearance for a gun dog.

Corgis with very little training will work in the thickest cover and retrieve with speed. The short, thick coat is a boon in this regard.

THE CORGI AND SCHUTZHUND WORK

In 1975 a new element was added to the Corgi's list of achievements. In April of that year Schulhaus Billy The Kid, CDX, TD, SchH II, became the first Corgi in the world to earn a degree in the sport of Schutzhund training. Billy went on two years later to gain his Schutzhund II degree. He was owned and trained by Margery Malseed of Olympia, Washington, under the direction of the Puget Sound Schutzhund Association.

Schutzhund training basically is threefold, specifically tracking, obedience and protection. The rules are stringent. The obedience section features such tests as retrieving over a forty-inch jump, heeling through a milling group of people and steadiness under gunfire. As there are no exceptions made for short-

Schulhaus Billy The Kid, CDX, TD, SchH II, performs a protection exercise in the Shutzhund training routine.

leggedness, Billy had to forfeit twenty points because he had to omit the sixty-four-inch scaling wall, and he touches the forty-inch hurdle, which he bounces over from a dead stop. The rest of his work had to be exemplary for him to pass.

It was in the protection section that Billy accomplished something new for the breed. In spite of his size and the skepticism of several Schutzhund fans used to working with more conventional guard dogs, Billy learned exercises involving locating and guarding a suspect, attack on command and defense of his handler who is under attack. The illustrations of Billy at work leave no doubt that a Corgi can be formidable. It certainly is one more example of the old adage, "A Corgi is a big dog in a small package."

HEARING EARS

While a bit short of leg to be satisfactory as a guiding eye dog, the alert Corgi is just the ticket as an aid to a person with impaired hearing. In several areas of the country Hearing Ear Dog organizations are training Corgis to function as a deaf owner's companionable alarm system.

One such accomplished Corgi is Tika, bred by Jane Rainsford and Leslie LaChance of Avalon Kennels near Boston. Her bright, inquisitive nature and dedicated, attentive attitude indicated she was a promising candidate for this work. After six months of intensive training at the Red Acre Hearing Dog Farm in Stowe, Massachusetts, Tika was teamed up with Mrs. Joan Rizzo, an active businesswoman in New York City with a weekend home in the country. Tika has been taught to touch/signal Joan and direct her to a ringing phone or door bell, for example, then wait in a down stay position until Joan releases her. She is comforting assurance the fire alarm will never be unobserved. And of course, Tika provides her own lick and bounce version of a wake-up call once the clock's bell has rung.

Joan and Tika travel everywhere throughout the city in taxis, on the subway and to restaurants, where Tika wears a bright orange vest and leash as a symbol of her status as a certified Hearing Ear Dog. Joan has been instrumental in the effort to establish the same rights for Hearing Ear Dogs as are afforded to guide dogs for the blind.

In many parts of the country Corgis have brought cheer to hospitalized patients young and old through the auspices of two national organizations, Therapy Dogs International and The Delta Society. These canine social workers must be certified and trained in order to be welcome in the institutions where their owners take them. Many are the heartwarming stories of smiles, gestures and voices evoked from previously unresponsive patients. A friendly, furry greeting is healing indeed.

Tika alerts her deaf owner, Joan Rizzo, to the sound of the doorbell.

The soft life . . .

. . . and the hard.

10

The Pembroke Welsh Corgi—a Companion

THE STANDARD for the breed describes a Corgi as "Outlook bold, but kindly. Expression intelligent and interested. Never shy nor vicious." This nutshell version of Corgi personality cries out for elaboration when the dog's whole entity is being considered—not just his conformation.

To begin with, the Corgi is an energetic dog, full of life, quick in movement and mind—a lover of activity. Yet, while a Corgi is always ready for the task at hand or a rollicking game with a friend, human or otherwise, he does not indulge in tiresome perpetual motion. Rather he is happy to enjoy as well quiet moments of companionship.

The Corgi's quick intelligence expresses itself in many ways. Just to look at a Corgi's face is to sense his bright mind. Curiosity, a component of intelligence, coupled with persistence, will lead a Corgi to explore and discover new meanings and solutions. An object when first confronted will be evaluated with an inquisitive nose, tactile whiskers and searching paw. Of course, there are variations in the minds of individuals and in their reactions to something new. One clever bitch coming upon a temporary barrier to protect wet paint pushed by it quite obviously thinking, "Humph! What is this for?" Others in the family inspected the barrier but sensibly realized it was to serve some purpose and pressed no further.

Whether they are house dogs or kennel dogs, Corgis love a routine. A friend's story about her first Corgi, Casey, not only illustrates what creatures of habit we and our Corgis can be, but it also demonstrates how unbelievably observant the Corgi is. It was this friend's custom to watch one particular soap opera on television every day and then call another friend to discuss the events of the day's program. Casey, upon hearing the start of the commercial at the end of the program and before his owner had moved from her chair, would dash to the phone and bark in anticipation of the inevitable phone call he knew would be made to the friend.

Corgis eavesdrop on phone conversations as well. The dogs here are up and stirring the instant they hear the "Well, I have to" without even waiting for the "go now" which means the end of a long call and signifies a possible trip outside for them.

The typical Corgi takes a particular pride in knowing, practically before you do, exactly what your next move will be. Small actions you may not even be aware of tip the dog off as to your plans. For instance, there is the Corgi who would run to the front door and bark because he knew his mistress was going out and chances were good he would get to go with her. It took the dog's owner a long time to figure out how the Corgi knew when she was ready to leave, but she finally discovered that the dog was responding to the click of her lipstick case as it was being closed. And sure enough, the last thing she always did before going out was to put on her makeup.

A Willets puppy shows that inquisitiveness begins at an early age.

A Corgi's curiosity is never-ending.

Dinner time here is a time of high voltage excitement, as the Corgis can barely stand to wait for the food to be served once it has been prepared. One would hardly think that in the fervor of the moment a dog would ever notice whether he was given his food from the left or right hand. Corgis are aware of every little detail, though, and one dog here will balk at eating from a dish put down with the left hand. He knows his daughter eats at his left side, therefore it is her dinner, not his. Pick the same dish up and put it down with the right hand, and the dog will dive in without a moment's hesitation.

Miss Caldwell writes in the *1955 Welsh Corgi League Handbook* of another observant Corgi:

> A well-loved bitch of an earlier generation used to enjoy showing off to visitors. She would strum on the piano keys, delighted with the inevitable applause rolling her eyes round and laughing with her audience. She was a great *poseuse*, and everybody spoilt her. This dog was the only one I have known who could really see a picture or photograph. She showed special interest in pictures of dogs, and was indifferent to those of people or scenery. She was tested many times. We tried out our other Corgis, but it never worked; they only sniffed politely at what was to them merely a piece of paper.

The ability to learn easily is another Corgi trait. However, there is a difference between learning and training. John Holmes of Formakin fame comments:

> So far as the Corgi is concerned, I cannot put it very high on the list of those easy to train. Of the breeds capable of being trained to do almost anything and do it well I put it right up near the top. My experience has been that it is easily trained dogs who are often stupid dogs who do what they are told because they are too dim to think of anything else.
>
> The Corgi is far from stupid. Although it is biddable, a working dog must be self reliant and able to think for himself in an emergency.

Corgis can let self reliance play into the tendency to be independent. They are not above being too busy to heed a command—at least not the first command. Although vagrancy is not usually a problem, some easily become engrossed in their own pursuits just a bit beyond the perimeter that is allowed. The best control is to guard against relegating a Corgi to a boring existence that drives him to find activity elsewhere.

Speaking of boredom, when training a Corgi it is important to maintain a brisk, variable schedule of exercises. Endless drill quickly bores and brings out a strong streak of balkiness. Along with an independence of spirit goes an independence of mind. That equates with stubbornness when handled inadroitly.

Most Corgis have a great sense of humor. Many games are devised for self-amusement when things get a bit dull. And when frolicsome ways elicit a laugh, the trick is repeated. Anyone who has lived with a Corgi can tell of many individual versions of mirth—eyes laughing, paws waving, rolling and woofing, dashing and darting. Playfulness prevails. Two Corgis carry out boisterous games

"Get it!"

"I got it!"

of tag, ambush, tug and tussle. Fun loving and fun giving, that is a Corgi! Humor stems from a bright mind.

Swimming is popular too. It begins with sloshing and pawing in the water dish and leads to summer dips in any available puddle or stream. For the lucky Corgi it is great sport to circle around the head of one's owner who has been herded purposely into the lake, or to attempt to pursue the water skiers.

This sense of fun can spill over into teasing and heckling. According to Mrs. Lynn Brooks, one of the reasons her dogs are good herders is that they tease the cattle and thereby move them. One scamp overdid, though, and decided ". . . to keep the feeder calves away from the feeder. She'll guard it for hours if she's not reprimanded. She does this with the horses and their water tank, also."

All this cleverness can have its disadvantages, and a Corgi's energy, like any energy can become disruptive if it is misdirected. Mrs. Beryl Morgan writes of Corgi naughtiness in her article "Corgi Traits" in the *1946 Welsh Corgi League Handbook*:

> Some Corgis develop an annoying habit of nipping ankles and I understand this is the working instinct coming out. Not being a cow myself I fail to appreciate it and think it a habit to be checked at once. I find some of them also get the trick of "minding" things. This is excellent if kept within bounds. Once when I had given a seven-months puppy a dose of medicine, I carelessly left the bottle in the kennel. In the morning I found him sitting in the corner growling quietly and couldn't understand what the trouble was about. He was "minding" his medicine, and as soon as I picked up the bottle, which he allowed me to do without demur, he came out of his kennel and seemed glad to be relieved of his self-appointed task.
>
> I don't think any dog without plenty of intelligence and reasoning power would respond to obedience training in the way the Corgi does, and in my opinion six weeks is not too young to begin teaching a puppy manners. Corgis are definitely not one of the breeds that can bring themselves up. To get the best out of them they must have a master. Once they understand they cannot do exactly what they like, they take pleasure in obliging, even sometimes forestalling their owners' demands, and quite often even a look is enough. But if not checked as youngsters they are likely to turn into bossy little dogs that will rule a whole household with a rod of iron.

Mrs. Morgan continues:

> This hard streak in them is what appeals to me personally. I could never like an animal without the brain to discriminate between the things he may and may not do, and I so admire that look in his eye when sometimes he just wonders if you still remember you said "he must NEVER . . ." whatever it is, and then the sedate way he semi-apologizes.
>
> Some people call the breed noisy, but I have never found them so. Good house dogs, yes, but when properly disciplined they never indulge in that aimless yapping which is so infuriating.

Miss Patsy Hewan, of Stormerbanks fame, supports Mrs. Morgan's assessment of Corgi temperament when she writes in the *1949 Welsh Corgi League Handbook* the following:

Although a Corgi is a sensitive dog, and can be ruined with ill-treatment, he is also extremely intelligent and determined, and will do his best to get the better of you, so you must be firm, and sometimes even strict with him if you are to get good results from your labours. Always make him realize that you are the master, and he will respect you ever afterwards.

An adaptable dog, the Corgi will accept kennel life with all the eagerness and energy typical of the breed. If bored, he will find his amusement fence running, hurling insults at a kennel mate in another run, or in the creative pastimes of making a mud hole of his water bucket (and a mud ball of himself) or playing barber. A barber in the kennel busies himself by neatly chewing off the lovely show coats of his kennelmates.

Unless he has plenty of freedom outside the kennel to develop both mentally and emotionally, the kenneled Corgi remains just a dog, whereas there seems to be no limit to the depth of the personality and character of a Corgi lucky enough to have at least one human companion to live with and look after. The much-loved Corgi becomes almost human, but without the human foibles that make the friendship somewhat less than perfect.

11

The Pembroke Welsh Corgi in Obedience and Other Performance Activities

CORGIS AIM TO PLEASE and like to be doing something. With active, intelligent minds they quickly learn and eagerly approach a job that brings them praise. They work cheerfully at the designated task, relishing success as much as their owners do. Their trainability has attracted obedience fans to the breed, and some splendid performers have emerged.

THE RIGHT APPROACH

Whether being trained for a specific job or for the formal exercises required in Obedience Trial competition, a Corgi should be handled with clear, consistent commands, gentle firmness and lavish praise. The heavy corrections often used on some larger working breeds or inattentive individuals definitely will have a negative effect upon a Corgi. They are anxious to comply but resent bullying and become balky or apprehensive. It is much better to encourage with pats and words, making only well-timed, light corrections with the lead or with a stern-sounding voice when necessary.

Eng. Ch. Rozavel Red Dragon, a leading show dog of his day, demonstrates the Corgi's natural aptitude for Obedience work.

Ch. Rozavel Rufus of Merriedip, a Red Dragon son, was the first Corgi to earn a CD both in England and in the United States.

Ch. Capt. Jinks Wiggs, UDT, an early West Coast Obedience worker, owned and trained by Margaret Downing.   *Lineer*

Corgis also thrive on variety. They rapidly become bored when subjected to ho-hum routine or repetitious drilling on one exercise. Training sessions should be brief, interesting and fun for the dog. The result will be a happy worker. And just because a Corgi is busy on the obedience routines should not relegate him to his work-a-day attire. At any Obedience Trial a Corgi in the limelight should be well groomed, for his own sake and that of the breed.

Many excellent books have been written on training dogs in obedience. Most libraries will have a good selection which give detailed advice. *The Pearsall Guide to Successful Dog Training* by Margaret E. Pearsall (Howell Book House, New York) is particularly recommended. Mrs. Pearsall and her husband Milo were prominent obedience trainers, handlers and teachers for many years, and they shared their lives with Pembroke Welsh Corgis.

In more recent years a number of training techniques have been developed, and books have been written that define these methods. Carol Lea Benjamin, who writes ''The Dog Trainer's Diary'' for *Pure-bred Dogs—American Kennel Gazette*, has done several excellent common-sense books and articles on the subject with emphasis on canine behavior.

EARLY OBEDIENCE CORGIS

Back in the early days of competition it was easy enough for the Corgi to step over from farm work to the more rarified obedience exercises. However, Corgis were given no special treatment just because they were small. They were required to retrieve two-pound wooden dumbbells and scale four-foot jumps in competition with German Shepherd Dogs and Great Danes. Later, concessions in the rules were made both in the United States and England to shift the emphasis in trials to the quality of training in a small dog rather than almost impossible physical capabilities. Jumps and dumbbells now are tailored to size.

The first Corgi shown in English Obedience tests was Chalcot Bruin, owned by Mr. W. R. Lee. In spite of the odds against a dog of his stature, Bruin managed to win a Certificate of Merit.

An excellent description of early Obedience Corgis on this side of the Atlantic is given by Mrs. Thelma Gray in the *1952 Welsh Corgi League Handbook*:

> The first Corgi to demonstrate obedience in the U.S.A. was Am. Ch. Rozavel
> Rufus, CDX. Owned by Mrs. Gray and trained and handled by Mrs. Montgomery,
> he made history by being the first Corgi to win an obedience class in England, and
> had qualified as a CDX at the Associated Sheep, Police and Army Dog Society
> (ASPADS) working trials. Bought by Mrs. E. P. Renner, as Am. Ch. Rozavel
> Rufus of Merriedip he made his title in the beauty ring, and then won his American
> CD degree, becoming the first international CD Corgi and, his owner believes, the
> first Corgi to win an obedience class in the U.S.A. All his performances were
> characterized by very high scores. He drew an enormous number of people to the

breed when he took part in a multi-breed demonstration at the Westminster show in New York, where he was handled by the late Miss Esther Bird, and his performance almost "brought the roof down." Rufus was followed to the U.S.A. by Torment of Sealy, also trained and handled in England by Mrs. Montgomery and bred by Mrs. Victor Higgon. Torment did a lot of winning at trials and in obedience classes, and distinguished himself on arrival in the U.S.A. by winning the first obedience class in which he competed. These two Corgis were the breed's pioneers of obedience work in the U.S.A.

Another noted English Obedience Corgi was "James," the Kenneth Butlers' Sinbad of Wey, TDX, UD, CDX, by Ch. Rozavel Scarlet Emperor out of Jill of Pem. Born May 12, 1946, he was an "only child" and soon developed a personality that merited him the ranking position of house dog with bed privileges. His obedience career was impressive, and he went on to sire several top Obedience workers as well. He qualified for his UD in 1949, was the first Corgi to do tracking, and made TDX in 1950, often in competition with the top working police dogs. James served double duty, for as a gun dog he put to practical use his ability to retrieve, track and jump.

The first Corgi bitch to gain a TD in Britain (1951) was Mr. and Mrs. Harrison's Bunty of Buzzard, CDX, UD. Bunty, when bred to Sinbad of Wey, produced the Harrison's Chorister of Fentimen, TD, UD, CD. Obviously brains as well as beauty can breed on.

To become an Obedience champion in England a dog must win three Challenge Certificates for Highest Scoring Dog in Trial. The first Pembroke Corgi to gain this most distinguished honor was Obed. Ch. Ambrose of Kingstead, whelped March 13, 1954, and trained by F. Strutt. "Johnny Boy" began in competition by winning the Novice class at the Welsh Corgi League's championship show in 1955. He had over forty tickets (prizes) between that first show and his first CC. The third and final CC was earned at the Southern Alsatian show in June 1959.

The first Corgi Obedience champion bitch was Obed. Ch. Dawnway Busy Bee, owned by Mr. A. E. Hutchinson. A granddaughter of Sinbad, she was linebred to Bunty of Buzzard.

To return to early Obedience Corgis in the United States, Mrs. William B. Long, whose dogs carry the famous Willets prefix, owned and trained one of the outstanding Obedience Corgis in the East, Waseeka's Megan. In 1940 Megan earned the breed's first UDT and was also the first small dog to win this combined degree. It was not until about 1947 that Tracking became a separate event from the Utility routine, and the UD degree was established. Megan and three other dogs competed as the New England Dog Training Club's team against six other clubs for large cash prizes at the 1940 Westminster show.

Obedience Corgis scored high marks in other parts of the country. In the Southwest, Mr. and Mrs. Jack Liecty's first Corgi, Sierra Penryn, entered three Arizona Obedience Trials in March 1948. She won Novice B in each of the three shows, received High Score of all entries in two and tied for High Score in the third.

In the late 1940s a Canadian dog amassed a string of titles longer than his name: Int. Ch. Windrush Redwing, Int. CD, CDX and UD plus UDT in the United States. He was the first dog of any breed to win all the Obedience Trial degrees then offered in two countries. With his American championship he became the first international bench champion and Obedience Trial degrees winner combined. He was never defeated for Best of Breed in Canada. This remarkable dog was bred by Dr. A. R. B. Richmond and owned by Mrs. M. H. Page of York Mills, Ontario.

On the West Coast Miss Margaret Downing had excellent success with her ''Cappy,'' or more formally, Ch. Capt. Jinks Wiggs, UDT. This famous fellow, born in 1944 from a family of obedience Corgis, began his Novice work in 1948 and had finished all four degrees two years later. Due to the small number of Corgis being exhibited in those days, Cappy did not win his majors until he was ten years old, thereby finishing his championship in 1956.

Cappy was the first Pembroke Welsh Corgi champion to earn a UDT once tracking had been separated from Utility. Cappy lived to be fourteen and a half years of age.

Mrs. Phyllis Young's bitch, Cymmwyn II, finished her UD with a third leg score of 199 out of a possible 200 points. ''Kim'' gained her Utility degree one year and ten months after entering her first Obedience Trial despite time out to raise a litter. She was originally enrolled in an obedience training class to learn basic manners, but did so well she completed her CD before the twelve-week-class was over. For her Novice work she was given the Dog World Award of Canine Distinction for gaining scores over 195 in three straight shows. She was eleven months old at the time.

Mrs. Young writes:

> We then formed a tracking class ourselves, and she got her degree at the very first local tracking test, just before her fourth birthday. The amazing part about passing it was that about a quarter of the trail through, she sat down and sneezed and sneezed and sneezed. Practically sneezing her head off. Then while still sneezing, she continued to work the remainder of the track and passed with flying colors! The test was held in a very dry field . . . and she had picked up a foxtail in her nose! It had to be surgically removed the next morning! We truly marveled at this fantastic girl, continuing to ''do her thing'' with a painful, hazardous foxtail up her nose.

MORE RECENT STANDOUTS

Several other California dogs have proven to be outstanding workers and have brought fame to themselves, their trainers and the breed. High on the list are three bitches owned and trained by Douglas and Gladys Bundock, Am. Can. Ch. Bundocks Mellow de Rover Run, Am. Can. UD, and her two daughters, Am. Can. Ch. Bundocks Rover Run Concerto, Am. Can. UD, and Bundocks Sonata de Rover Run, Am. Can. UD. Between them these three girls racked up a total of thirty-five Highest Scoring Dog in Trial awards in the United States

Cymmwyn II, UDT, owned and trained by Mrs. Phyl Young, with a classmate. *Phyl*

and Canada. Mellow and Sonata each had a 200 score; and Concerto earned no less than an incredible six perfect scores! At one show under judge Margaret Downing there was a runoff for first place in Open B between Sonata and Mellow, with Doug Bundock handling them both as a brace. The tied score was 199½. Sonata won.

Am. Can. Ch. Bundocks Mellow de Rover Run, Am. Can. UD, owned by Douglas Bundock, was nine times Highest Scoring Dog in Trial.

Am. Can. Ch. Bundocks Rover Run Concerto, Am. Can. UD (left) and Bundocks Sonata de Rover Run, Am. Can. UD.

Ch. Merwyn's Proud Patrick, UDT, owned and trained by Irene Enger.

Ch. Merwyn's Proud Patrick, UDT, a tri owned and trained by Mrs. Irene Enger, also had a notable career in California. "Riki" was whelped in January 1968 and had completed his UD by August 1970. The bench championship and T were added by September 1972. He won fourteen Highest Scoring Corgi in Trial honors, was several times Highest Scoring Champion of Record and passed three Tracking tests.

A well-known tri father and daughter combination belonging to Miss Olive Gardiner of Los Angeles was Ch. Gardiner Jones, UDT, VC, and Gardiner Djinn, UDT. "Djinn" earned three Obedience titles in a period of seven and a half months at an early age. Her father, "Jones," finished his championship in 1972 and four weeks later completed his UD. After seven months of training he passed his tracking test. Jones has always been a high-scoring Obedience dog and a happy, speedy worker. Miss Gardiner says:

> Crowds always collect to see the "funny, little black dog" in the ring. I don't think I've ever left a trial without being asked: "Where can I get a dog exactly like yours?" He is really a ham, and he passed this on to his daughter. Recently, Djinn got a standing ovation, but her score was 58!

Another family of Obedience whizzes descended from the late Mrs. Roz Hart's Ch. Devonshire's Royal Flush, UDT, Can. UD, Bda. CD. "Royal" and his son, also trained by Mrs. Hart, carrying the title of Ffafryn Cyntaf O Brenhinol, UDT, Can. Bda. UD, won many of their degrees in three straight shows.

To be a consistent scorer of 197 or better is rare, and Royal's daughter, Thurlow's Little Lizajane, UDT, deserves accolades. This bright little lady, owned

Ch. Gardiner Jones, UDT, and his daughter Gardiner Djinn, UDT, owned and trained by Olive Gardiner.

and trained by Joan and Virgil Thurlow, set a fantastic record of several 200 scores, many 199 and 199½ scores and a number of Highest Scoring Dog in the Regular Classes (as the HIT award is now known) awards—six in 1976 alone.

In Colorado a family of top performing Corgis has been trained by Mrs. Carole-Joy Evert. The first champion UDT bitch in the country, Ch. Larklain Katy-Did, UDT, shone in the breed ring as well as in Obedience. Her daughter, Ch. Larklain Red Venus Amour, UDT, is the only second-generation champion UDT bitch to date. "Venus," herself, has produced champions and Obedience titleholders and has a Stock Dog I Certificate of Working Ability. Venus's son, Am. Can. Ch. Katydid's Top Von Bart Starr, UDTX, VB, has had an exemplary career, becoming a third generation champion UDT.

Bart began his training as a 4-H project for Mrs. Evert's son, Thom, but later was handled to his many titles by Carole-Joy. As he was quite a clown in the ring, it was at the age of nine and a half that he finished his last title. Although not used extensively at stud, his daughter, Katydid's Bart Starr's Katy, UDTX, HC, VB, continued the line. Other accomplished Katydids going back to Bart Starr are champion, Obedience, Tracking Corgis and carry on the tradition.

The Pembroke Welsh Corgi Club of America offers an award for Obedience Breeder of the Year for the most titles completed during the year. So great has been Mrs. Evert's involvement, over a span of fourteen years she has won this coveted honor eleven times, often with eight or nine titles per season.

In 1977 the American Kennel Club initiated the Obedience Trial Championship (OTCH) to honor the elite of the sport. Dogs with UDs worked to earn points for top placements in Open B and Utility classes plus Highs in Trial. The first Pembroke Welsh Corgi to achieve this pinnacle was OTCH Welshberi Belle of the Ball, UD, owned and trained by Tatiana Nagro. "Wicky" completed her title at the PWCCA National Specialty in 1981 to the cheers of the crowd. She had earned all of her basic titles within nine months. Her singleton puppy, also an outstanding worker, became OTCH Tempe Wick By Invitation Only, UD.

The first male Pembroke OTCH was Garvins Grandmaster Freddie, UDT, trained by Evelyn Bock, DVM. Freddie was the first to include a Tracking title in his laurels. As of 1993, a total of eight Corgis have received this superlative award for countless hours of training, exhibiting and excellence. Two of these are breed champions as well.

Ch. and OTCH Aberdare Eliza of Taliesin, UD, and her owner-trainer Peggy McConnell had a spectacular record. During their career Liza went High in Trial fourteen times, earned a perfect score of 200, and accumulated 707 OTCH points—264 in 1987 alone. (It takes 100 points to earn an OTCH.) She passed on her penchant for Obedience, as four of her offspring have titles, and three are bench champions.

In 1990 Ch. and OTCH Backacres Bud In Ski, UD, became the first male breed champion at the top of the Obedience ladder. Owned and trained by Barbara Morris, along the way Buddy had earned the Dog World Award for his high scores in Novice and Open. His breed wins include a Group First.

Another level of Obedience Trials is promoted by the Gaines dog food

Ch. Devonshire's Royal Flush, UDT, Can. UD,
Bda. CD, the sire of two UDT offspring, owned
and trained by Mrs. Oliver J. Hart, Jr.

A daughter of Royal Flush, Thurlow's
Little Lizajane, UDT, a spectacular
worker with several 200 scores on her
record. She was owned by J. and V.
Thurlow.

Ch. Larklain Katy-Did, UDT, the first champion UDT bitch in the United States. Owned and trained by Carole-Joy Evert.

Am. Can. Ch. Katydid's Top Von Bart Starr, UDTX, HC, VB (left), and his dam, Ch. Larklain Red Venus Amour, UDT, a Katy-Did daughter, both owned by Mrs. Evert.

OTCH Welshberri's Belle of the Ball, the first Pembroke Welsh Corgi to become an Obedience Trial champion. In 1981, "Wicky" ranked third of all Obedience dogs in the nation, the only Pembroke Welsh Corgi ever to place in the top ten all-breed rankings.

company. For two years in a row, 1989 and 1990, Daniel B. Lewitzke's Danny's Little Darryllic, CDX, won first place in Novice at the Gaines Eastern Regional over huge entries with average scores of 198½ and 198. In 1989 he went on to place third of seventy top dogs from the entire nation, bringing honor to himself and his breed.

Ch. and OTCH Aberdare Eliza of Taliesin, UD, and her owner-trainer, Peggy McConnell.

Ch. and OTCH Backacres Bud In Ski, UD, is pictured with his owner-trainer, Bobbe Morris.

167

Ch. Briarwood For Heaven's Sake, TD, hot on the trail.

Two additional records must be mentioned. Am. Can. Ch. Calusa's Brandy Alexander, CDX, TD, owned by Mrs. Jacobsen in Florida, passed his Tracking test at the tender age of seven months. And at the age of twelve and a half years Munna of Greenshome was trained by her owners Donald and Eva Green to complete her CD degree with such high scores that she was awarded the Dog World Award of Canine Distinction.

There have been many extremely successful obedience Corgis across the country. As of mid-1993, the UD degree has been earned by a total of 232 Pembrokes, many of which are champions, and 66 have added a Tracking degree or two. Twenty-six dogs have qualified for the elusive TDX, with three of them Ch., UDTX. The records leave no doubt the Pembroke Welsh Corgi has the ability to star in the ever-demanding field of Obedience and Tracking trials.

NEW COMPETITIONS AND AWARDS

Over the years the opportunity for herding dogs of all breeds to use the talents innate to their kind has virtually disappeared. With the burgeoning of suburbia, gone are the many small farms and herds of livestock common a century ago. Herding breed clubs have sought ways to recapture and channel the natural talents of their dogs through herding instinct tests and herding trials. The American Herding Breed Association was formed in response to this effort.

Naturally, many Pembroke Welsh Corgi fanciers quickly started testing and working with their dogs on ducks and sheep, the animals of choice for these activities. Soon the PWCCA began to offer the Herding Instinct Certificate (HC), to those Corgis who showed sustained interest. In 1989 HCs were awarded by the club to 247 dogs.

In March of that year, representatives of various herding breeds met with the AKC, and plans for a Herding Test/Herding Trials program were formulated and put into effect in 1990. Currently there are five different Herding classes:

Tyler, known formally as Ch. Heronsway Free Style, UDT, HT, ROMX, VC, moves the sheep on.

two test classes and three trial classes. The titles given for the two tests are Herding Tested (HT) and Pre-trial Tested (PT). Both are judged as pass/fail, and each dog must qualify under two different judges to earn a title.

The next level involves trial classes with scoring along the same lines as Obedience. Titles to be earned are Herding Started (HS), Herding Intermediate (HI) and Herding Excellent (HX). A Herding Championship is also offered (H.Ch.). Of course, the skills needed become more and more difficult. The AKC provides three different types of courses to be run that are appropriate to the three herding styles, which vary among the breeds. The Corgi is a driving type worker, as opposed to the boundary or fetching type. When called upon to do so, a good working Corgi will fetch as well.

The PWCCA held its first licensed Herding Trial in 1990 in conjunction with the National Specialty in Graham, Washington. Twenty-six exhibitors participated and seven received the HT title. Advanced classes were not offered at this primary, historic event.

So far many Corgis in various parts of the country have earned their HTs and PTs, with several well into the trial classes. To date Ch. Ci Cymru Gwalchmai, CDX, HX, VC, owned, bred and trained by Kathy and Carl Graves, has gone the farthest in this exciting new but natural form of competition.

With all the interest and enthusiasm surrounding the performance activities open to the Pembroke Welsh Corgi, it is not surprising that the national breed club set up a Performance Events Committee to handle the management of the trials and awards. And to reward the excellence of those Corgis which have participated in three or four of the AKC's programs (Conformation, Obedience, Tracking and Herding), the PWCCA developed a new award system.

Starting in 1992 the Versatile Corgi (VC) Award and the Versatile Corgi Excellent (VCX) Award are offered. Dogs must have earned titles in three of the four programs for a VC, and in all three performance programs for the VCX. A

The first Versitility Corgi Excellent, Ch. Blu-Jor Sio Calako Kachina, CDX, TDX, HT, Can. CD, VCX, owned and trained by Lynda McKee. *Hanks*

Robert Bachman's Woody, Am. Can. Ch. Llandian Romp N Circumstance, UD, HT, masters an Agility obstacle.

170

schedule of points gives credit for each possible degree, and a certain total is required per award. As these awards are the ultimate achievement in versatility, they will be the crowns of super stars in the breed. For example, a requirement of the VCX is that the dog must have earned either an OTCH, a TDX or H.Ch.

Thirteen Corgis have been named VC at the first presentation, six retroactive to as early as 1973, and seven trained to their titles in 1991–92. Best of all, as of April 1993, the first VCX dog has finished her requirements. Ch. BluJor Sio Calako Kachina, CDX, TDX, HT, Can. CD, HC, VCX, is owned and trained by Lynda McKee, and bred by Neena VanCamp. Lynda writes, "Callie has done everything she has been asked to do—breed, obedience, tracking, herding, producing—and has done well in all. . . . It is a true honor and tribute to Callie to be the breed's first Versatile Corgi Excellent."

Shortly thereafter Ch. Pempono Just Joey, CDX, TDX, HT, VCX, became the first male to receive the new title. Joey was owned and trained by Susan E. Stanley. Others will surely follow.

The outstanding figure in Versatility training unquestionably is Deb Shindle, of Vero Beach, Florida. Three of her dogs have earned this prestigious title. Starting with her foundation bitch, Ch. Presqu'ile Bronze Caralon, UDT, HC, TT, VC, who is the grandam of Ch. Riverside Dream Addition, UDT, VC, who is the dam of Ch. Riverside Extra Addition, UDT, HC, TT, VC, Deb has been extremely busy. (TT stands for Temperament Tested, which is not an AKC title.) All these are house dogs, along with several others who are constantly winning more titles of all sorts. Riverside Kennels is the epitome of versatility.

And finally, there is a performance event designed for sheer fun—Agility. In 1977 in England a group of civilians thought it might be entertaining to train their dogs to scale walls, crawl through tunnels, and climb ladders just as police and military dogs did, except that the obstacles would be more lighthearted. The dogs were taught to jump through hoops, climb an A-wall, run through a long, round tunnel, walk a plank and master a teeter-totter, for example. The course is run and timed. The fastest dog clearing the most obstacles wins. The world-famous Crufts dog show sponsored an Agility exhibition that drew thousands of spectators.

Soon the sport spread to the United States, and in 1986 the USDAA (United States Dog Agility Association) was founded. Training classes and clubs sprang up. Of course, the fun-loving, adventuresome Corgi, in spite of, or perhaps because of, his shortness of leg was just the ticket. As there are few prerequisites in Agility training, all can participate, pet and show dog alike.

Care must be taken when introducing the Corgi to each obstacle with safety in mind. As always, time, patience, loads of encouragement and praise go into training a reliable Corgi who can manuever his way through, over, under and around anything . . . fast! Needless to say, dog and handler must be fit, as this is a high-energy sport; and it certainly is bound to develop a strong set of laughing muscles.

With so many activities to choose from, any Corgi owner can find something to stimulate that bright, doggy mind and enhance the quality of life for all.

H.M. Queen Elizabeth II holds Buzz, the great-grandson of Susan. *Studio Lisa Ltd.*

Sherry and H.R.H. Prince Andrew having a tête-à-tête. Sherry and Whiskey were the two nursery Corgis in 1962. *Studio Lisa Ltd.*

172

12

The Pembroke in the Spotlight

To WE WHO LOVE the breed it is not at all surprising that celebrated people share our admiration, for a Pembroke Welsh Corgi is certainly special. Quite a few Corgis have been in the spotlight with their renowned owners.

QUEEN ELIZABETH'S CORGIS

By far the most illustrious Corgi owner in the world is Her Majesty, Queen Elizabeth II, of England. The royal family long has been interested in purebred dogs of several breeds and always has had groups of dogs around.

It was in 1933 that the Duke of York, later King George VI, purchased a Corgi puppy from Mrs. Thelma Gray to be a playmate for his daughters Elizabeth and Margaret. The puppy was royally bred himself, as he was a son of Ch. Crymmch President out of Ch. Rozavel Golden Girl. His call name, Dookie, evolved during the month he was being housebroken by Mrs. Gray prior to his move to the royal household. It is a derivation of "The Duke," which he was dubbed to match his "snooty" airs supposedly assumed over his good fortune. Dookie, or more regally Rozavel Golden Eagle, soon joined the little princesses in all their play as well as during more formal occasions.

It is said the King, too, was captivated by the Corgi's great personality.

Dookie was such a success that Rozavel Lady Jane joined the royal dogs as his prospective bride. These two Corgis became dearly loved companions, but alas, no litter resulted. Eventually in 1938 Jane was bred to Mrs. Gray's Tafferteffy. The puppies arrived on Christmas Eve, and "Crackers" and "Carol" were added to the family.

Another early favorite was "Sue," who replaced Jane, tragically struck down by a car in 1944. Sue, or as an adult, Susan, had the honor indeed of joining the future Queen Elizabeth and Prince Philip on their honeymoon. Susan was mated to the renowned Int. Ch. Rozavel Lucky Strike, and two puppies were retained. Descendants of these Corgis and others surround the royal family today.

Although the Queen always has insisted on well-bred dogs of good quality, the royal Corgis usually are not shown. An exception was Windsor Loyal Subject, a Ch. Kaytop Marshall son bred by the Queen and owned by Mrs. Gray, who won a Challenge Certificate in 1973.

Queen Elizabeth has continued her interest in the breed. In 1978 one of her bitches produced a good litter bred to Miss Pat Curties' Aus. Ch. Scottholme Red Ember. No doubt Her Majesty's enthusiasm for Corgis will last a lifetime. After all, how many of us can say we have been "in the breed" since 1933?

The press has given a great deal of coverage to the palace Corgis, who are photographed accompanying the Queen on many of her daily activities. She mixes the food and feeds the dogs herself, and is concerned with their welfare and training. A charming portrait of the Queen commissioned by The Readers Digest Corporation shows a well-loved Corgi leaning comfortably against the royal lap.

Corgis also have graced the homes of other heads of state. In 1954 Mrs. Helen Sheldon sent a puppy by Critic of Cowfold out of Craythorne's Good Tender to General de Gaulle in Paris.

LARRY SULLIVAN'S CORGIS

Francis L. Sullivan, better known as Larry, gained fame on the stage and screen. Some of his most memorable roles were in *Witness for the Prosecution, Great Expectations* and *Oliver Twist*. Although London born, Mr. Sullivan moved to New York and ultimately became an American citizen.

According to Mr. Sullivan's close friend David Wainwright, in the 1930s Larry became a Corgi owner quite reluctantly. Upon returning to his dressing room on one special occasion, he found "a small reddish object with large paws, larger ears, and a still larger bow around his neck, with a yet even larger sign attached, 'I am Quoodle, please be good to me!' " In spite of a fearful fuss, this gift from his wife soon was ensconced in Larry's lap and in his heart. Quoodle lived in London and traveled with Larry all over Britain. He soon was joined by "Mrs. Quinn" and "Quirrip," the Sullivans' country Corgis.

In the late 1940s Mrs. Van Beynum, of the Connecticut Willow Farm

Actor Larry Sullivan with Willow Farm Quest
aboard ship en route to Europe.

prefix, offered the Sullivans Willow Farm Quest, who immediately set off with
them for Bermuda. Quest traveled back and forth between New York and California on the train with the famous actor, sharing the fanciest accommodations. He
crossed the Atlantic on the *Mauretania* to tour Europe, where ". . . he had *his*
dinner served to him in something like eight of the twelve 3-Star Michelin
Restaurants in the whole of France."

In Paris Mr. Wainwright, while walking Quest on the Champs Elysees,
noticed several people in front of Cunard's window, and discovered there was a
photograph of Larry and Quest on the *Mauretania*.

> . . . Quest with his dazzling "smile" had managed to upstage a famous actor,
> who certainly knew how to upstage any human soul. . . . The same picture stopped
> crowds in London, New York, and wherever Cunard had an office. The head of
> the NYC office of Cunard told us that if we ever took him on a Cunard ship again
> his passage was free.

Mr. Wainwright relates another story:

> At the Meurice . . . we got on [the elevator], Larry, Quest and I, and there was
> a small, rather pudgy woman already in the car, who exclaimed, "Oh my, a
> Corgi!" and promptly got down on her knees and had an animated conversation
> with Quest. As we got to the street, I asked Larry if he had realized who she was,
> and he said that he had not. "Dorothy Parker," I said. Larry remarked, "You
> mean that woman who is so brittle and tough in her writings?" "The same."
> "Good God."

175

There is also the story of Richard Burton reciting long Welsh poems in the native tongue to Quest; and of Jerry Lewis—". . . *he too* got down on his knees and had a long chat with Quest." Larry Sullivan died in 1956, but Quest lived on with David Wainwright to the age of seventeen as a true "Bon vivant . . . yet ever the gentleman."

TASHA TUDOR

In America the person with whom most associate the charming little red-and-white Corgi dog is artist-author Tasha Tudor. Her enchanting illustrations appear in many joyful books, including the tiny, leather-bound *The Twenty-third Psalm*. Prince Philip purchased a copy while visiting America, and the Queen ordered more through a British bookseller. The Corgi model for each of the illustrations is Mrs. Tudor's Megan.

Christmas and other holidays are featured in Tasha Tudor's work. At least sixty-five different designs showing Corgis have been circulated on colorful Christmas cards. She has prepared several books treasured by people the world over at Yuletide, particularly her version of *The Night Before Christmas* (Rand McNally & Co., Chicago). Completely unique and fanciful is *Corgiville Fair* (Thomas Y. Crowell Company, New York), wherein all the characters are animals, and every detail is worth studying. Tasha Tudor fans may indulge themselves through the Jenny Wren Press (Mooresville, Indiana), which offers a vast array of prints, cards, books and other items incorporating Corgis in the design. Mrs. Tudor lives in Vermont in a setting as quaint as the scenes she so artfully depicts.

Tasha Tudor and a *Corgiville Fair* Corgi.

Bundocks Sonata de Rover Run, as Candy in the film *Little Dog Lost*, pauses on the daily route in search of food to make sure the coast is clear.

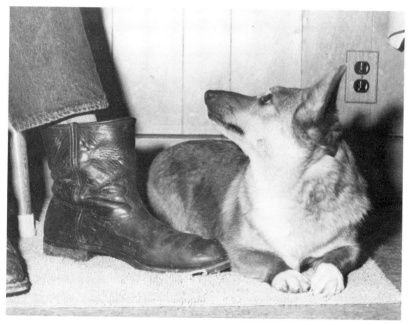

Bundocks Rover Run Concerto, as Candy, stares adoringly at the old man who befriended "him."

LITTLE DOG LOST

Undoubtedly the greatest publicity ever given the Pembroke Welsh Corgi surrounded the full-length Walt Disney color film, *Little Dog Lost*. First shown on television on January 13, 1963, the story concerns a Corgi puppy separated from his family and his adventures as he tries to cope on his own. The movie is an adaptation of Meindert de Jong's book *Hurry Home Candy*. Most of the scenes were shot in Northern California by Perkins Films, Inc. *Little Dog Lost* was an instant success, and the breed went straight to the heart of a vast viewing audience across the nation.

The star of the show, glamorous Am. Can. Ch. Bundocks Rover Run Concerto, Am. Can. UD, was owned, trained and handled by Douglas Bundock. Concerto was ably assisted by her littermate Bundocks Sonata de Rover Run, Am. Can. UD, who did many of the scenes demanding split-second timing between the "actress" and her handler. The girls' mother, Am. Can. Ch. Bundocks Mellow de Rover Run, Am. Can. UD, got into the act and even peeked through the camera used for the aerial shots.

Two other of Mellow's puppies contributed to the movie. Bundocks Cathl, CD, was called upon to howl on command, and Bundocks Colwyn supplied a tail-wagging scene with a somewhat longish appendage.

The beginning of the story called for pictures of the Corgi, Candy, as a puppy. Mrs. Marjorie Butcher sent out two Cote de Neige youngsters with similar markings named, appropriately, Candy Bar and Candy Tuft.

The major herding sequences were acted by yet another Corgi, Fferm Corgwyn Lucky Lady Bug, Am. Can. CD, belonging to Mrs. Jean Robocker of Kalispell, Montana. Lady Bug had been practicing by herding chickens and other animals on her farm and living up to the Corgi's reputation as a good ratter.

It is interesting to note that while the script called for a male Candy, almost all the Corgis participating were bitches. It is doubtful the public noticed the discrepancy as it became caught up in the drama of an endearing little dog.

13

An In-Depth Look at the Pembroke Welsh Corgi Standard

T HE PRESENT Pembroke Welsh Corgi Standard, which provides a comprehensive and realistic description of the desired breed characteristics, is the same as the Standard of 1972, but it has been reformatted to comply with AKC guidelines for all breeds. This latest version was approved by the Board of Directors of the American Kennel Club on January 28, 1993. The American Standard differs slightly from the Standard which is used in other countries, such as England, Canada, Australia and New Zealand. The official English Standard is presented at the end of this chapter.

The drawings accompanying the breed Standard are reprinted from the booklet, *An Illustrated Study of the Pembroke Welsh Corgi Standard*, prepared and published by the Pembroke Welsh Corgi Club of America.

OFFICIAL AKC STANDARD FOR THE PEMBROKE WELSH CORGI

General Appearance

Low-set, strong, sturdily built and active, giving an impression of substance and stamina in a small space. Should not be so low and heavy-boned as to appear

A study in general appearance. Note the lovely overall balance, good bone and substance, yet nice refinement throughout, and head and expression that illustrate perfectly the dictates of the breed Standard.

coarse or overdone, nor so light-boned as to appear racy. Outlook bold, but kindly. Expression intelligent and interested. Never shy nor vicious.

Correct type, including general balance and outline, attractiveness of head-piece, intelligent outlook and correct temperament is of primary importance. Movement is especially important, particularly as viewed from the side. A dog with smooth and free gait has to be reasonably sound and must be highly regarded. A minor fault must never take precedence over the above desired qualities.

A dog must be very seriously penalized for the following faults, regardless of whatever desirable qualities the dog may present: Oversized or undersized; button, rose or drop ears; overshot or undershot bite; fluffies, whitelies, mismarks or bluies.

Size, Proportion, Substance

Height (from ground to highest point on withers) should be 10 to 12 inches.

Weight is in proportion to size, not exceeding 30 pounds for dogs and 28 pounds for bitches. In show condition, the preferred medium-sized dog of correct bone and substance will weigh approximately 27 pounds, with bitches approximately 25 pounds. Obvious oversized specimens and diminutive toylike individuals must be very severely penalized.

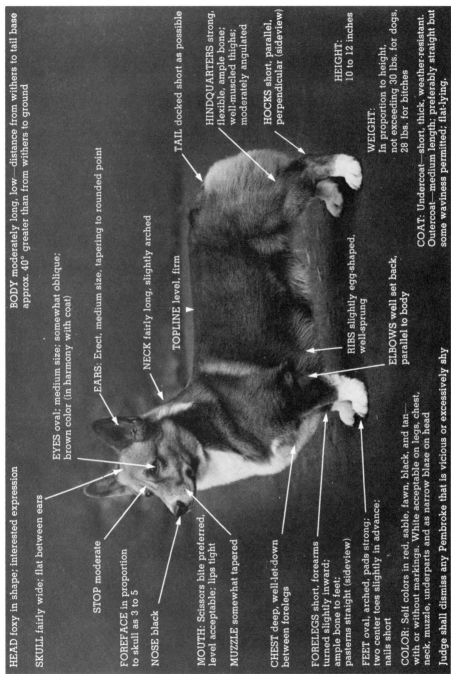

HEAD foxy in shape; interested expression

SKULL fairly wide; flat between ears

EYES oval; medium size; somewhat oblique; brown color (in harmony with coat)

EARS: Erect, medium size, tapering to rounded point

NECK fairly long, slightly arched

BODY moderately long, low—distance from withers to tail base approx. 40° greater than from withers to ground

TAIL docked short as possible

TOPLINE level, firm

HINDQUARTERS strong, flexible, ample bone; well-muscled thighs; moderately angulated

HOCKS short, parallel, perpendicular (sideview)

STOP moderate

FOREFACE in proportion to skull as 3 to 5

NOSE black

MOUTH: Scissors bite preferred, level acceptable; lips tight

MUZZLE somewhat tapered

CHEST deep, well-let-down between forelegs

FORELEGS short, forearms turned slightly inward; ample bone to feet; pasterns straight (sideview)

FEET oval, arched, pads strong; two center toes slightly in advance; nails short

RIBS slightly egg-shaped, well-sprung

ELBOWS well set back, parallel to body

HEIGHT: 10 to 12 inches

WEIGHT: In proportion to height. not exceeding 30 lbs. for dogs. 28 lbs. for bitches

COAT: Undercoat—short, thick, weather-resistant. Outercoat—medium length; preferably straight but some waviness permitted; flat-lying.

COLOR: Self colors in red, sable, fawn, black, and tan—with or without markings. White acceptable on legs, chest, neck, muzzle, underparts and as narrow blaze on head

Judge shall dismiss any Pembroke that is vicious or excessively shy

Visualization of the Pembroke Welsh Corgi Standard, reprinted with permission from *Dog Standards Illustrated* © 1975 by Howell Book House.

Proportions

Moderately long and low. The distance from the withers to the base of the tail should be approximately 40 percent greater than the distance from the withers to the ground.

Substance

Should not be so low and heavy-boned as to appear coarse or overdone, nor so light-boned as to appear racy.

Head

Head to be foxy in shape and appearance.

Expression—Intelligent and interested, but not sly.

Skull—Should be fairly wide and flat between the ears. Moderate amount of stop. Very slight rounding of cheek, not filled in below the eyes, as foreface should be nicely chiseled to give a somewhat tapered muzzle. Distance from the occiput to center of stop to be greater than the distance from stop to nose tip, the proportion being five parts of total distance for the skull and three parts for the foreface. Muzzle should be neither dish-faced nor Roman-nosed.

Eyes—Oval, medium in size, not round, nor protruding, nor deepset and piglike. Set somewhat obliquely. Variations of brown in harmony with coat color. Eye rims dark, preferably black. While dark eyes enhance the expression, true black eyes are most undesirable, as are yellow or bluish eyes.

Ears—Erect, firm, and of medium size, tapering slightly to a rounded point. Ears are mobile, and react sensitively to sounds. A line drawn from the nose tip through the eyes to the ear tips, and across, should form an approximate equilateral triangle. Bat ears, small catlike ears, overly large weak ears, hooded ears, ears carried too high or too low are undesirable. Button, rose or drop ears are very serious faults.

Nose—Black and fully pigmented.

Mouth—Scissors bite, the inner side of the upper incisors touching the outer side of the lower incisors. Level bite is acceptable. Overshot or undershot bite is a very serious fault.

Lips—Black, tight, with little or no fullness.

Neck, Topline, Body

Neck—Fairly long. Of sufficient length to provide over-all balance of the dog. Slightly arched, clean and blending well into the shoulders. A very short neck giving a stuffy appearance, and a long, thin or ewe neck are faulty.

Topline—Firm and level, neither riding up to nor falling away at the croup. A slight depression behind the shoulders caused by heavier neck coat meeting the shorter body coat is permissible.

Body—Rib cage should be well sprung, slightly egg-shaped, and moderately long. Deep chest, well let down between forelegs. Exaggerated lowness interferes with the desired freedom of movement and should be penalized. Viewed from above, the body should taper slightly to end of loin. Loin short. Round or flat rib cage, lack of brisket, extreme length or cobbiness, are undesirable.

> *Author's note:* It is impossible to have either a correct front or the desired front action with an incorrectly shaped rib cage. The desired egg-shaped rib cage will permit freedom of front action while providing ample heart and lung space.

Tail—Docked as short as possible without being indented. Occasionally a puppy is born with a natural dock, which is sufficiently short, is acceptable. A tail up to two inches in length is allowed, but if carried high tends to spoil the contour of the topline.

Forequarters

Legs—Short, forearms turned slightly inward, with the distance between the wrists less than between the shoulder joints, so that the front does not appear absolutely straight. Ample bone carried right down into the feet. Pasterns firm and nearly straight when viewed from the side. Weak pasterns and knuckling over are serious faults. Shoulder blades long and well laid back along the rib cage. Upper arms nearly equal in length to shoulder blades. Elbows parallel to the body, not prominent, and well set back to allow a line perpendicular to the ground to be drawn from the tip of the shoulder blade through to elbow.

Feet—Oval, with the two center toes slightly in advance of the two outer ones. Turning neither in nor out. Pads strong and feet arched. Nails short. Dewclaws on both forelegs and hindlegs usually removed. Too round, long and narrow, or splayed feet are faulty.

Hindquarters

Ample bone, strong and flexible, moderately angulated at stifle and hock. Exaggerated angulation is as faulty as too little. Thighs should be well muscled. Hocks short, parallel, and when viewed from the side are perpendicular to the ground. Barrel hocks or cowhocks are most objectionable. Slipped or doublejointed hocks are very faulty.

Feet—As in front.

Coat

Medium length; short, thick, weather-resistant undercoat with a coarser, longer outer coat. Over-all length varies, with slightly thicker and longer ruff around the neck, chest and on the shoulders. The body coat lies flat. Hair is slightly longer on back of forelegs and underparts and somewhat fuller and longer on rear of hindquarters. The coat is preferably straight, but some waviness is permitted. This breed has a shedding coat, and seasonal lack of undercoat should not be severely penalized, providing the hair is glossy, healthy and well groomed. A wiry, tightly marcelled coat is very faulty, as is an overly short, smooth and thin coat.

Very Serious Fault—Fluffies—a coat of extreme length with exaggerated feathering on ears, chest, legs and feet, underparts and hindquarters. Trimming such a coat does not make it any more acceptable.

The Corgi should be shown in its natural condition, with no trimming permitted except to tidy the feet, and, if desired, remove the whiskers.

Color

The outer coat is to be of self colors in red, sable, fawn, black and tan with or without white markings. White is acceptable on legs, chest, neck (either in part or as a collar), muzzle, underparts and as a narrow blaze on head.

Very Serious Faults:

Whitelies—Body color white, with red or dark markings.

Blues—Colored portions of the coat have a distinct bluish or smokey cast. This coloring is associated with extremely light or blue eyes, liver or gray eye rims, nose and lip pigment.

Mismarks—Self colors with any area of white on the back between withers and tail, on sides between elbows and back of hindquarters, or on ears. Black with white markings and no tan present.

184

Common Faults in General Outline

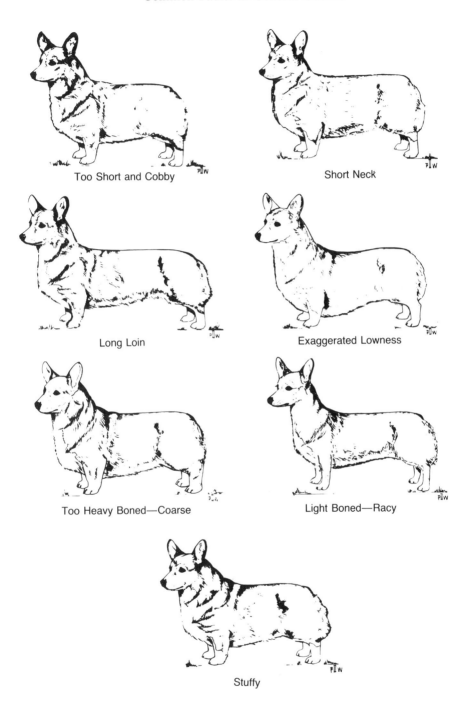

Too Short and Cobby

Short Neck

Long Loin

Exaggerated Lowness

Too Heavy Boned—Coarse

Light Boned—Racy

Stuffy

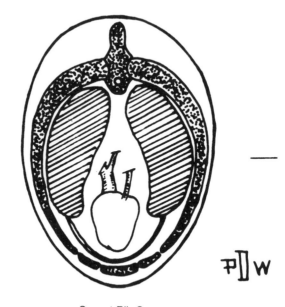

Correct Rib Cage

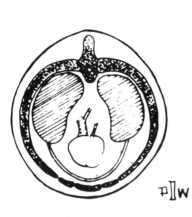

Round Rib

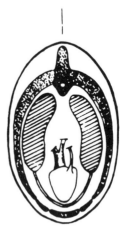

Flat Rib

Correct Head Proportions

The true foxy head, the intelligent and interested expression, and the kindly outlook are essential characteristics of the Pembroke Welsh Corgi. The four head studies presented here illustrate the desired head quality. Note the moderately wide spread of ears, the refinement under the eyes and the correct head and ear proportions that give the imaginary wide triangle.

Fronts

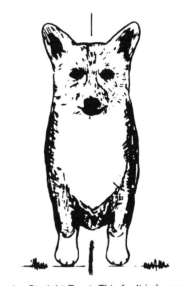

Correct Front. Note how the forearm turns in slightly to compensate for and fit around the deep brisket.

Terrier-Straight Front. This fault is becoming increasingly prevalent both in the United States and in England, with some judges mistakenly selecting it as a virtue.

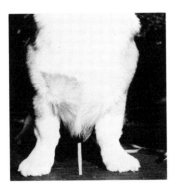

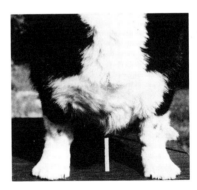

Crooked Front

Wide Front

Angulation

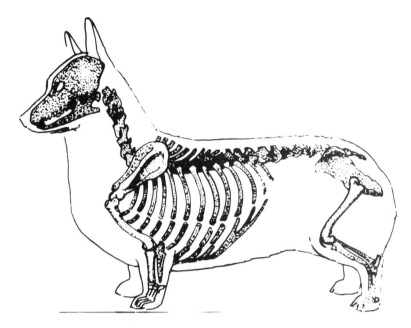

Correct Shoulder and Stifle Angulation

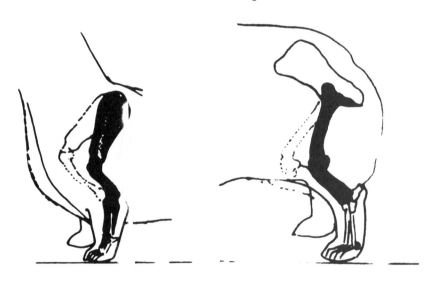

Straight Shoulder and Short Upper Arm   Insufficient Angulation—Straight Stifle

192

Gait

Free and smooth. Forelegs should reach well forward, without too much lift, in unison with the driving action of hind legs. The correct shoulder assembly and well-fitted elbows allow the long, free stride in front. Viewed from the front, legs do not move in exact parallel planes, but incline slightly inward to compensate for shortness of leg and width of chest. Hind legs should drive well under the body and move on a line with the forelegs, with hocks turning neither in nor out. Feet must travel parallel to the line of motion with no tendency to swing out, cross over, or interfere with each other. Short, choppy movement, rolling or high-stepping gait, close or overly wide coming or going are incorrect. This is a herding dog which must have the agility, freedom of movement and endurance to do the work for which he was developed.

Temperament

Outlook bold, but kindly. Never shy or vicious. *The judge shall dismiss from the ring any Pembroke Welsh Corgi that is excessively shy.*

Approved June 13, 1972   Reformatted January 28, 1993

(A) Desired line drawn perpendicular to the ground from the tip of the shoulder blade through to the elbow. (B) Well-developed forechest; brisket well let down between forelegs.   *Tauskey*

Elbows well forward of the desired line (A) drawn from tip of shoulder blade perpendicular to the ground; (B) denotes lack of forechest.

(A) Strong, level topline. Correct proportion of length to height.
Tauskey

(A) Correct turn of stifle. (B) Hocks short.   *Tauskey*

(A) Lacking the desired turn of stifle. (B) Overly long in hock by present-day standards. The straight stifle and long hocks account for the "high in rear" topline.

Two famous dogs in the history of the Pembroke Welsh Corgi have been selected to illustrate the Standard's specifications for forequarter and hindquarter angulation and correct topline. Eng. Ch. Rozavel Red Dragon, considered by many to have been the progenitor of the breed, represents the foundation from which our present-day Pembrokes stem. A more recent Pembroke, Ch. Willets Red Jacket, ROM, a top Best in Show winner, demonstrates the sound construction breeders are continually striving to obtain.

195

Hindquarters

Nice view of a champion Pembroke from behind, showing good hindquarters, short hocks, good bone, good tail set and finish, nice length of neck, good ear set and lovely coat.   *Phyl*

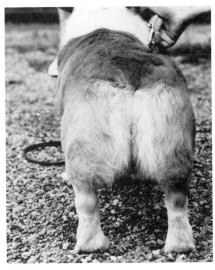

Overly wide behind.

Faulty Hindquarters

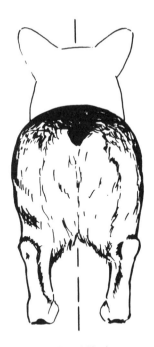

Barrel Hocks

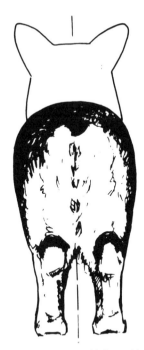

Narrow Behind with Long Hocks

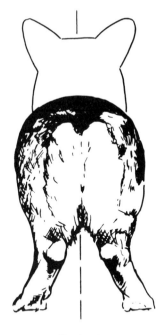

Cowhocks

Overly Angulated Hindquarters—Sickle Hocks

Double-Jointed Hocks

197

Side Movement

Correct side movement, with low, sweeping forward reach in front, the driving thrust behind, and the strong, level topline.

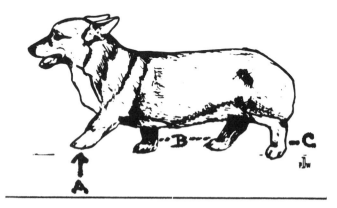

Short Stride. Note (A) lack of forward reach, (B) short distance covered in a single stride and (C) lack of thrust behind.

Front Movement

Correct Front Movement

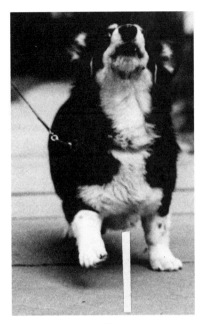

Wide Front Movement

Paddling

Plaiting

199

Rear Movement

Correct Rear Movement

Hocks Turning Out—Toeing-in Movement

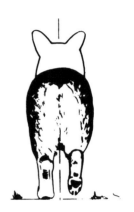

Close Hind Movement

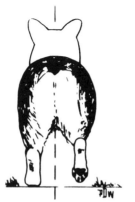

Wide Rear Movement

Weaving Rear Movement

200

Feet

Correct Foot

Round Foot

Long, Narrow Foot with Weak Pastern

Splayed Foot with Long Nails

A Very Serious Coat Fault

A typical adult fluffy.

NEW ENGLISH STANDARD OF THE PEMBROKE WELSH CORGI*

General Appearance

Low set, strong, sturdily built, alert and active, giving impression of substance in a small space.

Characteristics

Bold in outlook, workmanlike.

Temperament

Outgoing and friendly, never nervous or aggressive.

Head and Skull

Head foxy in shape and appearance, with alert intelligent expression, skull fairly wide and flat between ears; moderate amount of stop. Length of foreface to be in proportion to the skull 3 to 5. Muzzle slightly tapering. Nose black.

*Reproduced by permission of the Kennel Club.

Color and Markings

White marking on the body should not extend above dotted line.

Mismark. The side marking extends well up above the level of the elbow, and the stifle trim continues up to the base of the tail. This dog also appears to be short-coated as well as mismarked.

Color and Markings

This tricolor illustrates the maximum acceptable extent of white markings.   *Phyl*

Whitely. The white body color with red or dark markings. (Note the lovely eye and expression of this striking fellow.)   *Phyl*

Eyes

Well set, round, medium size, brown blending with colour of coat.

Ears

Pricked, medium-sized, slightly rounded. A line drawn from tip of nose through eye should, if extended, pass through or close to tip of ear.

Mouth

Jaws strong with perfect, regular and complete scissor bite, i.e. upper teeth closely overlapping the lower teeth and set square to the jaws.

Neck

Fairly long.

Forequarters

Lower legs short and as straight as possible, upper arm moulded round chest. Ample bone carried right down to feet. Elbows fitting closely to sides, neither loose nor tied. Shoulders well-laid, and angulated at 90 degrees to the upper arm.

Body

Medium length, well-sprung ribs; not short-coupled, slightly tapering, when viewed from above. Level topline. Chest broad and deep, well let down between forelegs.

Hindquarters

Strong and flexible, well-angulated stifle. Legs short. Ample bone carried right down to feet. Hocks straight when viewed from behind.

Feet

Oval, toes strong, well arched, and tight, two centre toes slightly in advance of two outer ones, pads strong and well arched. Nails short.

Tail

Short, preferably natural.

Gait/Movement

Free and active, neither loose nor tied. Forelegs move well forward, without too much lift, in unison with thrusting action of hindlegs.

Coat

Medium length, straight and dense undercoat, never soft, wavy, or wiry.

Colour

Self colours in Red, Sable, Fawn, Black and Tan, with or without white markings on legs, brisket and neck. Some white on head and foreface is permissible.

Size

Height: approximately 25.4 to 30.5 cm. (10 to 12 in.) at shoulder. Weight: Dogs 10 to 12 kgs. (22 to 26 lbs.); bitches 10 to 11 kgs. (20 to 24 lbs.).

Faults

Any departure from the foregoing points should be considered a fault and the seriousness with which the fault should be regarded should be in exact proportion to its degree.

Note

Male animals should have two apparently normal testicles fully descended into the scrotum.

14

Showing Your Corgi

A HEALTHY, properly conditioned and trained Corgi is an easy dog to prepare for the show ring and a joy to show. Even though the Corgi does not require the endless hours of brushing or trimming that many long-coated breeds must have before a show, the night before the show is not the time to wake up to the realization your Corgi is not looking his best. True, vibrant show condition is a product of months of good diet, ample exercise and conscientious health care. All the chalk powders, coat conditioners and coat dressings in the world, by themselves, will not give your dog true bloom. A lovely coat and sparkling good health come from within, not from a spray can or bottle.

GROOMING

If your Corgi has been kept in good condition right along, his nails have been trimmed routinely, and his teeth have been kept free of tartar, there is really very little you must do the night before. In fact, if the breed judging is not scheduled for the crack of dawn, our Corgis are permitted their usual run in the woods and even a session of frogging down at the pond if it is the appropriate time of year. It is not until they come back to the house and see the towels and soap out that they realize they are about to have a day's outing at a show.

What we do to ready our Corgis for a show is quite simple. First we wash the white parts on the feet, chest and collar with a mild soap. The soap is *thoroughly* rinsed out and the wet areas are vigorously dried with a towel. The dampened towel is used to give the dog a thorough body rub. This will remove

The Beauty Treatment

the surface grime and also fluff the coat out just a bit, adding to the overall impression of a luxuriant depth of coat. To bathe the entire dog the night before the show usually is a frightful mistake, as when the coat dries it will be unmanageably fluffy, curly and go every which way. If for some reason a dog has to be given a complete bath before a show, it should be done at least two or three days ahead. On the other hand, some top exhibitors routinely wash the entire dog just before the show and cope with the unruly hair by weighting it down with towels or through constant brushing. The Standard states the body coat should lie flat.

If the weather is uncooperative or if time is scarce, the coat may be dried with an ordinary hair dryer. Separating the wet clumps of fur with a comb both speeds the drying time and adds to the carefully groomed effect.

When the dog's white marked areas are nearly dry, white chalk powder can be brushed into the coat and left until just before show time. Some Corgis have crystal white markings. Others have markings that are a duller white. Yellowish white markings will be whitened somewhat with the use of chalk. When it is brushed out before the dog is taken into the ring, the chalk will carry with it the dirt and soot picked up on the way to the show. A slight chalk residue will remain after the brushing and will help give the white parts of the coat a fuller look, as the remaining chalk separates the individual hairs from one another.

Even though all Corgis being exhibited should have their nails trimmed at least once a week, there always seems to be a little bit of nail that can be sanded off before the dog is ready to go to the show. The excess hair on the foot is trimmed off at the same time. Uncared-for feet detract from the "Sunday best" look of a keen show dog.

Years ago most exhibitors removed the whiskers on their Corgis before a show. British breeders abhor this practice, as it does somehow alter the overall impression of the head and expression. It was not done with our dogs because we disliked the prickly face washes while the stubble is growing in, and whiskers are an impossible nuisance to keep short. Plus we learned eventually that few judges ever noticed whether a dog's whiskers were trimmed and the presence of whiskers certainly made no difference in the eventual placing of the dog. Additionally, scientific studies have shown that the tactile whiskers are important to the dog's perception of his environment. Nowadays most Corgis enter the ring with their whiskers intact.

The last and most time consuming part of grooming the dog for the show ring consists of an absolutely meticulous combing or brushing. We start at the back end of the dog, at the very bottom of his pants, and work up over his back and sides to the front and end with the chest coat. An English fine comb or a natural bristle brush is used, and the coat is worked from the skin out in the direction the hair grows. Be careful to not scratch the skin as you work. With a dense undercoat, only a very small section can be done at a time. Grooming the coat in this manner will get the undercoat and guard hairs all going in the same direction and will give a smooth, even, rich appearance to the coat. If the coat is full of static electricity, making it difficult to handle because of the flyaway hairs, dampen the coat slightly with a fine spray of water as you work. After all your efforts are done, the dog will give himself a good shake, letting you know he prefers to go dressed his own way, and you are ready to set off for the ring.

In recent years it has become the misguided practice of many handlers to use various means to alter the coat of their dogs in an effort to disguise a fault or enhance a virtue. However, it clearly states in the Standard of the breed that no trimming is allowed except to tidy up the feet or whiskers. Do not fall into the trap of trying to sculpture our natural breed.

Rough, ungroomed coat. *Spengler*

HANDLING

Even though the Corgi is a relatively easy dog to prepare for exhibition, he is not necessarily an easy dog to handle in the ring. The Corgi is a natural working breed and should be shown on an absolutely loose lead to give the dog a chance to show off his free, easy movement. Finding the right pace is important. He should be trotted fast enough to display his ground-covering ability, but too fast can exaggerate movement faults. Running with the dog is to be discouraged. And the Corgi should pose himself just as naturally. He should never be shown artificially posed or strung up by the neck on a taut lead.

It takes a little doing to train a Corgi to stand patiently in front of you all the while looking alert and full of energy. A Corgi will quickly learn to bait if you make a practice of giving him food treats only when he is standing squarely. The competition for the treats from other dogs will keep a youngster really on his toes. The baiting game will become great fun for the dog, and he soon will enjoy practicing his catching skills in the ring. Experiment with different foods to see which one is most certain to keep your dog's attention in the presence of many distractions. Dogs here do best with beef liver that has been thoroughly cooked—usually boiled and then dried slightly in a low oven. A modern variation is microwaved liver sprinkled with powdered garlic. Other dogs are known to prefer pieces of hot dogs, potato chips or a variety of tidbits.

Table training should begin during the puppy's early grooming sessions. Without making a big production of it, train the puppy to stand calmly on a table

210

Ready for the show ring. *Spengler*

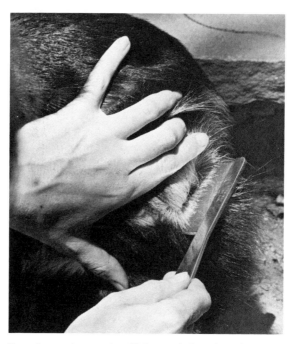

For a thorough grooming, lift the top hair and comb through the undercoat. *Spengler*

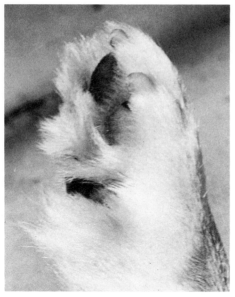

The foot before trimming. *Spengler*

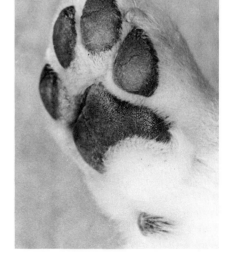

The foot after trimming. *Spengler*

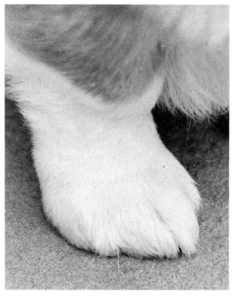

Correctly trimmed foot. Note the desired oval shape and the short toenails. *Spengler*

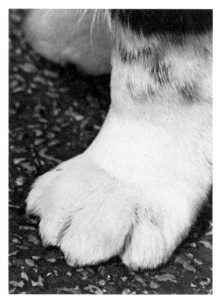

An overly trimmed foot, emphasizing the incorrect round shape. *Spengler*

A poor pose, illustrating a common handling error. The tall man is too close to the dog, forcing her to hold her head back so she can see his face, which throws her topline off. Rather, stand back and hold the bait low so the dog will stretch up and forward, thereby leveling the topline.

Phyl

Ch. Vangard Mister Ski Bum, ROMX, with his breeder-handler, Robert Simpson. Owner: Margaret Shepard. Whelped October 15, 1975, he was a winner of ten Bests in Show and sire of thirty champions.

Robert

213

while you examine him from head to tail. Take your time in training a puppy to allow his mouth to be examined. At first do little more than lift the sides of his lips and tell him what a good boy he is to have such pretty teeth. Gradually work him up to the point where you can have other people approach him while he is standing on the table and examine in his mouth in the way a judge will do at a show.

Lead training a youngster for the show ring need consist of little more than teaching him to take you for a walk. This does not mean he should be allowed to pull you all over kingdom come, but rather he should proudly step out ahead of you, though still to your left side, as you walk along.

The fun of actually going someplace rather than walking around in a circle, as in a show ring, in your backyard will make a vast difference to how your dog reacts to lead training. Often it helps to start out with an older, trained dog as a buddy. The puppy is caught up with his pal's excitment over the outing and is distracted from the new sensation of being on a leash. Once he is confident on the lead, he can be taught in a few brief sessions the patterns of gaiting used in the show ring, such as the straight out to the end of the ring with a U-turn and

This dynamic team of BIS winner Am. Can. Bda. Ch. Velour of Rowell, ROM, and owner-handler Janet Robinson achieved great success. "Spock" was always shown in impeccable condition, which contributed to his remarkable record of over 200 Bests of Breed.

Klein

URGIS
NEL CLUB
BER 31 1987
EST
IN
HOW
UDGE
N B PATTERSON

BEST IN SHOW

Ch. Walborah's Rugby V Marjoe (Ch. Snowdonias Black Knight, ROM, ex Ch. Beaujolais of Revelmere, ROMX). All-time top winning male Pembroke Welsh Corgi in America. Breeder: Deborah Harper; owners: Mr. and Mrs. Joseph Vaudo. Whelped in 1981, Rugby and his handler, Joy Brewster, set an amazing record of 44 all-breed Bests in Show, which stood for many years until it was broken in 1993. Included in his wins were 211 Group firsts and 185 other Group placings. In the highly competitive world of show dogs, it takes a good dog, a super handler, ample funds and perseverance to aspire to such goals. *K. Booth*

back, the L-shaped and the triangle patterns. More potentially good show dogs are ruined by overpractice at home than by lack of training.

A Corgi is easily bored, and what is worse, a Corgi will take special delight in letting the whole ringside know just how bored he is. The more you try to pep up a Corgi who refuses to show, the worse he will get. With luck he will come to life if you studiously ignore him and make him work to get your attention. If you find you have one of those few Corgis who simply cannot be tricked into being a ''showing fool,'' then it is best to put him aside and go with a dog who thoroughly enjoys the whole dog show scene. At the very least, give him a vacation from the ring.

If you decide to have a professional handler to show your dog, write the Professional Handlers Association for recommendations. When this book went to press, the address for the PHA was 15810 Mt. Everest Lane, Silver Spring, MD 20906. Another organization, The Dog Handlers' Guild, can be reached c/o Andy Moyer, 5390 Irene Road, Belvidere, IL 61008. If these addresses become obsolete, you will be referred to the current contact.

15

Breeding the Pembroke Welsh Corgi

W ITH BEGINNER'S LUCK you might find you have bred a top-flight puppy in your very first litter. Unfortunately, not all of us are blessed with beginner's luck, nor does such luck linger long with those it touches. Undeniably, there is an element of luck in the breeding of dogs, but the ability to breed successive generations of quality dogs depends largely on careful planning and judicious selection of the parents of every litter.

BREEDING PRINCIPLES

Most successful Pembroke breeders, people who have consistently produced quality stock over the years, some for as many as forty years, attribute their success to a program of linebreeding. Linebreeding is the mating of related dogs—such as grandson to grandam, niece to uncle, or cousin to cousin.

In recent years, the term linebreeding has become less rigid in its application. We hear of closely linebred, loosely linebred or distantly linebred animals. If a dog and bitch being mated together share one or more common ancestors in the first three generations, the resulting puppies are considered to be linebred. In assessing the strength of a linebreeding, it makes sense that the more times one or two particular dogs appear in the first few generations of a pedigree, the greater the influence of those dogs will be.

Linebreeding is usually the safest course for the novice breeder to follow as opposed to outcrossing or inbreeding.

Outcrossing is the mating of two seemingly unrelated dogs. Outcrossing can result in a lack of uniformity in the litter, thereby negating any attempt to establish a specific type characteristic of the line.

Inbreeding is the mating of two closely related dogs, such as father to daughter, mother to son, or brother to sister. Undertaken by a skillfill, truly knowledgeable breeder, inbreeding can be a most effective means of setting type. Misused, the results can be disastrous.

A number of the early Pembroke breeders in America embarked on breeding programs that involved intense inbreeding and linebreeding, the likes of which most breeders today would find quite alarming. Forty years ago, though, the nation watched the rapid decline of one of this country's favorite breeds, and the public grew to believe that all "highly bred" show dogs were neurotic or sickly. Influenced by public sentiment and not wanting to be guilty of ruining a fine breed, the majority of present-day Pembroke breeders have studiously avoided close breeding. For a time breeders would boast that all the leading bloodlines in England and America were represented in their kennel. Now, having realized the folly of trying to blend all the winning bloodlines into a single, perfect line, American breeders are concentrating their efforts on serious linebreeding.

SELECTION OF BREEDING STOCK

If you have decided you are interested in breeding Pembrokes before purchasing your first bitch, you are in a position to start off in the best possible way. You are not making do with what you have. Instead, you are free to select a nicely bred puppy from an established breeder, a person who can be of great help to you as you go on. If possible, purchase a quality, linebred bitch from breeding that is being widely used. You will want to have several alternatives of suitable studs to choose from for your bitch. The purpose of selecting a linebred bitch to begin with is lost if there are no appropriately related stud dogs available for your use.

Perhaps you have already purchased a Corgi bitch as a pet and have decided you would like to breed her. Before blindly plunging in, give some serious thought to the difficulties you may encounter and be sure you really want to have a go at it. Even if all goes well, raising a litter of puppies properly involves untold hours of work and a myriad of expenses. Few pet owners who raise a litter of puppies come close to breaking even on the venture, let alone come out ahead. Also interesting to note, few people who have bred their pet bitch ever care to repeat the whole performance.

If you are certain you want to breed your bitch, first contact someone with experience in the breed who can tell you if your bitch is suitable for breeding. Identify her best points and possible faults. You will need help in selecting an appropriate stud dog. It would be unwise to mate her to a dog carrying similar faults or to one from a line where one of her faults may be a problem.

THE BITCH IN SEASON

A Pembroke bitch can be expected to come in season, or heat, for the first time at about eight to nine months of age. An occasional bitch will come in a month or two earlier, and some stall around about it until they are over a year old.

A bitch should not be bred on her first season unless she is over a year old at the time. Even at twelve months, a Corgi bitch is still very much a puppy herself, and should not have to assume family responsibilities quite so soon. Ideally, a bitch should be bred for her first time at her second or third season.

Problems can arise if an older bitch who has never had a litter before is bred. If a bitch is going to be bred at all, it is best that she have at least one litter by the time she is three years old. There are exceptions to every rule, though, and there have been bitches who have whelped their first litter at six years of age with all going well.

The first indication that a bitch is about to come into season is usually a noticeable swelling of the vulva. If there are male dogs about, they will let you know things are about to happen by showing more than a usual interest in checking the bitch over.

Bitches kenneled together will often come in season close together. If this is about to happen, you may observe the girls being uncommonly sexy, to the point they think it is great fun to ride one another. That's the time to start watching closely for the first signs of the bloody vaginal discharge.

For the first day or so, the discharge will be light pink in color and the flow itself light. Unless the bitch is under close observation, the actual beginning of the season may be missed. As the season progresses, the flow increases, and the color of the discharge deepens considerably. Normally, the bitch is not ready for breeding while there is a dark, heavy discharge, and she will not accept the attentions of the male at this time.

A bitch is normally receptive and ready to breed from the tenth to, and including, the fourteenth day. This is not a hard and fast rule, however, as many bitches are successfully bred as early as the seventh day. At the other end of the scale, there have been occasional surprise litters from mating that occurred on the eighteenth or nineteenth day. Some successful matings happened even later, when the bitch was thought to be well out of season.

As a bitch approaches the receptive period, the vaginal discharge will normally change color from a deep, bright red to a paler, pink or straw color. The discharge seems to be thinner, more watery. If the bitch is kept on newspaper, you will be able to detect the change in the discharge more readily than you can seeing the discharge as it comes from the vulva. The swelling of the vulva also will subside a bit as the discharge lessens.

Ch. Cadno Melanie, ROMX (Eng. Ch. Winrod Peregrine ex Chloe of Cadno), whelped December 13, 1970. Breeder: Mrs. B. M. Tulloch; owner: Mrs. Joan L. Maskie. The dam of six champions by Eng. Ch. Kaytop Marshall, plus five others, Melanie was the top Brood Bitch for 1976. *Petrulis*

If you exercise a bitch in season on a lead rather than turning her out in a kennel run by herself, you will know how ready for breeding she is by the way she reacts to the sight of a possible male caller. A ready bitch is anxious, and she leaves no doubt about it. When you observe her eagerness, the time has come to let the stud dog have a try at mating her.

THE MATING

If the bitch is to go to an outside stud, make arrangements with the owner of the stud dog well in advance of when the bitch is due in season. You will need to know the stud fee, what tests the dog's owner may require and what accomodations are available for her while she is away from home. As soon as the bitch has actually come in season, notify the stud dog owner and set the date that the bitch will be either shipped or brought to the stud for mating. If the bitch is to be shipped, it is best to send her several days ahead of when she will likely be ready for breeding.

Prior to shipping, check the health regulations and requirements. A health certificate and record of a rabies vaccination may have to be sent with the bitch. If the owner of the stud dog requests that your bitch be tested for brucellosis, this should be done soon after the bitch comes in season. Brucellosis testing of canine breeding stock is becoming more widespread, and it is a wise owner who requests that it be done for both the dog and bitch prior to mating.

In that conception may not take place for several days after the actual mating, it is a good practice to not have the bitch shipped back for four or five days.

Some stud dogs just take charge when put to a bitch who is ready to breed. Such a dog needs little assistance other than to have someone firmly holding the bitch so that she cannot turn on him, pull away or roll over. After the dog penetrates the bitch, the dog's penis will swell tremendously, locking him in the bitch. At this point, both are said to be "tied." The bitch will typically feel discomfort as the dog swells and may turn on the dog or try to pull away. A tie lasts anywhere from a few minutes to a half hour or more. Most often, the dog can be turned after a few minutes so that he is standing next to the bitch rather than having his weight on her for the entire time. If turning a particular dog is known to make him pull away from the bitch prematurely, it is best to hold the dog on the bitch for a short while.

When the tie is completed and the dog pulls away from the bitch, both dogs should be returned to their quarters and rested. The dog, especially, will appreciate a drink of fresh water.

Not all matings are simple events, and how the matings are handled when a young dog is first started on stud work can determine how well the dog is apt to manage subsequent matings. An occasional Pembroke has sired a litter at seven months of age, but most breeders wait to start their young dogs at ten months or so, and then they are used sparingly for several months yet. A dog's first "bride" ideally should be a bitch who has mated easily before, thus instilling in the dog a confidence in his own ability. Regardless of whether a dog is to service a calm matron bitch or a maiden bitch, a person experienced in handling matings should be on hand. In most cases, it is a mistake for anyone to try handling a mating without help.

Procedures for handling matings differ greatly. Many breeders accustom their stud dogs to mate bitches on a firm table with a nonskid surface. This method allows better control of the dogs and makes it easier to give whatever assistance may be necessary. If the dog will not work on a table, the alternative would be to simply sit on the ground with the bitch placed across your legs, with your helper holding the bitch's front end steady while you manipulate the bitch's hindquarters to the appropriate height for the dog.

Whatever procedure is used, it is important that the stud dog be conditioned to let you handle him or the bitch as need be, so he is not thrown off if you have to assist.

Occasionally a bitch will be unpleasant about being bred without any obvious reason other than her pride is being hurt. If a bitch is threatening the dog with growls and bared teeth, you can try putting a cut-off nylon stocking over her head. Use the foot end and cut a piece about eighteen inches long. This seems to surprise the bitch into behaving. She can see what is happening, she can breathe easily and yet she is not so sure she could open her mouth to bite if she wanted to, making her reluctant to try. A really tough bitch will try to put an end to the shenanigans despite the stocking, in which case, she should be firmly muzzled with a long, thin strip of cloth.

A bitch can be bred without the dog actually achieving a tie. There are dogs who have sired a number of litters without ever tying a bitch, so do not be alarmed if this is the case when your bitch is mated.

It is a good idea to have the equipment right at hand to artificially inseminate the bitch if the mating does go awry and the dog ejaculates outside the bitch. With necessity being the mother of invention, we found here that a 10-cc plastic syringe with a puppy stomach tube attached served very well for inseminating a bitch artificially. The syringe and tube (a #8 French catheter) need not be sterilized, but they must be thoroughly rinsed if they have at any point been cleaned with disinfectant or detergent.

After the semen is collected in the barrel of the syringe or in a clean plastic cup (5 to 8 ccs is plenty to do the deed), and you have put the plunger back in the syringe, quickly, but gently, insert the tube into the vagina past the cervix. Slowly press the plunger until all the semen has been injected. If the fluid starts coming out of the vagina as you press the plunger, you do not have the tube inserted past the cervix, so gently try again.

After the tube has been withdrawn, hold the bitch rear end up in the air, head toward the ground, for a few minutes. This is done to encourage the flow of semen into the uterine cavity rather than letting it immediately drain out of the bitch.

A second mating is unnecessary if all appeared to go well with the first mating. For a young dog just starting stud work, though, a second successful mating may bolster his confidence. If there is doubt about the success of the first mating, or there is particular pressure that the bitch be successfully mated, a repeat mating about forty-eight hours following the first mating would be advisable.

An advantage to a single mating is that the date the bitch is due to whelp can be figured more closely. When sixty-three days pass, the average length of the gestation period, counting the day following the mating as the first day, you are not left wondering whether the bitch is going past her due date from the first mating or is only at her sixty-first day from the second mating.

THE PREGNANT BITCH

Some bitches will let it be known early on they are in a delicate way, while others will keep you guessing well into their fifth and sixth week.

An observant owner may notice several days after a bitch has been mated that she is urinating more frequently than usual. The increased frequency lasts a day or two at the most and may well be associated with hormonal changes that occur at the time of actual conception.

You can be fairly certain puppies are on the way when, two to three weeks

222

after mating, a high energy, always-on-the-go bitch becomes content just to snuggle in your lap, dreamily soaking up all the affection you give her. A bitch who demonstrates a marked personality change is responding to strong hormonal influences. Usually such a bitch will be a super "mum," being very attentive to her family well past the point when other bitches would have decided the time had come for their puppies to be someone else's responsibility.

It is not uncommon for a bitch to go off her food for several days between the second and third week of pregnancy. Also during the third week, the nipples will become noticeably pinker, this being most obvious in a bitch who has neither been pregnant before nor had a false pregnancy.

If a bitch is carrying a large litter, you may see a rounding of the abdomen during the third week, and it will also have a tight drumlike feel. Typically, slight distention of the abdomen will become apparent during the fourth week. The "potty" look will be more noticeable after the bitch has eaten or when she is lying down, and the apron of her belly hair spreads out to the side.

In some cases, a bitch can keep a trim figure throughout the entire gestation period and surprise the unexpecting owners with a puppy or two. If plans are such that it is necessary to know if a bitch is in whelp, a veterinarian can palpate the bitch near the end of the third week and into the fourth week, possibly detecting the presence of little hickory nut–sized embryos. With a positive finding, you know where you stand. Negative results can still fool you. To be absolutely sure a bitch is not in whelp, she can be X-rayed at the end of the eighth week. It is also possible to check the status of things with the very safe ultrasound procedure. Otherwise, keep track of when a bitch is due, and even though she has given no indication of being in whelp, keep an eye on her at that time—just in case.

Little, if any, change should be made in the bitch's diet or routine during the early weeks of pregnancy. A bitch should be at her ideal weight at the time of mating, pregnancy being neither the time for a crash diet nor the time to set right a poorly conditioned bitch.

Watch the bitch's weight closely during the pregnancy. If she begins to appear thin over the withers and along the spine, the amount of food given should be increased accordingly. Otherwise, the total amount of food intake should remain close to the usual, but with the percentage of meat and other protein foods, such as cooked eggs and cottage cheese, increased from the fifth week on.

Breeders used to add hefty amounts of vitamin and mineral supplements to the diet of a pregnant bitch, all in an effort to produce big, heavy-boned puppies. Whelping difficulties increase proportionally as the size of the puppies whelped increases. How much more sense it makes to encourage the puppies to grow on well after they are on the ground. If a bitch is fed a good, well-balanced diet and has access to plenty of fresh air and sunshine, she should not need any diet supplements other than, perhaps, a balanced multivitamin and mineral tablet. A great many experts insist that even the added vitamin tablet is unnecessary.

Having observed an obvious difference in the condition of adult dogs here, maintained on a vitamin supplement as opposed to when no supplements were given, it would be difficult to believe the added vitamins are without benefit. However, vitamin and mineral supplements can be as harmful when misused as they can be beneficial when properly used. A crucial balance between vitamins and between minerals is essential to their effectiveness.

Calcium is a popular supplement given to pregnant bitches yet is potentially harmful if not judiciously used. For many years it was thought that in order to have well-boned puppies, the bitches should be given a calcium supplement in the form of bone meal or calcium lactate tablets. We now know heavy calcium supplements can destroy the delicate balance of calcium within the body. Breeders also know that genetic influences largely determine the bone and substance of a puppy. A puppy genetically destined to be fine-boned will always be such, regardless of how much calcium is given either to the dam in whelp or later to the puppy.

If you just wish to add something, you might try a teaspoonful of ground raspberry leaves to the main meal a soon as the bitch is known to be in whelp. Many believe this ingredient is helpful during gestation and parturition. Generally, however, the fewer additives given to the pregnant bitch, the better.

As the pregnant bitch increases in size, she will appreciate several small meals a day rather than a single large meal. Two regular feeds plus a bedtime bowl of milk with a few dog biscuits on the side will do nicely. Canned milk or goat's milk is less likely to cause looseness of stool than regular cow's milk, which is not recommended.

Nan Butler, who with her husband, Ken, is well known for their famous Wey Corgis, wrote some years back that she considered the nighttime milky feed to be one of the most important meals for helping puppies to grow on well and for bringing youngsters into good bloom. We could not agree with her findings more; likewise we feel the milk feed is every bit as beneficial to the pregnant bitches, who quite relish this end-of-the-day treat.

Plenty of free exercise is essential to the physical and mental well-being of any animal and is especially important in the care of pregnant bitches. Some whelping problems may be eliminated altogether if the bitch receives adequate exercise. In other instances, the properly conditioned bitch has the stamina and vigor to see her through a difficult whelping situation should it occur.

You can generally let the bitch determine how much exercise she wants to have. Most bitches will look after themselves pretty well, slowing down considerably as their load grows heavier. Despite the increased effort required, bitches accustomed to going on daily walks will want to continue their usual routine until nearly the last minute. Care must be taken if a pregnant bitch is exercised with other dogs that she is not run down or jostled about by the group.

Under no circumstances should any jumping be permitted. This rule can be difficult to enforce with house pets and may mean the bitch will have to be confined in an area where she does not have access to inviting furniture.

A large load in combination with a short-legged build makes stairs an impossible obstacle course for most pregnant Corgis. Again, make certain that an in-whelp bitch simply does not have access to stairs lest she should make the decision that one way or another, she can cope with them.

By the last week of a bitch's pregnancy, she should not be allowed outside on her own. As her time approaches, she will begin nosing around for a suitable den in which to have her puppies. Unsupervised, she just might find an unreachable hideout under the garage or an old tool shed.

WHELPING PREPARATIONS

At least a week prior to the date the puppies are expected, set up the whelping quarters so all is in readiness should the puppies arrive earlier than expected.

Choose a quiet place out of the main stream of activity. It seems that nearly all Corgi breeders have their bitches whelp in their own bedroom, a guest bedroom or a bathroom adjacent to either. This makes it possible to have the bitch close at hand during the night so frequent checks on how things are going can be made easily.

A whelping box that is about thirty inches square and fourteen inches high is ideal. Such a box is sufficiently large to provide ample room for a big litter, yet not so large that the puppies wander off and cannot find mother. An opening at least fifteen inches wide should be cut out in the front of the box. A piece of wood about five inches high can be fastened with small latches across the bottom of the opening to keep the puppies in the box while enabling the bitch to go out at will. When the puppies are old enough to toddle out of the box, the bottom piece can be removed.

If two upright pieces of wood are placed directly inside the box, one in each corner on either side of the front opening to form a slot, a nine-inch-wide slat of wood can be dropped into place, closing the front side completely. During the first few days after the puppies have arrived, the front should be kept entirely closed to keep heat in the box and to prevent any possibility of even slight drafts on the puppies.

A very satisfactory box can be made out of a good-grade, lightweight plywood. Put several coats of a plastic finish, recommended for use on children's furniture, on the inside of the box, sanding with a fine paper between each coat. The resulting hard, smooth surface will protect the box from dampness and is easily cleaned. The outside of the box can be painted with a nontoxic enamel paint or can be finished in the same manner as the inside.

If the whelping box is put inside a portable exercise pen the bitch can be free to leave the whelping box to stretch her legs or get a drink of water, but will be confined while she is having the discharge that follows whelping.

The floor of the exercise pen should be covered with a plastic sheet; shower curtain liners serve the purpose nicely. The whelping box is set on a piece of the rubberized padding that is used under carpets. This keeps the box from sliding on the plastic, and if the bottom of the box is at all uneven, the matting prevents the box from rocking. The entire area of the exercise pen is covered with newspaper, as is the bottom of the whelping box. Have stacks of newspaper on hand, as you will go through layers of paper during the whelping. As the puppies grow, it will take bundles of papers to keep the puppy pen clean.

Another arrangement is to use a remnant piece of vinyl flooring several inches greater on all sides than the dimensions of the pen. During the whelping and until the puppies are old enough to venture out of the box, there is no need to put down newspapers, which are hard to keep neat. Any mess can be wiped up and cleaned with paper towels.

Over the years further refinements to this setup have been devised. When preparing the pen, cinder blocks and bungee cords can be used to secure the position of the sides. And as older puppies are not above demolishing walls they can reach through the wire, a two-by-four board can be placed between any adjacent baseboard and the bottom of the pen.

Perhaps the dandiest invention is a solution to bedding for the newborn. First cut two pieces of stiff vinyl flooring to fit the bottom of the whelping box. Then sew an envelope on three sides from imitation sheepskin (top) and any other scrap material (bottom) into which the piece of vinyl can be slipped. Allow a little extra bottom material on one side of the opening to form a flap, which can be pinned closed. A piece of padding the same size completes this simple project. Make at least two or three envelopes.

Once all the puppies have been born, the dirty newspapers are removed and the piece of vinyl and padding in the envelope is placed in the whelping box. A heating pad may be positioned in one corner. The flap is pinned along the open edge. The bitch and her babies now can be settled in the nest, which provides warmth and good footing for newborns, is washable and will not allow disarrangement by the dam. When the bedding becomes soiled, it is replaced easily with the second piece of vinyl, all readied with its snug envelope. The first envelope and pad are washed and prepared for the next change.

If any form of sewing is not possible, other accommodations can work out well. The foam pad made for a crate fits nicely into the whelping box, serving as a comfortable bed until labor actually begins, at which time the pad is removed. After the new family has arrived, the box is cleaned and the newspapers are replaced with the foam pad and a piece of carpet. Pad and carpet are then covered with a section of blanket. The edges of the blanket are tucked well under the pad and carpeting so the puppies cannot crawl under the blanket.

Mothers really appreciate the comfort of the foam pad in the whelping box, and newborns like to line up along the side, resting their heads on the pad. The puppies very quickly learn to squirm their way up to mother to nurse, sliding back down to the warmth of the heating pad when they are finished.

Breeders differ in their preference for using a heating pad or a heating lamp for newborn puppies. The preference here is for the heating pad, simply because the amount of heat can be easily regulated, and the bitch can get away from the heat if she is uncomfortable. The argument in favor of the heating lamp is that a higher ambient temperature can be maintained, and the puppies are not receiving heat just from underneath.

Regardless of method, some form of heat is beneficial during the first few days when the puppy's own mechanism for regulating body temperature is not fully functioning. Care must be taken, though, not to make the bitch and her puppies uncomfortable with too much heat. Puppies who are either too warm or too cold will be restless and continually crying as they move from side to side in the box. About 80° to 85°F in the nest is about right.

When the puppies are four to five days old, they will usually start avoiding the heated area of the whelping box. Gradually lower the heat, dispensing with the heating pad altogether by the time the puppies are a week to ten days old. Obviously, the time of year and the climate will be factors in maintaining the correct temperature.

By placing the whelping box in a pen that is only slightly wider than the box, it is possible to cover the entire area of the whelping box with a blanket or spread. In a cool room, especially, this is a satisfactory way of keeping the puppies in a warmer environment with less temperature fluctuation. The cover is not only added protection against possible drafts, but it provides the bitch with welcomed, denlike privacy.

WHELPING

There are a few almost invariable signs to watch for that will indicate the imminent arrival of the new litter.

During the last week or so of pregnancy, the presence of a clear, glassy, odorless vaginal discharge is perfectly normal. Should the discharge become cloudy, discolored or have an odor, consult your veterinarian immediately.

Also at this time it is exciting to observe movement of the puppies as the bitch seeks a comfortable position on her back. Her nipples should be wiped clean, perhaps with a small amount of mineral oil to loosen the dirt, and she should be introduced to her whelping box.

A check on the bitch's temperature will show a drop in temperature as much as five days ahead of whelping. It may hover around 100° to 99.8°F, a drop from the normal range of 101° to 102°F. The lower temperature seems to be associated with the pre-labor changes taking place within the bitch. A day or so before the pending whelping, the bitch will appear thinner and the hip bones will become more prominent as the weight shifts lower in the body. An internal examination now would likely show that the dilation of the cervix has begun.

When the temperature takes a sudden nose dive down to the 99°F to 98°F range and stays there, watch for the initial stages of labor to begin. Now is a good time to notify your veterinarian that you may be needing his assistance within the next twenty-four hours. Thus he will be prepared for your possible middle-of-night call, or if he is not going to be available, you will be able to establish contact with someone whom you can reach if you need help.

It is highly recommended that a second person be lined up to attend even a normal whelping. Sometimes puppies come so fast it takes four hands to cope. And should things go wrong, the moral support is invaluable. Novices should have a knowledgeable assistant at hand.

Coinciding with the final temperature drop will be another very obvious change in the bitch's appearance, as she becomes what can be best described as "lumped up." The sides of her abdomen will be tense and hard as they seemingly constrict around the laden uterus. The lumps you can feel at this point are the puppies about to be born. Once a bitch has started to lump up, she will most likely refuse any food, no matter how tempting you have made her favorite meal. Should she eat, despite her better judgment, do not expect the food to stay down for long.

Labor begins with shivering, trembling and panting. The bitch, though obviously unsettled and wanting the reassurance of your company, has a faraway, withdrawn look about her, as though she had returned to the wilds of her ancestors and was giving birth to her young all on her own. This preliminary stage of labor with the panting, the shivering, the digging and shredding of papers, all interrupted with occasional periods of rest, can continue quite some time before the final stages of labor begin. Some bitches will carry on for ten hours or more before getting down to business. Others will have a puppy out within two hours of tossing up a dinner they really should not have eaten.

When the actual whelping appears to be starting, put a heating pad or hot water bottle wrapped in a towel or piece of blanket in a small cardboard box and cover the carton with a blanket. Place the heated box near the whelping box so the first-born puppies can be put in the box to be kept warm and out of the bitch's way when she is occupied with the delivery of later arrivals. Let the bitch see the puppies being placed in the box, and if she becomes bothered when a puppy in the box squeaks, put the puppy back with her. It is of utmost importance throughout the entire whelping that the bitch feels totally secure, private and not fussed.

Keeping in mind the old adage "A chilled puppy is a dead puppy," remember to take your "incubator" box with you should you have to take your bitch to the veterinarian for assistance with the whelping. Opinion is divided as to how much assistance should be given to a bitch during whelping. Bitches of some breeds resent any interference to the point where they will prove to be poor mothers unless they are permitted to deliver and care for their young in complete privacy.

Corgi puppies are often slow to start breathing, and most breeders, being reluctant to trust to luck that the bitch will get the puppy going in time, will take the puppy away from the bitch as soon as it is born. The puppy is then returned to its dam after it has been dried off and is breathing easily. Fortunately, most Corgi bitches are quite tolerant of any help given during whelping.

Ch. Northwoods Song and Dance, ROMX (Ch. Braxentra Michaelmas, ROMX, ex Ch. Maravon Sally Forth), whelped August 23, 1975. Breeder-owner: Pamela Bradbury. As runner-up all-time top Brood Bitch in the United States, she produced thirteen champions from four litters, all by different sires. "Cookie" is pictured at ten years of age winning the Veterans Bitch class under judge Pat Curties at the Canadian Ontario/Quebec section Specialty.

When hard labor begins and the contractions become strong and regular, stand by with a towel (an absorbent bath towel is best), ready to lift the puppy away as it emerges from the vulva. If it is an easy birth, and the cord is still attached, you can ease the placenta out immediately after the puppy is born. Quickly break the membrane sac over the puppy's head, open the mouth with your little finger, and dry the puppy briskly with the towel. As soon as the puppy is breathing easily, tie the cord about an inch from the body with strong thread and cut on the placenta side with sterilized scissors. Put the puppy with the bitch so she will realize the newborn is her responsibility.

There are definite pros and cons to letting a bitch eat the afterbirths. Many breeders find the bitches will vomit or have diarrhea if allowed to eat the afterbirths, so they quickly remove each afterbirth when it is passed from the bitch before she can get to it. Other breeders contend, perhaps rightly so, that

Ch. Vangard The Last Chance, ROMX (Ch. Stokeplain Fair Chance of Cote de Neige, ROM, ex Ch. Vangard Maid of Honor). Bred by Robert Simpson in 1975 and owned by Marge Bennett, "Prune" is the dam of twelve AKC champions, including multiple all-breed BIS and Specialty winners. She is shown winning Veterans Bitch at the 1984 Cascade Specialty when she was almost nine years old.   *Carl Lindemaier*

Mother Nature is not wasteful in her design and the afterbirths contain nutrients that are beneficial to the bitch after whelping.

Having seen many bitches clean up all the afterbirths from a large litter with no ill effects whatsoever, it would be easy to claim the most natural procedure is best. By the same token, though, bitches who have undergone caesarian sections without having the chance to devour a single placenta seem to do well by their puppies without the added elements stored in the afterbirths. Thus it becomes a matter of your preference and experience as to your procedure here. In any case, it is important to account for the placenta of each puppy, as some may be retained and not appear until later.

The time interval between the delivery of each puppy varies from fifteen or twenty minutes to several hours. If the bitch is resting for most of the time, all is well. Two hours of intermittent, unproductive contractions, though, is a different matter entirely. Hard, prolonged labor will wear a bitch down quickly. If labor is allowed to go beyond three hours, the bitch may have a difficult time of it if surgery is required.

Some puppies are presented breech, meaning the hind feet come first. A breech puppy must be freed as quickly as possible as chances are the sac has already broken, and there is danger that the puppy will suffocate. Wrap a piece of toweling around the hind end of the puppy, and holding the body with one hand, get a good grasp on the tail with the other. With each contraction pull firmly on the puppy in a downward direction if the puppy is coming tummy down. Pull in an upward direction if the puppy is on his back.

Puppies who have had a difficult birth are often extremely difficult to revive. Their tongue, mouth membranes and even the pads of their feet may have turned blue. Even though a puppy may appear to be dead, do not give up on it too quickly. Sometimes a puppy will come around after fifteen to twenty minutes of seemingly futile attempts to revive it.

Take the apparent stillborn puppy to another room to work on it so the bitch will not be alarmed by what you are doing to the puppy. If vigorously rubbing the puppy against the hair up the back and neck with a towel does not elicit a response, try briskly swinging the puppy to free the air passages of fluid that may have collected. To do this, use both hands to firmly hold the puppy on its back in a towel. With its head away from you, your arms outstretched, quickly swing the puppy down between your knees. Repeat several times, wiping away any mucous and fluid expelled from the nose. Alternate swinging the puppy with sessions of mouth to mouth resuscitation. Breathe into the puppy's mouth, then press gently on the ribs to force the air back out. Rhythmically repeat the procedure for a minute or two before swinging the puppy again.

If your efforts are successful and the puppy starts to gasp for air, start massaging him with a towel. Rubbing a puppy against the hair up the back of the neck will goad him into crying. Once he has let out with a lusty yell, you can take him back to his mother.

One of the most difficult situations to be encountered with a whelping is one where you are able to haul the puppies out of the bitch, but because of the difficult whelping the puppies are stillborn. It is not uncommon for all but maybe one or two puppies of a litter to be lost this way. With the old adage of hindsight being better than foresight proving to be ever so true, you will realize after such a loss that had a caesarean been performed after the first one or two puppies were lost, you may have saved the rest of the litter. If you let the bitch struggle through a rough delivery for a number of puppies, the odds will be that much less in favor of her surviving the surgery. Here is where you are indeed fortunate if you have a veterinarian who is as interested and determined to save the bitch and as many of the puppies as possible as you are. Despite the fact the time taken to perform a caesarean will play havoc with the office schedule, a competent veterinarian will not waste time while you are losing puppies. You can expect to pay good money for the considerable time the veterinarian will give to your whelping bitch. It is well worth it, though, to know if the bitch does not respond to the usual whelping aids, such as intravenous calcium injections or pitocin injections, that surgery will be performed before all is lost.

If it appears that a caesarean is necessary, be sure there are several people handy to rub the puppies as they are taken from the dam. The veterinarian will be busy with the surgery, and it is imperative that the whelps be brought around and kept warm. Often these babies are almost lifeless at first and need considerable attention to get them going.

It is difficult to determine when a bitch has finished delivering a litter. The swollen horns of the uterus can feel hard and lumpy, and consequently can be taken for another puppy.

One possible indication that the bitch has finished whelping is that she will usually relax and quietly settle down to nurse her new family after the last puppy has been delivered. If you get all the soiled wet papers in the whelping box replaced with fresh dry bedding and the heating pad, only to have yet another puppy arrive, just remember you are far from being the only person who has been fooled this way.

The bitch will do the best by her puppies if she is allowed to have absolute privacy and quiet after she has settled in with her family. This is difficult when there are small, curious children in the family. If the bitch shows no uneasiness about the children coming into the room where her puppies are, no harm will be done by letting the children quietly look at the puppies. Be even more cautious about permitting outsiders to see the puppies, gauging your restrictions on the bitch's reactions.

CARE OF THE BROOD BITCH

During the course of the whelping, a bitch will be eager for small drinks of cool fresh water. Some breeders add a bit of honey to the drinking water, making a drink that is rather similar to glucose in water. High carbohydrate foods such as honey, sugar, and glucose, or stimulants such as milky tea with glucose, will give a short-term energy boost that can get a bitch through a single crisis. When a whelping is nearing completion with perhaps one puppy to go, the honey- or glucose-in-water drink may provide a tiring bitch with the necessary energy to finish up.

Feed the new mother lightly for the first day or so after whelping. Small milky feeds, such as milk with cereal, can be given three or four times a day, with a raw egg yolk added to one of the meals. (Remember to avoid regular cow's milk.) Small bland meals of rice with cooked chicken can be used to make the transition from the milky feeds to the bitch's regular fare. By the second or third day after whelping, most bitches will welcome their usual meals of fresh meat and cereal or biscuit.

Fresh drinking water should be available at all times. This is a must that is all too frequently overlooked.

By the second week after whelping, the demands on the bitch by her rapidly growing family rise quickly, and her food intake has to be increased proportionately. At least three meals a day, preferably four, should be given. Two of the four meals should consist of the bitch's regular food with an ample allotment of fresh meat. The other two meals can be milk and cereal feeds, with or without additional protein supplements such as cottage cheese or a raw egg yolk.

A bitch's milk production is at its absolute peak when her puppies are between three and four weeks old, despite the fact that by this time the puppies are beginning to eat from a dish. Although one seldom hears of a Pembroke bitch having eclampsia, be aware that this is the critical time period when eclampsia is most apt to occur. Eclampsia, a disorder involving the calcium balance in the body, is characterized by obvious weakness, staggering and possible convulsions. Should a nursing bitch act at all peculiarly, play it safe and call your veterinarian.

It is wise to continue taking the bitch's temperature for a few days after the whelping. Should it rise above 103°F, contact the veterinarian. Also, a dark discharge is common for the first week or so. If it does not gradually disappear or becomes bloody, again seek the advice of the doctor.

For the first few days after whelping, the bitch will be reluctant to leave her puppies even for the few minutes necessary to take care of her needs outside. By the end of the first week, she will enjoy going on a few brief walks, letting you know when she thinks she had better hurry back to her family. By the time the puppies are two weeks old, most bitches are eager to join the other dogs on their regular daily walks. The exercise, fresh air and a chance just to be themselves provide a welcomed change from the confines of the whelping box.

Few bitches want to stay on around-the-clock duty after the puppies are four weeks old. Most ask for time off before then. Generally the bitches will stay with their young at night until the puppies are six weeks old. During the seventh week, the bitch may want to visit the puppies occasionally if she still has milk. It is best, though, to start keeping the puppies away from Mum at this point so her milk can dry up completely. Usually by the time the puppies are eight weeks old, the bitch will be completely dry, and she can go back with her puppies for playtime. Most bitches love to play with their puppies, and the puppies benefit as well from her discipline as from her love.

Within two months after whelping, the bitch will begin to shed heavily, to the point where she will become as naked as a billiard ball. One cycle has ended, and her system is preparing for a new one to start, with a season due in about two months.

The bitch has put her all into giving you a fine litter. She richly deserves a rest, and except under unusual circumstances, should not be bred at the season immediately following a litter of puppies.

A litter of six-week-old puppies born in the early 1950s. The solid red coloring is seldom seen today. Note the difference in type of these puppies from those in the other photographs.

Six-week-old bitch puppies.

Spengler

16

Puppies

PUPPIES. A joy to watch whether they are newborns only a few hours old or roly-poly, eight-week-old bundles of energy clowning about in a pen.

There is a deep, indescribable satisfaction that comes with rearing a litter of healthy, personable puppies of good quality. The effort, the heartache, the disappointments encountered along the way fade when you see the bright future shining in the eyes of the happy puppies you have bred and raised.

Healthy, newborn puppies are quiet puppies. All that is heard from a contented new litter will be an occasional squeak as a puppy is nudged away from a teat by a tougher littermate, or when another puppy is frustrated at not being able to locate a teat as quickly as he would like. When not busy nursing, very young puppies will sleep stretched out on their sides. By the time the puppies are a week or so old, they will sleep on their tummies more frequently, often crawling into a heap rather than sleeping all spread out from one another as newborns do. Twitching in their sleep is normal and a sign of good health.

All is not well if the puppies are restless and crawling from one end of the box to the other while fussing constantly. Puppies will behave in this manner if they are too warm or too cold, if the bitch has insufficient or poor-quality milk or if an infection is brewing. A veterinarian should be consulted if the puppies remain fussy and restless for more than eight hours.

Well-nourished puppies will feel plump and firm to the touch. Any puppy who is not nursing, or is falling behind his littermates in size and weight, should be examined for a physical defect such as a cleft palate.

SUPPLEMENTAL FEEDING

Newborn puppies will benefit from supplemental feeding if they have been separated from the bitch for any length of time during the whelping, or if the bitch's milk is slow to come in. Also the smaller, weaker puppies can be helped along with several supplemental feedings a day for a few days, as can the puppies of a very large litter.

There are prepared canned formulas for puppies available, but a simple homemade formula has proven to be the most satisfactory for supplemental feeding, or for rearing orphan puppies. The formula consists of 1 can condensed goat's milk diluted with 2 to 3 cans of boiled or distilled water; 1 raw egg yolk, 1 tablespoonful honey (or light Karo syrup), and a few grains each of table salt and "lite" salt (potassium chloride).

Fresh goat's milk can be substituted for the diluted condensed milk if available. Powdered goat's milk will do as well. Canned cow's milk can be used in a pinch, but goat's milk, said to be the closest to bitch's milk in composition, is least likely of the substitute milks to produce gas in the puppies. Canned goat's milk is readily available at most health food stores. It would be wise to have a supply on hand before the litter is due. What is not used as formula for the nursing puppies can later be used for weaning the puppies.

Be careful when adding the egg yolk not to let any of the egg white slip into the milk mixture. Somehow egg whites in the formula, however small the amount, manage to gravitate to the nipple of the bottle and completely clog the opening.

Warm the formula slightly before feeding. The formula can be fed with a regular baby's bottle and full-sized nipple rather than with the small nipple provided with pet nurser kits. Make sure the milk will flow easily from the nipple without pouring out. To get the puppy to take the bottle, hold him gently by the head, lifting him both up and slightly forward so his front feet are off your lap or the table where you are holding him. With the hand holding the head, gently press the sides of the puppy's mouth open and insert the nipple. As the mouth closes on the nipple, pull up and back slightly on the bottle. As the puppy tries to hang on, suction is created. Hold the bottle tilted upward. The puppy should do the rest.

Tube feeding has become a widely used method of feeding very young puppies. It takes infinitely less time to tube feed an entire litter than it does to feed each puppy with a bottle, a factor that lends appeal to this method of supplemental feeding. For puppies not nursing on their dam, though, tube feeding removes what little form of exercise is left for such puppies. Also with tube feeding, puppies are fed a specific amount of formula regardless of whether or not they are hungry. Surely the very young must benefit from the nursing behavior, or we would hear of busy human mothers tube feeding their infants.

While bottle feeding is preferred here for routine supplemental feeding, small puppies who are too weak to nurse either on the dam or the bottle can often be saved with tube feeding. The process of tube feeding may seem scary until you actually try doing it. The instructions that come with the puppy tube-feeding kit, available through most animal supply houses, are quite clear, and if you follow closely the amount to feed a puppy, being careful to not overfeed, all should go well.

There is one word of caution, however. Never tube feed a chilled puppy. First warm the baby. The traditional method is to place him under your shirt as you move about, thereby encircling him with natural warmth. A few drops of glucose solution given every half hour will provide energy until he is warm and strong enough to start the milk. Homemade glucose, wise to have on hand before the onset of whelping, consists of one teaspoon of light Karo syrup dissolved in four tablespoons of boiled or distilled water plus a few grains each of table salt and ''lite'' salt.

ORPHAN PUPPIES

Rarely are puppies raised by hand truly orphans. Most have been taken away from their dam because she has either developed an infection that can affect the puppies, or she has proven to be one of those unfortunate bitches who will try to kill her puppies. Perhaps just one puppy needs special attention.

The puppies to be raised by hand can be kept in a cardboard carton large enough to have a heating pad at one end with sufficient room remaining for the puppies to sleep away from the heat if they are too warm. Place a piece of blanket or toweling over a thick layer of newspapers on the bottom of the box. If the edges of the blanket are tucked in under the newspaper, the puppies will not be able to crawl under the blanket. Cover the box with a towel or light blanket to provide a constant ambient temperature for the puppies.

Experts vary in opinion as to how often the puppies should be fed. Some people believe newborn puppies should be fed every two hours day and night. Others suggest one feeding every eight hours. Puppies here have done well with a feeding every four hours day and night for the first week. Thereafter, the middle of the night feeding is eliminated.

During the first week each puppy will take an average of one ounce of formula every four hours. Some puppies are much greedier than others and may have to be limited in the quantity of formula consumed if they show signs of distress after an overly large meal.

If a puppy refuses to take the formula, it may need to relieve itself. Young puppies who are not being cared for by their dam need to be massaged in order to urinate and defecate. After every feeding gently stroke the puppy in the pelvic area with cotton moistened with warm water to stimulate urination. Lift the tail (if it has not been docked yet) and gently wipe the anal region with cotton to induce the puppy to empty. If the skin on the abdomen appears red and dry from urine irritation, apply baby oil or a soothing hand cream several times a day. Once you begin to find stools and damp spots on the bedding, you can be sure the puppies are capable of tending to business themselves, making one less chore

Pembroke Welsh Corgi puppies at various ages. The puppies in the top photo are ten weeks old; the tricolor in the center is three months old; and the puppy at the bottom is four months old.

for you to look after. Constipation can be a chronic problem with orphan puppies. A pinch of Senecot granules added to the formula will serve as a mild laxative. Regulate the amount of Senecot used in accordance with its effect on the puppies after one or two feedings.

A hand-raised litter is usually introduced to solid foods earlier than is a litter nursed by the dam. By the time the puppies' eyes are open, usually around the fourteenth day, the puppies can be given small amounts of solid food. The puppies will greedily suck in small pieces of lean ground beef moistened slightly with warm water. Be careful not to overfeed. Baby cereal or meat can be mixed with formula to make a thickened gruel the puppies can lick from a dish. The puppies are still too wobbly at this age to hold themselves up long enough to eat from a dish, so each puppy will have to be held to the dish for a turn at eating. This is a messy business, with the puppies getting more gruel on themselves than in them. Within a few days the puppies will become more adept at eating, and feeding them will be much easier.

Unlike puppies who put considerable energy into nursing on their dam and who benefit from the exercise obtained when competing with littermates to nurse at the bitch's most productive teats, hand-reared puppies get very little exercise. Consequently, as fat, sloppy, pancakelike puppies, they are less well coordinated for their age than puppies raised under normal circumstances. This difference will gradually diminish as the puppies become old enough to start playing with each other. Heavy puppies will have an easier time getting up on their feet if they are kept on a textured surface (blanketing, washable matting) than if they are kept on newspaper.

One last but very important point to be concerned about with hand-raised puppies is the matter of distemper-hepatitis-parvo immunity. Puppies receive a high concentration of antibodies in the colostrum, which is the milk produced by the bitch during the first few days after whelping. Orphan puppies who have not nursed on the dam at all will lack the usual antibody protection. Consult your veterinarian for his recommendations as to what immunization program should be initiated.

TAIL BANDING

The vast majority of Pembroke Welsh Corgi breeders now remove their puppies' tails with rubber bands rather than having them surgically docked. The advantages of banding over docking are many. The pain and shock caused by surgical amputation is avoided with banding. All the puppy appears to feel is an annoyance at the tingling, pins-and-needles sensation as the tail becomes numb after the rubber band has been tied in place. The banding method eliminates the worry about possible bleeders and minimizes the concern over removing too much tail.

Over the years the banding method of tail docking has been viewed with considerable skepticism by veterinarians or breeders who have either not seen

Tail Docking by the Rubber Band Method

Litter of three-day-old Corgis with tails of various lengths. Two are natural bobs. *Phyl*

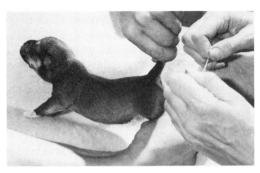

Holding the tail up . . . *Phyl*

. . . place the rubber band firmly against the tail. *Phyl*

Be careful to place the rubber band above the anus. *Phyl*

Tail Docking by the Rubber Band Method

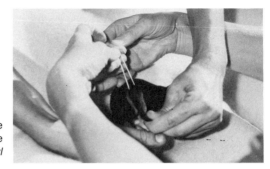

Pull the tail down while holding the ends of the rubber band over the back. *Phyl*

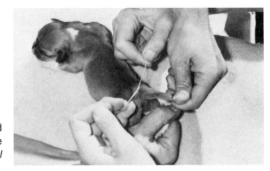

With the rubber band going around the tail only once, tie a knot at the top. *Phyl*

Snip off the ends of the rubber band to ¼ inch. *Phyl*

Within an hour or so after banding, the tail will go limp and gradually shrivel (middle puppy), and by the fourth or fifth day it will drop off (right puppy). Should seepage occur, the tail area can be swabbed with a mild disinfectant. Check any tail that is slow to come off to make sure it is not simply hanging on by hairs caught up in the band. *Phyl*

241

the tail banding procedure being done, or have not seen it performed correctly. The main objection these people have had is that banding may cause an infection and, worse yet, gangrene. Apparently infection is commonly associated with banding of lambs' tails, and the assumption is made it will be likewise with banding puppy tails. Numerous veterinarians who have become acquainted with the banding procedure, as illustrated here, readily concede that it is a simple, efficient method that subjects the puppy to less stress than would be encountered with surgical docking.

No breeder looks forward to the chore of "doing tails and dewclaws," but the sooner done and forgotten about the better. Full-term puppies born early in the day usually are sturdy and vigorous enough to have their tails banded and dewclaws removed on the following morning. Puppies born late in the day or at night should not be done until the second morning. Small puppies off to a slow start need not be done until they are three to five days old. If the decision has been made to have the tails surgically docked, make an appointment with the veterinarian for when the puppies will be approximately three days old.

Ideally tail docking, regardless of method, and dewclaw removal should be done early in the day. This permits the puppies to settle in with their dam and forget the whole mean business before your bedtime. Plus it is easier to make frequent checks on the puppies during the daytime. While most puppies quiet down and are happily nursing on Mum even before the last puppy in the litter has been banded, an occasional litter is encountered in which all of the puppies will fuss and fret at great length. The puppies' crying and constant restless motion around the box is wearing on the puppies and trying on the dam as well as her owner, but it does stop.

Have a supply of fresh elastic bands on hand. Old rubber bands will snap in two with aggravating frequency just as you are tying the knot. Use a band that is approximately one-sixteenth inch wide and long enough to handle easily, about two inches when cut open. The width of the band is important, as it is the extremely narrow area of pressure on the tail that makes this docking procedure work so well.

The tail banding and dewclaw removal operation should be carried out well away from the bitch. It sometimes helps to play the radio at full volume near the whelping box to keep the dam from hearing the puppies' distressed crying. If it is a large litter, it works well to take two puppies away from the dam at a time, keeping them warm in a box with a hot water bottle, and exchanging them for two more when they are ready to be returned to Mum. A small litter can be done quickly while Mum is outside, oblivious to your activities.

SURGICAL DOCKING

The following explicit description of surgical tail docking was published in the PWCCA *Newsletter* (March 1967). If your veterinarian has not had consid-

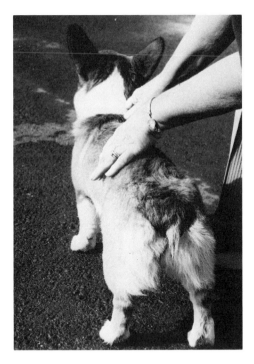

A natural bobtail at six months. (The subject is second from the right in the photo of the three-day-old litter.) It is usually necessary to remove surgically any tail stump. Left undocked, the heavy, brushy stump will detract from the overall appearance of the adult.   *Phyl*

erable experience with the Pembroke breed, he may well appreciate having information on the procedure as written by a fellow practitioner.

The unique demands of the fancy for tail docking in the Corgi requires certain special techniques based on these objectives:

1. Painless and bloodless procedure
2. Prompt and uncomplicated healing
3. Total elimination of any tail "stump," with a nice finish to the rump in the mature dog

Procedure

Prepare the base of the tail by shaving with a surgical clipper and swabbing with merthiolate or a good antiseptic. Infiltrate above and below the base of the tail with 2% procaine and 1:100,000 epinephrin for anesthetic and hemostatis. Using a sharp, curved scissors, and by placing the tip of each blade at the immediate junction of the tail with the body of the puppy, holding the scissors almost perpendicular to the puppy, make a slightly crescent-shaped cut through the skin on top of the tail. Similarly, make a cut through the skin above the anus to intersect with the original incision and to provide a somewhat shorter and straighter line of incision. Snip the tail between these two incisions flush with the contour of the rump. Secure the skin with two sutures to provide a neat, smooth closure. Gentle digital pressure over the amputation site for two or three minutes will preclude any oozing of blood.

243

This procedure, done with aseptic technique and a minimum of trauma, will provide a painless expedient for tail docking the Corgi, prompt uncomplicated healing and a symmetrical *widow's peak* effect over the anus in the grown dog.

REMOVAL OF DEWCLAWS

While it is not required by the Standard, Corgi breeders, almost without exception, remove all dewclaws on their puppies at the time of tail docking. Check all puppies for dewclaws on their hind legs as well as on the front legs.

Have the following materials ready before you bring in the puppies:

Thin, curved manicure scissors
Sterilized cotton
70% rubbing alcohol
Coagulant powder or liquid (Nail Clot) or silver nitrate sticks.

Cover the work area with newspapers and have a box of tissues handy in case a puppy urinates or messes during the banding or dewclaw surgery. Disinfect the scissors thoroughly with a piece of cotton saturated with alcohol. Repeat after each puppy has been done.

Using a slightly fatter rubber band than used for the banding, make a tourniquet by tying a piece of rubber band around each front leg just below the elbow. Have your assistant who is holding the puppy push with his thumb against one of the puppy's elbows to force the leg out taut, dewclaw facing up. With the curve of the manicure scissors slipped under the dewclaw and resting on the leg, pull up slightly and snip off the dewclaw. Push back the skin to expose the round, white ball of cartilage that lies beneath the dewclaw. Cut this core of cartilage out to prevent the possible return of a stunted dewclaw. Dab with coagulant powder and slowly remove the tourniquet. Remove the other dewclaw in the same manner. The nail clot powder made by Four Paws has been found to be exceptionally effective for this purpose. Normally at this point there will not be any bleeding where the dewclaws were removed. If bleeding starts again when the tourniquets are removed, reapply the tourniquets, wipe off the excess blood and quickly put more coagulant powder on the wound. Give the coagulant a minute to form a seal, and remove the tourniquet. The tourniquet should not be left on any longer than absolutely necessary at any point in this procedure.

Dewclaws on the hind legs can just be snipped off without benefit of a tourniquet. These dewclaws usually are more like skin appendages and are much easier to remove than are front dewclaws.

It is a good practice to trim each puppy's nails at this time, and then trim the nails regularly once or twice a week. Keeping puppies' nails short will prevent the bitch from being scratched by busy little feet during nursing. Proper foot care while puppies are young will help achieve the desired neat, tight foot in the adult.

WEANING

If at all possible, postpone any attempts to wean the litter until after the puppies are twenty-eight days old. If the litter is large and the bitch has little milk, you must, of course, start weaning earlier.

Clarence Pfaffenberger in his excellent work *The New Knowledge of Dog Behavior* (Howell Book House, New York) emphasizes the necessity of not subjecting a puppy between the ages of twenty-one to twenty-eight days to any abrupt changes, as it is an extremely critical period in a puppy's development when he needs to feel absolute security. Mr. Pfaffenberger writes:

> At twenty-one days of age the puppy not only can start to learn, but will start whether he is taught or not. This change is so abrupt that whereas the puppy does not see (at least very much) or smell or hear at all on his twentieth day of age, within twenty-four hours he does all of these quite well. Naturally, he needs the security of his mother.

Mr. Pfaffenberger continues:

> This period of twenty-one to twenty-eight days is so strange to the puppy that at no other time in a puppy's life can he become so emotionally upset, nor could such an upset have such a lasting effect upon his social attitudes.

In fact, the observation of many Corgi litters seems to indicate that this breed reaches the critical point as early as nineteen days old.

To understand how best to care for your puppies during the three- to four-week period, consider how the young in the wild, raised in the dark, silent warmth of their den, become slowly aware of their environment. First there is the warmth and smell of their mother and littermates; the perception of motion as the dam comes and goes; and the hearing of the quiet, distant woodland sounds. Only when the young are physically, mentally and emotionally ready to cope with their surrounding environment will they cautiously make brief exploratory ventures away from the security of the den. Then contrast this with what a litter of puppies raised in the family kitchen face as their senses spring to life— bright lights, the clatter of pots and pans, a blaring television or radio, a lot of chatter and coming and going of people. The confusion of family life is ideal when it comes to socializing an older puppy, but not a baby. If your puppies have to be moved out of their first accommodations, put them in their new quarters before or after the critical twenty-one- to twenty-eight-day period.

SUGGESTED DIET AND FEEDING SCHEDULES

Four-week-old puppies are physically quite able to stand and eat from a dish, which makes them far easier to wean than younger puppies. They will catch on right away to lapping up milky feeds such as milk mixed with baby cereal. By thickening the milk slightly with the cereal, the puppies are less apt to snort the milk up into their nostrils. Ring salad mold pans make excellent puppy feeding dishes. The food is kept close to the outside edges so the puppies will not crawl through the food to reach it all.

Puppies can be fed milky feeds from one dish, or more if it is a large litter, until they are about seven weeks old. At this point or sooner, puppies should be fed separately to discourage squabbling over the food. The meat meals should always be fed in individual containers to ensure that each puppy gets his full portion. To avoid a mad scramble, place all the dishes on a tray, put the tray on the floor of the puppy pen, and guide one face per bowl. Once the puppies are eating, ease the bowls off the tray and apart, and supervise until the meal is completed.

A suggested feeding schedule is as follows (remember, ''milk'' means goat's milk, commercial puppy formula or canned milk, never regular cow's milk):

4 to 6 weeks:
Morning	Milk and baby cereal (start with rice cereal)
Noon	Scraped or minced lean raw beef, 1 to 2 teaspoonfuls. Milk and cereal.
Supper	Repeat noon feeding
Bedtime	Milky feed

Start off weaning with one milky feed in the morning and one meat feed later in the day. Build up to the four-meal-a-day schedule by the time the puppies are five weeks old. Reduce the amount of food that is given to the dam and keep her away from the litter for longer periods each day. When the puppies are six weeks old, the dam should be visiting them only briefly morning and night. She should be completely dry of milk shortly after and can return to her puppies to get on with her maternal duties of training and disciplining her young.

6 to 8 weeks:
Morning	Milk and cereal. Cooked oatmeal, farina, or hard-baked (rusked) wholewheat bread can be substituted for baby cereal. Good quality commercial kibble soaked with warm water until soft can be introduced. 1 tablespoon whipped cottage cheese
Noon	2 to 3 oz. lean raw beef cut in small chunks or ground Soaked kibble or cereal ¼ teaspoonful corn oil (optional) ½ teaspoonful wheat germ (optional)
Supper	Repeat noon meal, omitting the corn oil and wheat germ
Bedtime	Milky feed, including 1 raw egg yolk per four puppies, plus enough baby cereal to thicken slightly

As the puppies depend less and less on the dam for their supply of essential vitamins and minerals, these nutrients must be provided in the basic diet you are feeding. The use of a multivitamin-mineral supplement is recommended for all growing puppies.

A vegetable oil high in polyunsaturated fats is used to provide the essential fatty acids the puppies had been previously obtaining from the bitch's milk. Safflower oil with its high fatty acid concentration is also a good oil to use, but a lesser amount should be given than is specified for corn oil. Vitamin E requirements are higher when safflower oil is used, so increase the amount of the daily wheat germ supplement accordingly. Do not substitute hydrogenated oils for the corn or safflower oils.

8 to 12 weeks: *Morning*   Milk and cooked cereal or kibble. At this point the kibble may be moistened very slightly with warm water and should not be fed sloppy wet nor sticky and pasty. Start with ¼ cup dry kibble per puppy. Buttermilk or evaporated milk may be substituted for goat's milk.
1 heaping tablespoonful cottage cheese

Noon   2 to 3 oz. raw beef. Other meats such as beef heart, tripe, liver, cooked chicken or fish can be gradually introduced
Kibble as above
½ teaspoonful wheat germ
1 teaspoonful grated raw carrot, chopped parsley or other vitamin A-rich vegetables such as tomatoes, green beans (cooked) or baked sweet potatoes can be added on occasion

Supper   2 to 3 oz. raw beef
Kibble, as above
¼ to ½ teaspoonful corn oil

Bedtime   Milk and egg mixture with a few chunks of kibble

Now is the time to begin adding a well-balanced vitamin-mineral supplement to one of the meals. There are many excellent products available from pet supply companies or veterinarians. A minimum amount is ample as long as the overall diet is nutritious.

In selecting a commercial food, avoid those which have an unusually high protein and fat level. As a rule Corgis do not tolerate foods that contain large amounts of certain fats or tallow for any length of time.

In following any feeding schedule, allow the puppies some individuality in their eating habits. If ten-week-old puppies toy with their midday meal but seem hungry at night, then rearrange the schedule to give a more substantial meal at night while providing a light meal, if any, of milk at noon.

3 to 6 months: *Morning* Buttermilk and ½ to ¾ cup cooked cereal
or kibble, gradually decrease the milk
1 tablespoon cottage cheese
Vitamin supplement

Noon Milk, kibble and meat

Evening 1 heaping tablespoon fresh meat
½ to ¾ cup kibble or meal (measured before soaking in warm water)
½ to 1 teaspoonful corn oil
1 teaspoonful wheat germ
Vegetable supplements

Bedtime Milk feed can be eliminated if desired, but a couple of biscuits would be appreciated

6 to 12 months: Same as for 3 to 6 months with the elimination of the noon meal. The suggested amounts may be altered to suit the individual puppy, who should not be allowed to become pudgy. Extra weight can seriously affect the developing bone structure and lead to problems as an adult.

WORMING AND VACCINATION

Virtually all puppies are born with roundworms (ascarids), even though the dam has been checked and cleared just prior to mating. Do not neglect to ask your veterinarian when and how to worm the litter. The worming process usually is begun at about three to four weeks of age. The vet will also recommend what immunization program should be followed. Every puppy should have a veterinary examination at least once before leaving for its new home.

EARLY TRAINING

The best training a breeder can give a litter of puppies is accomplished by taking the puppies on short, fun walks as soon as they are old enough to go outside, usually at about five weeks of age. At this age the puppies stay close by your feet (usually under them!), as they are too uncertain of themselves to stray off. If you take some older dogs with you, their enthusiasm for the walks quickly passes to the puppies, and the puppies are soon looking forward to this daily activity. The walks provide excellent opportunities to reinforce a puppy's positive behavior of coming to you. Each time a puppy runs to you either to make sure he has not lost track of you, or because you called him, let him know how pleased you are that he came to you. Show him you love him and that you are enjoying his company. Not only will the puppy never forget that you made him feel extra special for coming to you, but a pattern of rapport and companionship will be established that will remain with the puppy for the rest of his life.

To such a dog an open door will signify an invitation to join you, not a temptation to bolt from you.

Another form of early training comes as a matter of course if you start grooming the puppies at an early age. Corgis are independently Welsh! They abhor restraint. Ask any veterinarian who has been the first human being to ever restrain an otherwise docile, well-behaved Corgi when medical attention was required. If a puppy learns to accept physical restraint early, many problems will be avoided later on.

When the puppies are about six weeks old, once or twice a week take each puppy to a room by himself and quietly hold him in your lap or on a table. Gently start combing him with an English fine comb. Keep the first sessions very short, perhaps two minutes or so. Try to stop before the puppy starts to squirm to get away. Whatever you do, do not put the puppy down if he struggles to escape. To do so only teaches the puppy forever that all he has to do to get out of any unwanted situation is to scream, growl, bite or otherwise resist.

If a difficult situation arises, calm the puppy by rubbing his chest and tummy. At the same time, talk to him as though nothing was wrong while pretending to still comb him. As soon as the puppy has settled, put him down and play a bit with him before returning him to his littermates. Never let the puppy so much as guess that you did not accomplish exactly what you set out to do. Properly handled, the puppy will soon look forward to grooming sessions and will even try to cut in on someone else's turn if given a chance. He will have learned there are times when he has to submit to your will, and he will respect you all the more for having that authority.

Trimming the nails all too often can become a struggle. Once a week, pick up a sleepy puppy and place him in your lap. At first cat claw clippers are easiest to use on the tiny nails. When the puppy is five to six weeks old, the guillotine-type nail cutters are more satisfactory. At twelve weeks a puppy can be introduced to the electric grinder, which does the best job. Each session should be approached calmly, with a firm but cheerful attitude. Take all the time you need to reassure and quiet the puppy, and stop only when he is not struggling to get away. Always reward him with a few moments of cuddling until the tension leaves his body. This becomes a bonding experience and paves the way for easy nail care throughout his life.

EVALUATING PUPPIES

From the minute puppies are born, the evaluation process begins. It cannot be helped. With each look at a litter, your eyes will gravitate immediately to the particular puppy or puppies that appeal to you the most. As the puppies grow on, you will continue to match the progress of your favorites against the rest of the litter. Many breeders make a point of keeping a puppy they find instantly appealing. If you are a lucky gambler, this method of selecting the best puppy will probably work. The best you can do any other way is to make an educated

A normal-coated puppy at five weeks. *Phyl*

A fluffy puppy at five weeks. Note the long, silky hairs on the forehead and under the forelegs.
Phyl

Yes, eight-week-old fluffies are cute.

guess, and you still may finish up with a dog you dearly love, but that is no show dog. In other words, there are no guarantees.

The first concern in appraising a litter is to determine whether any of the puppies possess shortcomings described in the official Standard (see Chapter 13) as "very serious faults." Puppies with very serious faults are generally sold without registration papers or with the AKC's limited registration at a considerably lower price than more promising littermates. These puppies should be neutered.

Occasionally the buyer of a puppy with a very serious fault may later decide to enter the dog in Obedience or Tracking trials. He cannot do so, however, unless the dog is registered with the American Kennel Club. Dogs with limited registration may participate in AKC Performance Events but not breed competition. Or, if papers are withheld, depending on the nature of the fault, the breeder may agree to provide registration papers upon receipt of proof that the animal has been neutered.

Several very serious faults specified in the Standard involve coat color or coat quality. The color faults—whitelies, mismarks and usually bluies—are obvious at birth. The whitelies (white predominating with red, sable or tricolor markings) and mismarks (more than the acceptable limit of white markings, or white markings in places other than where listed as acceptable by the Standard) are disappointing to the breeder but these dogs make excellent pets. Bluies are usually more difficult to detect. A smoky gray cast to the coat accompanied by liver-colored eye rims and nose pigmentation is indicative of the bluie's coloring.

Mature color of the puppies cannot be determined with any certainty at an early age. Tricolors are obviously black, but whether they will be red-headed tris or tris with very pale tan markings may not be apparent for some months. Reds vary tremendously in their development. Some puppies are such a dark brown at birth they appear almost black when they emerge from the sac. These dark puppies can clear to any shade of red or sable, ranging from a pale fawn to a dark, heavily sabled red.

As the puppies grow on, their thick, woolly puppy coats often appear more gray than red. At about three months the adult guard hairs begin to come in, the gray puppy fuzz is shed out and the coat slowly clears to its adult coloring. The color of the new guard hairs growing in at the tip of the docked tail will give a good idea of the puppy's eventual color.

Usually the overly long, soft coat of a fluffy is readily apparent by the time the puppy is five weeks old. By paying close attention to the condition of the hair on newborn puppies, some breeders can detect future fluffies with a fair amount of accuracy. The hair on the skull and back of the neck of a newborn fluffy will appear to be silkier and much shinier than the hair of puppies with acceptable coats. Often a "Schnauzer" look on the bridge of the nose is a sign of a future fluff. At three to four weeks of age winter puppies or puppies from heavily coated lines will be carrying such heavy coats the entire litter could look as though they were going to be fluffies. If the hair appears stiff rather than soft and silky, and if there is no decided difference in coats between puppies, there is little reason for concern.

White head markings are accentuated in young puppies. The wide blaze gradually diminishes as the puppy grows. The tan markings of the adult tricolor are just light shadings in the three-week-old puppy.   *Phyl*

At eighteen months the marking has narrowed to a pencil-thin blaze. Also, the eyebrow markings and cheek patches have become prominent. The black muzzle markings of a puppy will be replaced by the tan of the typical "black-headed" tricolor pattern. *Phyl*

252

Puppies should be checked occasionally for overshot or undershot bites. A grossly overshot bite, sometimes called a shark mouth, is often apparent at birth. A puppy with a severe, unattractive mouth fault often is put down at birth. This individual would have difficulty nursing, and later eating. It will most likely have serious dental problems as an adult as well.

Before a puppy loses his milk teeth at about five months, he may appear slightly overshot. An allowance of about an eighth to a quarter of an inch between the inside of the upper baby teeth and the outside of the bottom teeth permits room for the larger permanent teeth to come in with the desired close-fitting scissors bite.

Unfortunately, monorchid or cryptorchid puppies cannot be identified early. If both testicles have not fully descended by seven weeks, there is reason for concern. Even though missing testicles have shown up in some dogs as late as a year of age, the percentage of puppies who become entire after nine weeks is low. Occasionally a puppy will have a testicle that goes up and down like a yo-yo. This condition usually corrects itself by the time the dog is a year or so old.

Because of the uncertainties involved, a monorchid puppy is usually sold at a reduced price with the understanding that should the second testicle come down, the buyer may have registration papers for the puppy upon payment of the balance of the full purchase price. There need not be any such arrangement for a cryptorchid puppy, as it is not expected that both testicles will descend at a later date.

Ear faults are a problem in that generally they are not apparent until well after a puppy reaches a salable age. If thick, heavy ears are not erect at three months, it may be a good idea to tape them up, even though there are doubts as to the actual benefits of taping. Many people believe ears will stand when the physiological conditions are right and not before. This theory is supported with the evidence that very often problem ears will come up on their own after the puppy has completely finished teething at five to six months of age. Favoring early taping, starting at three months, is the concern that the hanging weight of a heavy floppy ear will cause actual structural changes within the ear that make it difficult for the ear to ever stand erect.

There are many ear taping procedures, and each breeder seems to have his or her own favorite method. A very simple technique has worked well here in uncomplicated situations. To tape the ears, shape each ear into a little devil's horn by gently folding the ear around your index finger and tape into place with a five-inch-long strip of half-inch-wide Scotch packaging tape or masking tape. Place the tape as far down the ear and close to the head as possible. An alternative is to tape the ear flat with no curl. Free any hairs caught up in the tape that appear to be pulling on the puppy's skin.

Several taping sessions may be necessary. Leave the ears taped for several days. Then remove the tape for a day in between tapings to give the puppy a chance to use his ears on his own, as well as to prevent ear irritations resulting from continual taping.

If it were to come down to selling off every puppy who has some obvious minor faults, you would undoubtedly find yourself with nothing left to run on for showing and breeding.

Instead, select for overall quality. Look for the nicely proportioned puppy with proud, effortless movement, in contrast to the puppy who pounds along, moving as though his legs are wrapped in splints. A certain handiness of motion more often than not leads to a well-coordinated adult stride. A good length of neck blending well into the shoulders adds a touch of class.

Keep in mind the word "moderation" when selecting a puppy. The heaviest-boned puppy is not necessarily the best puppy any more than is the longest puppy of the lot always a desired length. Refinement in head is essential to maintain the desired foxy look, but neither should a Corgi be so refined that the overall impression is of a toyish dog with a weak, snipey muzzle.

Miss Anne Biddlecombe has provided some excellent guidelines for selecting the best puppies in a litter in her article "Champions in Embryo," published in the *1951 Welsh Corgi League Handbook*. Miss Biddlecombe suggests:

> The mistakes most commonly made by experienced and inexperienced alike, is to hang on to a puppy, hoping against hope, when definitely things have begun to go wrong; and, less often, to discard a puppy unnecessarily when it goes through that awkward age most puppies attain at about four or five months.
>
> Although we generally pick our puppies at three days old, it is really wiser for the novice to wait till they are weaned and wormed, say about eight weeks. The good puppy should by then be beginning to show his points.
>
> He should stand sturdily on thick short legs, with a straight front and his feet forward, a front foot that turns out at this stage nearly always means a bad front later on. Never mind if he is a bit cow-hocked, provided he is not exaggeratedly so, as young puppies seldom stand square behind, and are generally either slightly cow-hocked or slightly barrel-hocked. As the pup grows this should correct itself.
>
> The length of back should be in proportion to height even at this age, and a very short or very long backed puppy can be discarded at once, bearing in mind that a thin puppy will look longer in the back than a fat one.
>
> If the pup's ears are not yet up, a good idea of his future head and expression can be obtained by rolling the puppy over on to his back, the ears will then fall into place.
>
> There should be no tendency to thickness or coarseness in the skull, as this is much more likely to increase rather than decrease as the pup grows older. If, instead of being flat between the ears the skull is slightly domed, this is an advantage, as it will flatten out in time and will ensure plenty of width. A puppy with a domed forehead, i.e. domed immediately above the eyes (apple-headed) can, in general, be discarded, as this will seldom correct itself.
>
> Length of foreface is a bit difficult to judge in a young puppy, one with a long nose can be turned out at once, one with a rather short nose can be kept on till the second dentition, as it may easily grow.

Of eyes and ears, Miss Biddlecombe writes:

> All puppies' eyes are blue when they just open. An eye which is going to be light coloured is a much more clear and intense blue than one which will be darker.

The true colour shows first around the pupil and gradually spreads outwards. It should be quite possible by eight or nine weeks to judge the eventual colouring. The size of the ear cannot be judged with safety until later. I prefer a big-eared puppy to a small-eared one, as little triangular cat ears seldom grow enough, and small ears spoil the whole expression.

In concluding her article, Miss Biddlecombe writes:

Generally speaking, in my opinion, the puppies that make into the best dogs in the end are the loose, floppy, slow developers—often unshowable under nine or ten months. There are, of course, exceptions, outstanding ones, but I am convinced that the slow developers are the better in the end.

SELLING PUPPIES

As with other issues, opinion is divided on the best age for selling puppies and sending them off to their new homes. There are now state and interstate regulations that prohibit the sale of puppies under eight weeks of age. Many breeders let puppies leave the kennel at eight weeks of age. Others prefer to hold puppies back until they are at least ten weeks old, preferably twelve weeks. The span of a few weeks makes a considerable difference in the puppy's emotional development and its ability to cope with new situations. Also, because it is physically more developed, the older puppy has a much easier time complying with the house training rules than it would have had a few weeks earlier.

It is the breeder's responsibility to provide the proper registration papers and an accurate three-generation pedigree when a puppy is sold. Litter registration forms are obtained by sending a request to the American Kennel Club. After the puppies arrive, the litter registration application should be filled out by the owner of the dam and sent to the owner of the stud dog for his or her signature. The completed form is returned to the American Kennel Club with the appropriate fee. The owner of the litter will then receive an individual registration application for each puppy in the litter. It is this blue slip that is transferred to a new owner unless the breeder, himself, applies for the individual registration. In the case of the new option, limited registration, the breeder must indicate the puppy is to be registered in this fashion and then transfer the dog to the buyer. A dog with a limited registration may not be shown in conformation, and any puppies he or she produces are ineligible for AKC registration.

Remember, when selling your puppies you are responsible for the fact that your particular puppies even exist. Consequently, you are obligated to see that, to the best of your knowledge, each puppy will go to a home where he will be well loved and well taken care of, and where he will have companionship and security. Never hesitate to refuse a sale if you have any reason to believe a family is not right for the puppy, or vice versa. Families with well-behaved, enjoyable children usually make super Corgi families. However, if the children are ill mannered and disobedient, you would only be placing a Corgi puppy in jeopardy by subjecting him to the whims of such children. The puppy, too, could become equally unruly and of no credit to the breed if he were to be raised without understanding and discipline.

A little preparation beforehand, on the breeder's part, can make a puppy's transition to a new home ever so much easier for all concerned. Puppies here are crate-trained before they go off with new owners. Thus they are accustomed to spending the night away from their littermates before they are taken into a totally new environment. Also, because even young puppies are reluctant to mess their sleeping quarters, crate-trained puppies have a head start on their house training.

Starting at eight weeks, our puppies are fed at least one daily meal by themselves in a wire mesh show crate or airlines carrier. At night a crate is placed at each end of the puppy pen and, on a rotating basis, two puppies are selected to spend the night in a crate. They can commiserate with their buddies through the wire so do not feel abandoned while becoming accustomed to the crate as their sleeping quarters. As the time nears for the puppies to be leaving, they learn to spend the night quietly in a crate in a room by themselves away from their companions.

We strongly recommend to purchasers of our puppies that they continue to use a crate (approximately 27 inches long by 17 inches wide by 22 inches high) for the puppy in his new home. The advantages of a crate are many. The presence of a crate will help a puppy feel more secure in his new surroundings and will provide a place to put the puppy when his activity in the house cannot be supervised. In a crate, the puppy does not have to be shut off from the family in the way he would be if he were put in a room with the door closed. The crate is not used just for confining puppies, for crate-trained adult Corgis are a blessing as well. When you entertain or have workmen in the house, it is handy to know your Corgi is in his crate, conveniently out from under foot. There will be no danger of his being let outside by mistake. There are occasions, too, when a dog has to be confined to small quarters to recuperate from perhaps a minor injury or surgery. A crate-trained dog finds this much less of a hardship than does a dog that has not learned to accept confinement. Once accustomed to a crate, the Corgi will seek it out as he would a den and can often be found snoozing there surrounded by his collection of belongings.

THE PUPPY IN THE NEW HOME

If you are buying a new puppy, plan to bring him into the home when you can concentrate for two or three days on his introductory training. It is far easier to work at establishing desired behavior patterns right at the start than to struggle later on to break unpleasant habits.

Obtain a diet schedule from the breeder when you purchase your puppy. If the puppy has been weaned on a food that is not readily available in your locality, ask the breeder to supply you with a small amount of the food to use while making a gradual shift to another brand or type of food.

Also ask the breeder for a list of what vaccines the puppy has had, the dates they were given, the dates of wormings and types of worming medications

A promising five-month-old bitch puppy.   *Vahaly*

used. Your veterinarian will want to have this information when you take the puppy in for a routine checkup and any follow-up vaccines he may need.

Give the new puppy a warm welcome to your home and then let him take his time in becoming acquainted with his whole new world. Keep in mind that the new puppy is very much a baby, and like a human infant, he still needs numerous rest periods. Scientific studies have determined that the body produces growth hormones only during sleep periods. This explains why so many times a promising, well-up-to-size puppy will go off so badly when he goes into a busy home where he is kept constantly on the go with little chance to get the sleep a growing puppy requires. Not only is a puppy's growth affected by inadequate rest, but as with the overtired child, a tired puppy becomes a bratty puppy. Unfortunate behavior, such as nipping and yapping, can become routine if a puppy is encouraged to be a hyperactive play toy.

A Pembroke Welsh Corgi puppy is bright, extremely adaptable and highly impressionable. The personality of your adult Corgi will reflect the care, understanding and training you have given him during his puppyhood. If after meeting your Corgi, friends express a wish to have a dog just like him, you can take satisfaction in knowing that your early training efforts have molded to perfection in your dog the many wonderful personality traits inherent in the Pembroke Welsh Corgi breed.

17

Care of the Adult Corgi

_____

WITH HIS SMALL SIZE and tidy coat, the Corgi is an easy dog to care for and maintain in good health.

FEEDING

The adult Corgi can do well on the same basic diet he was fed during his puppyhood. The question arises, though, whether it is better to feed one or two meals a day. Many dog owners have found it is easier to maintain a desired weight on both young, active dogs and the older, more sedentary dogs, including spayed bitches, by feeding two meals a day. When a weight gain is desired, the total amount of food fed in a day readily can be increased when split into two meals without causing the intestinal upsets that may occur when just one heavy meal is fed. By feeding the overly "good doer" his total ration for the day in two meals instead of one, the calories contained in a small meal are burned off as usable energy and are not stored as fat.

There has been a tremendous increase in both the number and quality of commercial dog foods on the market today. Kibbled, canned or fresh frozen products abound. During the 1980s, researchers realized soy beans substituted as an inexpensive source of protein could be detrimental to the health of dogs eating foods containing it. Concurrent with the health food movement and in reaction to the dangers of soy, several excellent, well balanced products have emerged. Now owners can choose from foods tailored to the specific needs of growing puppies, average house pets, senior citizens or high-energy working or show dogs. There are even specialized diets available through veterinarians for maintenance of dogs with particular health needs.

Usually the prime dog food brands are in stock at pet supply shops as opposed to supermarket shelves. The somewhat higher price of the best foods is offset by the optimum condition your dog deserves. In any case, beware of cheap generic brands that are poorly balanced and use inferior ingredients, and actually may cause illness.

With so many options, the owner should select a quality product that is appropriate to his dog's needs and stick with it as a basis of the daily menu. Nonetheless, as nothing is perfect, if one single food is fed day in and day out, the imbalances within that food, however slight, can have a cumulative effect on the dog. Thus a basic diet providing some variation of protein and vegetable supplements is recommended.

Keep in mind, however, it is totally unwise to jump from one brand of dog food to another. Severe diarrhea usually results from such indiscriminate feeding.

GROOMING

The Corgi's grooming requirements are few. A regular once- or twice-weekly combing will usually keep the coat in top form. During periods of heavy shedding (and every Corgi seems to have his or her own shedding schedule), more frequent and thorough combings are needed.

A healthy coat is a naturally clean coat. If a Corgi is receiving a well-balanced diet with sufficient amounts of fatty acids present, his coat will not be at all oily nor too dry. Bathing a Corgi disturbs the natural balance in the skin and only leads to more bathing. If at all possible, complete baths should be infrequent. Surface grime can be removed easily by briskly rubbing the dog down with a damp towel. Toweling the dog off after he has been outside on a rainy day will have the same cleansing effect.

The regular grooming sessions should include a quick overall inspection of the dog for latent problems. Examine the ears for a possible buildup of wax and dirt, and teeth should be free of tartar. Check the anal area for any skin irritation due to the presence of dried fecal matter. The Corgi's heavy "pants" can camouflage any accumulation in the anal region for long periods of time. Fluffies will need special attention to keep them tidy in this area. Owner awareness will preclude problems.

Nail trimming is a must for most Corgis. Corgis exercised on hard pavement may wear their nails down sufficiently and need no further attention. Ideally, nails should be trimmed once a week to keep the quick (vein) in the nail well back. Not only is a dog more comfortable with short nails, but its feet are more attractive, and inadvertent scratches inflicted by long nails can be avoided. Nails can be trimmed with any of a variety of canine nail clippers, filed with a metal file, or ground down with a drill with a sanding attachment. If the dog proves impossible to cope with during nail trimming sessions, it is better to have your veterinarian or a groomer trim the dog's nails regularly than it is to simply forget the whole business.

POSSIBLE HEALTH PROBLEMS

The average Corgi is a sturdy, healthy little dog. Relatively few encounter ailments any more serious than a brief intestinal upset resulting from a dietary indiscretion.

There are some conditions that occur in the Corgi with sufficient frequency to warrant being mentioned here, so Corgi owners will be aware of their existence should their dog be having a problem.

The ruptured disc syndrome is perhaps the most common disorder known to occur in Corgis. In this condition, the spongy disc, which acts as a buffer between one bony spinal vertebra and the next, ruptures out of its encasement, so to speak. The pressure of the ruptured disc on the spinal cord causes the animal severe pain, and in extreme cases, the pressure on the spinal cord can cause varying degrees of hindquarter paralysis. Obviously, a veterinarian should be consulted if the dog shows evidence of pain along its back or is walking in a peculiar manner.

Experts used to associate the disc syndrome with long-backed dogs, but since some long-backed breeds have a low incidence of ruptured discs and a number of short-backed breeds are commonly affected, it seems a matter more of individual sensitivity. Possibly there is an inherited susceptibility within the bloodline involved. Ordinary exercise and activities such as climbing stairs or scaling stone walls will not cause a disc to rupture in a dog who is not already predisposed to the condition. In a disc-prone dog a disc can rupture when the dog is simply turning around in his crate or rolling over in his sleep. Care should be taken, though, with a dog whose medical history indicates disc problems. The dog should not be allowed to climb steep stairs or jump over and off furniture, as excess exertion can trigger a rupture.

Often, serious complications from a ruptured disc can be avoided if the condition is spotted right away, and in conjunction with veterinary care, the dog is confined to a crate immediately. Knowing that disc syndrome does occur in Corgis, it is wise to be alert to the signs of an impending problem. If a dog shows any reluctance to get up and walk, hangs back on an outing with you or noticeably hesitates before going up or down stairs (providing he is accustomed to stairs), play it safe and restrict his activity for a few days.

Some Corgis are inclined to urinary tract disorders. Urine sediment that in more severe cases leads to stone formation can be responsible for recurrent bouts of cystitis or bladder inflamation. Frequent urination, blood in the urine or unsuccessful attempts to urinate call for immediate veterinary attention.

Most cases of cystitis can be promptly relieved with antibiotic therapy and the administration of urine acidifiers. Dogs with chronic cystitis can generally be maintained on urine acidifiers.

GENETIC SCREENING

There are three disorders of genetic origin which are prevalent in many breeds and which conscientious breeders are working to control. They are hip dysplasia, eye abnormalities such as PRA (progressive retinal atrophy), juvenile cataracts, PPM (persistent pupillary membranes) and von Willebrand's disease, a bleeding disorder. Many excellent articles and books have been written on these topics, and it is not within the scope of this volume to delve into detailed descriptions of these diseases. In addition, there is a great deal of controversy as to the degree to which the Pembroke Welsh Corgi breed is affected by these problems. Nonetheless, it is necessary to briefly describe each and list what action should be taken to prevent further infiltration of the undesirable traits into the gene pool.

Hip Dysplasia

Hip dysplasia occurs when the head of the femur does not fit into the hip socket properly and the shape of the bones is remodeled. Pain and lameness results. Genetic predisposition and environmental factors are believed to cause the condition. A dog can be carefully positioned and X-rayed to determine the condition of the hips. The Orthopedic Foundation for Animals (OFA) is an organization to which X-rays may be sent for evaluation by a team of three specialists. One of seven grades from excellent to severely dysplastic is assigned, and an OFA number is given to each dog over age two and deemed clear of the disease.

Compared to most large breeds that can have major problems with hip dysplasia, Corgis are on the low end of the scale of dogs X-rayed and found to have questionable hips. Still, a significant number of X-rays do not pass OFA's standards. Most importantly, however, very few Corgis show any clinical signs of discomfort at all. Dogs known to have X-rayed poorly have become big winners noted for excellent movement. With all this in mind, for the sake of the breed as a whole and the well-being of any resulting puppies, it would be wise to have all Corgis checked before breeding.

Eye Abnormalities

A similar situation exists for eye abnormalities. Several other breeds have a high incidence of PRA, for example, which leads to total blindness at an early age. Juvenile cataracts and PPM are not as disastrous, and either can be corrected or cause no sight impairment. Still, when the disease can be avoided through careful breeding practices, it behooves us to take advantage of testing facilities.

The Canine Eye Registration Foundation (CERF), working with the American College of Veterinary Ophthalmologists, certifies dogs examined by diplomates of the ACVO. These veterinarians, with their specialized equipment, are available throughout the country. Recent studies indicate PRA is almost nonexistent in the Pembroke Welsh Corgi, although some of the other abnormalities have been found. Again, breeding stock should be examined.

Von Willebrand's Disease

In the late 1970s the third genetic disorder, von Willebrand's disease (VWD), was recognized in the Pembroke Welsh Corgi. In VWD, affected dogs have difficulty clotting when cut and may bruise easily. Due to complicated genetics, there is a wide range of expression of the disease, and most carriers of the gene are clinically normal and never have any problems whatsoever. But a dog who is a carrier bred to another carrier can produce affected puppies that might not survive. Your veterinarian can draw blood, process it and send it to a lab specializing in VWD diagnostic assay procedures. Once more, this is a good idea for all Corgis with parenthood in their future.

It must be emphasized that while these diseases do exist in the breed, the average Corgi is highly unlikely ever to be bothered by them. However, owners of popular stud dogs and brood bitches should have their Corgis checked and be aware of the genetic potential they carry.

ROUTINE HEALTH CARE

To maintain your Corgi in the best of health, annual visits should be made to the veterinarian to keep your dog up to date with its distemper-hepatitis-parvo-parainfluenza booster vaccines and rabies vaccine. In regions where heartworm is known to exist, annual blood checks also should be made to make certain your dog is free of this parasite. At the time of annual boosters, it is advisable to also have a stool sample from the dog checked for the presence of eggs from intestinal parasites. Bitches to be bred should be checked for worms several times before they are due in season. A single negative stool check does not necessarily mean the dog is free of worms, as the worms do not always shed eggs every day. It is important to determine whether or not a bitch has worms. If she does she should be wormed before she is mated.

There is currently a battery of vaccines that may be injected against the ravages of a host of diseases. Yet caution is advised. Overdosing a dog with these man-made chemicals is proven to have dire consequences due to immuno-suppressive complications, especially if the animal is stressed by his environment. The Corgi is a breed susceptible to this syndrome.

Finally, good care of your Corgi does not consist of feeding a satisfactory diet, periodic grooming and occasional attention to health care alone. Exercise is paramount to the well-being of any dog. This is an area where a great many dog owners fail badly. Neglect is truly unfortunate, as both dog and owner would benefit not only from the exercise but from the companionship as well. Teaching your Corgi to play ball, developing a regular walking routine, exercising via obedience training—all of these things will enhance his health and quality of life and your pleasure in him.

18

The Senior Citizen

Corgis CAN and often do live to a ripe old age. The average lifespan of the Corgi seems to be between twelve and thirteen years. Corgis of fourteen and fifteen years are not at all uncommon, and occasionally we hear of Corgis still getting about at age eighteen.

EXERCISE

Common sense should be your guide in taking care of your aging dog. Exercise should be less strenuous. The length of time an older dog is kept outside in inclement weather, too, should be limited. More care must be taken that an aged dog is thoroughly dried off with a towel after he has been in the rain or snow.

As your dog begins to lose his sight and his hearing fails, he will need to be accompanied on his outings, for there is a greater risk that he will get in the road or will wander off and not be able to find his way home. Some Corgis really do get quite senile with old age, and these dogs, particularly, need to be supervised outside if they are not enclosed in a fenced yard.

And do not forget to groom the older dog. His coat should be kept tidy and washed should he soil himself due to incontinence. Often trimming the foot hair will give the dog welcome traction on slippery floors. Overly long nails are a special hazard for the older fellow. Your veterinarian can help with the inevitable bad breath of aged teeth.

Ch. Beaujolais of Revelmere,
ROMX, at twelve years of age. From
her three litters came eleven champions, many of whom bred on.
Owner: Deborah Harper.

A young fifteen-year-old, Ch. Cyclone of Cowfold, one of the foundation dogs of Cappykorns Kennels. He was imported and owned by Margaret Downing. *Phyl*

FEEDING AND SPECIAL SUPPLEMENTS

Old dogs generally benefit from several small meals a day rather than one large meal. There is less stress both on the digestive system and on the weakening kidneys with the feeding of small meals. High-quality protein foods (chicken, beef, cottage cheese and eggs) in limited amounts with cooked cereals will provide the older dog with essential nutrients while taxing kidney function as little as possible. Several excellent commercial ''senior'' diets are on the market today that can serve as the base instead of cereal.

Although some experts have questioned the effectiveness of the prescription canned foods available for dogs with kidney problems, many Corgis have benefited from the use of such foods. Your veterinarian can not only supply you with the appropriate prescription diet, but he can also provide you with geriatric vitamin-mineral supplement tablets for your senior citizen. These tablets usually contain some hormones and dessicated thyroid, which together will help make up for the diminishing output of an older dog's endocrine glands.

Mild, old-age stiffness can be helped considerably with the daily addition of vitamin E to the dog's diet. A 100 I.U. capsule per day will suffice.

Another helpful dietary supplement for aged dogs in the initial stages of nephritis, or loss of kidney function, is sodium ascorbate, the acid-free form of vitamin C. Corgis with early nephritis have responded well to treatment with 200 mgs of sodium ascorbate twice a day. Excessive water drinking and frequent urination, especially during the night, have been markedly reduced in dogs receiving the sodium ascorbate tablets. While the sodium ascorbate seems to slow down the degenerative process in the kidneys, it can in no way be considered a cure. Also, it may not be advisable to give sodium ascorbate to a dog with a heart condition, so check with your veterinarian first.

An older dog can be expected to spend most of his day sleeping quite soundly, and it takes a moment for him to become alert upon awakening. A soft bed, well padded and with a washable blanket, will be appreciated. He will need to take more trips outside. It may be necessary to make special arrangements for his comfort should you have to be away from home for a lengthy stretch of time.

MORALE BOOSTING

In caring for your aging friend, above all else, do not neglect to spend some time with him just because he no longer makes demands on your time in the way more boisterous young dogs do. A meaningful hug, a quiet pat, a gentle game of ball playing will let your old dog know you still love him every bit as much as you did when you were enjoying his puppy antics; the communication will give a boost to his morale and help him stay with you longer still.

19

Breed Organizations

$\mathbf{A}$LL AROUND THE WORLD, Welsh Corgi fanciers have joined together to form organizations to protect and promote both the Pembroke and the Cardigan. At this point in the Corgi's history, many such organizations exist that support all the aspects of Corgi activity covered in the foregoing chapters. Here you will read of many of them and learn how they figure into breed development where they operate.

THE WELSH CORGI CLUB

The first banding together of Corgi enthusiasts was in 1925, when a group of Welshmen in Carmarthen under the leadership of Capt. J. H. Howell and Capt. Checkland Williams formed the Corgi Club. As described in an earlier chapter, this club, later named the Welsh Corgi Club, was comprised of fanciers of both Cardigan and Pembroke Corgis. The organization, which is active to this day, was the only Corgi club until 1938 that included Pembrokes.

THE WELSH CORGI LEAGUE

Interest in the Corgi soon spread beyond the confines of its Welsh homeland. The breed prospered in England, and gradually Challenge Certificates were offered at many Championship shows. Mrs. Thelma Gray of Rozavel Kennels felt a club should be formed with more accessible headquarters near London, and in June 1938 the Welsh Corgi League was formed. Over the years it has grown to well over 775 home members. Its worldwide membership, open to all Corgi fanciers, numbered close to 1,260 in 1993.

Perhaps the most significant contribution of the League, and one that is appreciated around the globe, is the annual *Welsh Corgi League Handbook*. First published in 1946 with Miss Edith Osborne as the pioneer editor, the Handbook is distributed free to all members, and it is the model for similar volumes in other countries. It gives pictures and pedigrees of Challenge Certificate winners and overseas titleholders plus numerous kennel ads. The collection of volumes from 1946 on has provided the Corgi world with a permanent record of the breed and its progress.

A major project was the making of the 16 mm, 25-minute color film, *Corgwn Sir Benfro*, said to be the first documentary made by a breed society on either side of the Atlantic. The idea was originated by Miss Anne G. Biddlecombe, secretary of the League for many years. Miss Biddlecombe thought it would be valuable for people in years to come to see the Corgis of the present day. The well-known BBC personality, Leslie Perrins, then president of the Welsh Corgi League, was instrumental in its preparation.

Eng. Ch. Luther of Wey (Eng. Ch. Wey Spearmint ex Dundryview Gemma), whelped June 2, 1984. Breeder: Miss J. Harvey; owner: Mrs. Nan Butler. Luther was Best of Breed at the prestigious Welsh Corgi League Silver Jubilee show over a record entry of 363 Pembrokes. He has won nineteen CCs. *Sally Anne Thompson*

Each year the League offers a huge number of commemorative cups for wins at Championship and Open shows. The top honor is the Leslie Perrins Memorial Trophy, initiated in 1963 for the Pembroke Welsh Corgi of the Year. Two other coveted awards are the Formakin Stud Dog Cup, given to the top producing sire of the year, and similarly for the bitches, the Coronet Brood Bitch Cup.

In 1988 the League celebrated its Silver Jubilee by holding a gala Championship show complete with many special events and activities. Corgi lovers from all over the world assembled to view the tremendous entry and the spectacular parade of champions. Of enduring value is a booklet compiled for the occasion by Simon Parsons, *British Pembroke Corgi Champions 1928–1987*. A picture and pedigree of every champion during those years is included.

Although the Welsh Corgi Club and the Welsh Corgi League are the main breed organizations in the British Isles, there are smaller groups in existence that often include both Corgi breeds. A listing of these local clubs is available from the secretary of the Welsh Corgi League.

THE PEMBROKE WELSH CORGI CLUB OF AMERICA, INC.

It was not long after the arrival of Little Madam with Mrs. Roesler that a group of Pembroke fanciers on this side of the Atlantic were drawn together over their interests in the Corgi. At first there was a Welsh Corgi Club composed of both Cardigan and Pembroke fanciers. On February 12, 1936, at the time of the Westminster Kennel Club show, the Pembroke Welsh Corgi Club of America was founded. Although none of those appearing on the original roster are still active in the breed, Derek G. Rayne, now a prominent all-breed judge, joined the PWCCA in 1938 and was listed as a Corgi Club judge in 1939.

A Standard for the breed, only 120 words long, written by the Welsh Corgi Club in 1925, was adopted by the PWCCA and approved by the American Kennel Club in March 1936. In 1951 the PWCCA went to a slight variation of the 1934 English Standard for the Pembroke Welsh Corgi. For over fifty years this document stood as the official yardstick of the breed. After a careful and thorough revision by the Club, a new Standard for Pembroke Welsh Corgis in the United States was approved by the AKC on June 13, 1972. Then, to comply with the AKC's desire for more uniformity between the breed Standards, the format of the Pembroke Corgi Standard was revised in 1993.

Annual meetings at first were held when exhibitors gathered for the Westminster show in New York City. Early PWCCA minutes tell of a hiatus of club activities during the war that was ended in 1946 by a meeting

> . . . in the center of the Madison Square Garden arena which was practically deserted due to the postpon[e]ment of the show because of the brownout. During the meeting the arena lights were extinguished which caused a hasty adjournment after the last items of business were discussed in semi-darkness.

The PWCCA has several publications. In 1961 Mrs. Gladys Orlowski initiated the quarterly *Pembroke Welsh Corgi Newsletter*, which has grown from a mimeographed news sheet to a professionally printed, well-illustrated magazine. An introductive brochure on the breed was prepared in 1968 for the general public. A handbook, *Pembroke Welsh Corgis in America*, was originally edited by Mr. and Mrs. Ronald Shakely, with yearly supplements ably compiled by Mrs. Friend Kierstead from 1972 to 1979. Since then Mrs. Mary Miner has continued the tradition of excellence.

In 1975 the booklet *An Illustrated Study of the Pembroke Welsh Corgi Standard* was completed and distributed to Corgi fanciers throughout the world as well as to all approved judges of the breed in the United States. The leaflet *A Judge's Pictorial of the Pembroke Welsh Corgi* was published in 1990. Most recently, in order to educate the general public, the Club has prepared a flyer to be sent through the AKC to each person who registers a Pembroke Welsh Corgi with them.

The highlight of the PWCCA year is the National Specialty show. Exhibitors gather from all across the country and from Canada to compete and socialize. In 1988 a record 444 dogs were entered. The Sweepstakes, a popular feature for Corgis between six and eighteen months of age, has had as many as 185 youngsters exhibited. In conjunction with the conformation classes, an Obedience Trial, Tracking Test and Herding Trial now are part of the Specialty week. The National rotates to different geographical areas and is hosted by a regional Corgi club.

PWCCA AFFILIATE CLUBS

Application to the PWCCA is through a sponsorship system. The number of members has always been relatively small in relation to the national interest in the breed, with the current mark being around 400 in the early 1990s. However, representing various parts of the country, there are nine affiliate clubs plus a host of forming clubs each with an enthusiastic following. The affiliate clubs hold their own annual Specialties.

The Golden Gate Pembroke Welsh Corgi Fanciers, Inc., was founded late in 1956 in the San Francisco area, and has always been a forward-moving group. It held the first independent Pembroke Welsh Corgi Speciality in the country in 1963 attracting a large entry of 79 for judge Miss Pat Curties. GGPWCF was also the first Corgi club to issue a newsletter, which was launched by Mrs. Gladys Bundock in 1959. Five years after the club's formation a 148-page handbook became the first American publication of its kind. In 1967 a second, double-sized handbook followed. The club continues to grow, and attracts about 175 Corgis to its Specialty.

By the 1960s there was a sufficient increase in Corgis in southern California to warrant the formation of a second regional club, and the Pembroke Welsh Corgi Club of Southern California, Inc., came into being. A highly coveted

Ch. Northrun Sea Goin' Magic, HC (Ch. Garvin's Magic Marker, ROMX, ex Ch. Nebriowa Exquisite), owned by Gertrude Ferriday and his breeder, Cathy Donovan. "Zorro" won the PWCCA National Specialty in 1986 and in 1988 in an entry of 444 dogs—the greatest ever. Although other Corgis have won the National Specialty two or more times, it was at a time that the entry averaged well under 100 dogs.

Ch. Garvin's Magic Marker, ROMX, owned and bred by Gayle K. Garvin, a dominant sire of twenty-six champions, including "Zorro."

Ch. Howbout Welsh Wonder Boy (Howbout Rhythm 'N Blues ex Howbout Mandolyn). Breeder: Sally Howe; owners: Jill and Lonner Holden and Joan Jensen. "Basil" won the PWCCA National Specialty two years in a row, 1991 and 1992.   *Vahaly*

Ch. Nebriowa Greenforest Ranger (Ch. Nebriowa Oleg Cassini ex Greenforest Diedre). Breeder: August Ludwig; owners-handlers: Thomas Mathiesen and Larry Cunha. Winner of five Specialty Bests of Breed in thirteen months, he is pictured with his handler, Tim Mathiesen, and judge Rutledge Parker.

271

trophy at the Southern California Specialty is the Pembroke Seal of Excellence given to Best of Winners. This special award by the County Council of Pembrokeshire, Wales, is a plaque with the Pembroke County Coat of Arms, and was arranged for by Mr. Lee Pitt.

Another unique feature of the southern California club is a tree with branches of copper on which engraved medallions of the Club's Obedience degree winners are hung. The club produces a prize-winning newsletter.

California has not been the only area of burgeoning Corgi activity. In the Midwest, on July 10, 1965, Pembroke fanciers met for dinner and agreed a local club was desirable. The club they formed eventually became known as the Lakeshore Pembroke Welsh Corgi Club, Inc. The first issue of *Corgi Capers*, the LPWCC quarterly newsletter, was published in 1966.

The year 1970 marked the holding of the first Lakeshore Specialty show. This popular event, which boasted an entry of over 100, was topped by Ch. Cormanby Cadenza. Cadenza set an unequaled record by winning the same honor for three straight years. Since then entries have risen to an average of near 175.

In the northwestern corner of the United States the fourth PWCCA affiliate club took root during the late 1960s and became the Cascade Pembroke Welsh Corgi Club, Inc. This club has a particularly active number of obedience trainers in its membership. It was the first club to hold an annual tracking trial exclusively for Pembroke Welsh Corgis.

The Middle Atlantic states was the area served by the next PWCCA affili-

Ch. Vangard Briarwood Magnolia was bred and owned by Robert L. Simpson and Shirley M. Zapf. "Maggie" was shown at five U.S. Sweepstakes, starting the day she was six months old, and won them all.   *Vajdik*

ate, the Pembroke Welsh Corgi Club of the Potomac. Established in the mid 1970s, this successful club now holds the largest Specialty next to the National. In 1993, 291 Pembrokes were in conformation and Obedience competition.

Texas claims two thriving PWCCA affiliate clubs. The North Texas Pembroke Welsh Corgi Fanciers joined the parent club in 1985, and the Greater Houston Pembroke Welsh Corgi Fanciers was added in 1990. Both clubs hold popular, independent Specialties and provide their members with other Corgi events and newsletters.

The eighth PWCCA affiliate, also joining in 1990, is the Pembroke Welsh Corgi Club of Greater Atlanta. Another club serving the southern tier of states is the Southeast Pembroke Welsh Corgi Club, which is not affiliated.

The latest club to be aligned with the PWCCA is a New England club named the Mayflower Pembroke Welsh Corgi Club. For years the AKC would not recognize this club because the distribution of its members was too large. Nontheless, its spirited membership organized a Specialty-like weekend called the Corgi Classic, complete with a Sweepstakes, Obedience and a New England clambake. Supported classes at a local all-breed show served to offer AKC championship points. Eventually the AKC recognized the Mayflower club, which held its first Independent show in 1992. Its newsletter also has been awarded first prizes in writing competitions conducted by the Dog Writers' Association of America.

Although not yet affiliated with the parent club, several other groups are in various stages of development. Corgi owners in Oregon, Colorado, New Jersey, Ohio, the Carolinas, Iowa, Illinois and Florida all have clubs where they can share their enthusiasm for the breed and attend Specialties, matches and other events. It is hoped these regional clubs will continue to prosper and proliferate as the breed itself gains strength in various sections of the country.

PEMBROKE WELSH CORGI ASSOCIATION (CANADA)

The first Pembroke Welsh Corgis crossed the seas and a great land beyond to find themselves in Sundance, Alberta, in 1932. The breed remained relatively scarce, however, for years despite several enthusiastic exhibitors and a growing number of breeders across Canada. Finally, in November 1966 the Pembroke Welsh Corgi Association (Canada) was inaugurated in the Vancouver/Victoria area of British Columbia. The PWCA newsletter, now named *The Corgi Courier*, started publication two years later.

Membership in the PWCA increased across Canada until in 1972 the Association was divided into several sections. There are two sections in British Columbia—the B.C. Mainland Section and the Vancouver Islands Section. Moving east, we find the Southern Alberta Section, the Manitoba/Saskatchewan/Northern Ontario Section, the Ontario/Quebec Section and the Maritimes Area. During 1992 Specialty shows were held in all but the Maritimes.

AUSTRALIA

On the other side of the world, at about the same time Corgis first appeared in North America, the first Pembrokes reached Australian soil. In 1934 in the state of Victoria a nucleus of Corgi interest grew and eventually pressed north into New South Wales. Presently there are Corgi associations in almost every state. These associations are for both Cardigan and Pembroke fanciers.

The Welsh Corgi Club of New South Wales is the oldest Australian club, as it was founded on May 29, 1950, in Sydney. The great popularity of the breed in this state is reflected in the tremendous number of Corgis at the club's Championship shows. A total of 369 entries (including 88 Cardigans) was reached in 1969.

Other, more regional clubs are active in New South Wales. These are the Illawarra Welsh Corgi Club, the Newcastle and Northern Welsh Corgi Club and the Welsh Corgi Club of Canberra. In 1969 the first handbook, *The Welsh Corgi in Australia*, was prepared and underwritten by the Welsh Corgi Club of New South Wales in cooperation with the other Australian clubs. To date seven volumes have been published.

The Welsh Corgi Club of Victoria was formed in 1953. The number of Corgis in that state soon was sufficient to top the entries at the Royal Melbourne show. Western Australia, South Australia, Queensland and Tasmania all have active Corgi clubs, although Corgi populations are not as large as in New South Wales and Victoria. A complete listing of these clubs appears in the 1974 edition of *The Welsh Corgi* by Charles Lister-Kaye, edited by Mrs. Dickie Albin (Arco Publishing Company, New York).

Although many of the Australian clubs hold their own annual championship shows, a National Australian Specialty is held every few years and is all important to serious breeders and exhibitors.

NEW ZEALAND CLUBS

Across the Tasman Sea in New Zealand Pembroke Welsh Corgis began to arrive from England in the late 1930s. Pembroke Corgi fanciers in the Auckland vicinity of the North Island inaugurated the Dominion Welsh Corgi League in 1951. With the importation of the first Cardigan in 1953, the League embraced both breeds. Now there are four Specialist clubs in New Zealand. The Dominion Welsh Corgi League, Inc., serves North Island and the Auckland area. The South Island Welsh Corgi League, Inc., is self explanatory; the Central Welsh Corgi League operates around Wellington; and the newest, the Waikato Welsh Corgi League, also is active on the North Island. There is *The New Zealand Welsh Corgi Handbook*, which was published yearly. The most recent edition, produced by the Central Welsh Corgi League, is a joint effort entitled *The New Zealand & Australian Welsh Corgi Handbook*. All four clubs hold Championship shows.

SOUTH AFRICAN CLUBS

The Corgi followed the British Empire to South Africa. There three clubs flourish. Established in the southern section is the Cape Welsh Corgi Club, to the north is the Welsh Corgi Club of the Transvaal, and the Natal Welsh Corgi Club serves its region. The Welsh Corgi Club of Zimbabwe and the Welsh Corgi Club of Mashonaland are also active organizations.

CLUBS IN CONTINENTAL EUROPE

Considering the relatively short distance from the original source, it is interesting that Welsh Corgis have not been quicker to gain popularity in continental Europe. In Holland, Dutch owners returning from England with their dogs after the war began the influx of Corgis there. In 1950 the Nederlandse Welsh Corgi Club was established.

Corgis were rare in Sweden before 1953. It was not until 1963 that the Swedish Welsh Corgi Club was founded at the suggestion of Per-Erik Wallin. The Pembroke Welsh Corgi is still relatively uncommon in Sweden, but the ratio of dogs shown to dogs registered is high, and the Swedish Club now has drawn over 250 members. One special feature is the annual Corgi Walk around the parks of Stockholm, where fifty Corgis running loose attract much attention.

Corgis did not appear in Norway until about 1950. Yorken Gallant Knight arrived in 1967, and his spectacular show career helped the breed make strong gains. Corgi popularity has grown steadily, stabilizing at 110 to 120 registrations per year. The Norsk Welsh Corgi Klubb was founded in Oslo in 1971. Membership now numbers over 200. Each year a Championship show with approximately fifty entries is judged by an English specialist.

There are other Corgi clubs that have formed or are forming in Europe. The Finnish Welsh Corgi Club is active and holds its own Championship show. A club in Switzerland, founded in 1969, is thriving. The Danish, German, and Austrian Welsh Corgi Clubs are all active. As Pembroke Corgis have been imported into Poland, Czechoslovakia, France, Gibraltar, Italy and elsewhere, more clubs may be organized by the breed's followers.

To reach any of these Specialty clubs, contact the national kennel club in each country for direction to its Welsh Corgi club. Most of these associations are for both Pembrokes and Cardigans.

Delila, a Swedish Pembroke Welsh Corgi owned by Pia Bekkhus and bred by Mr. and Mrs. Hans Viden.

A puppy by Nord. Ch. Jofren Nabob.

20

The Tail End— a Quandary

As THIS BOOK goes to press, the hottest topic in the Corgi world is the tail docking ban that went into effect in England on July 1, 1993. The British Parliament passed a law in 1991 stating that as of the above date only "qualified persons" would be allowed to dock puppy tails. It is now illegal for English breeders to do newborn Pembroke tails themselves. Only veterinarians can do it.

At the same time, the Royal College of Veterinary Surgeons (RCVS) has declared emphatically that it is unethical for any veterinarian to dock tails except for therapeutic reasons. Any of their colleagues caught docking puppies could be severely censured. Apparently the issue is not because docking is cruel, as it always is done when the babies have not yet fully developed a sense of pain. Rather the objection is to the "unnecessary mutilation." Cropped ears long have been banned in England and other European countries. Sweden and Norway have not allowed docking for several years. Pembrokes in these countries sport their full appendage.

Needless to say, the fanciers of the many breeds that always have docked tails have tried to forestall the ban. A group named the Council of Docked Breeds has been instrumental in getting the English Kennel Club to pass a motion supporting docking where called for in the official Standard. Many of the Standards of these breeds have been revised to say the tail is "customarily docked," thereby opening the door to those which may not be.

Yet the law has been passed, and the RCVS is adamant. The only hope left is that the government will designate certain laymen as "qualified persons" to perform the procedure, as the law does not state that tails cannot be docked at all. Everyone is waiting for the outcome of this extremely important issue.

It is of historical interest that this is not the first time the Pembroke Welsh Corgi has had a docking ban imposed on it. Back in 1931, at a time when there was much rivalry between the proponents of the two Corgi types, the Cardigans and Pembrokes were lumped together as the Welsh Corgi. Perhaps in a effort to standardize the one breed, the KC ruled there could be no docking of Pembroke tails. Nonetheless, the trait for a natural bob was a definitive characteristic of the Pembroke. It is reported that about half of the puppies were born with short tails. What is more, natural-bob Pembrokes cross-bred to dogs of other breeds with normal tails (including Cardigans) would produce bobtailed puppies. When natural-bob Pembrokes appeared in the ring, their breeders were accused of not complying with the rules. Finally the Pembroke enthusiasts convinced the Kennel Club it was folly to go against the natural tendency of the breed, and the ban was rescinded in 1934. The Pembroke then was given full status as a separate breed from the Cardigan, and was placed on the list of breeds allowed to have docked tails.

Over the intervening years the incidence of natural-bob puppies has greatly diminished, as breeders have selected for other attributes that would improve their stock. Now, with the 1993 docking ban upon us, it has become desirable to recover the buried trait without losing the quality of the present-day Pembroke.

Fortunately, there is at least one eminent breeder in England working to this end. For several years the foresighted Peggy Gamble of Blands Kennels in Yorkshire has made natural bobtails her pet project. Calling upon the tremendous strength of her kennel, in 1986 she bred a bobtailed bitch, Stormerbanks Bobs, to Eng. Ch. Blands Status Symbol, and produced natural-bob puppies. One of these, Vaquera of Pemwell, has been most useful. Peggy put her Eng. Ch. Blands Expectations to him and got Blands Revelation of Malsis, a bobtail, who won her Junior Warrant in 1989. Revelation, bred to Eng. Ch. Pemland Magnus, produced Malsis Gilt Edge of Blands, another winning bobtail. Two of the six puppies out of Revelation by Eng. Ch. Belroyd Nut Cracker were bobtails. Vaquera and Eng. Ch. Blands Starlight Express had three bobtailed puppies in a litter of six. Blands Specialty, a CC and JW winner, and Vaquera had four out of seven. From a repeat breeding of Starlight Express and Vaquera Peggy kept Blands Simply Simon, another promising puppy. There are others.

All the puppies Mrs. Gamble has run on in the 1990s have been bobtails, and she writes, "Now quality is such that they are equal to others for competition." She has begun bobtail to bobtail matings.

Mrs. Gamble contends that the bobtail gene is just a single dominant gene, not two genes, as some have thought. If one of the parents of a litter is a true bobtail, there will be bobtail puppies born. A controlled mating of a Boxer bitch to a bobtail Corgi produced five bobtails out of seven.

The length of the short tails as birth varies somewhat. Our Standard accepts up to two inches on an adult. The legendary Eng. Ch. Rozavel Red Dragon was endowed with a perfect example. Nowadays a stub as long as that would be docked to comply with the current style. Other puppies have virtually no tail at all.

Sometimes a puppy is born in a litter where neither parent is a natural bobtail. Mrs. Gamble does not consider such a puppy a true bobtail and claims it will never produce bobtails. Rather, the taillessness is a deformity, and may be coupled with additional abnormalities. Yet apparently healthy bobtails do appear unexpectedly with enough regularity for one to believe that there may be more to the genetics surrounding this characteristic of the Pembroke. In the future, blood tests from the sire, dam and all the puppies may be checked for DNA fingerprinting. After a generation or two the bobtail gene should be isolated from those that go to make up the rest of the Corgi. Peggy Gamble is confident that only true natural bobtails will carry the gene and therefore the ability to produce it.

Now that the docking ban in England is a reality, the importance of Mrs. Gamble's work will become very apparent. She and others have proven that it is possible to breed modern Pembrokes of high quality who will not carry a long tail. But it will take much perseverance and skill to achieve such an end. Many may not be willing to continue breeding Corgis if they have to compromise their lines to comply with the ban. Valuable bloodlines are bound to be lost or diluted.

For those who abide by the law and refrain from docking the puppies, what sort of guidelines are they to follow? Who will decide what the Standard of the breed should say about desired length and tail carriage? The Cardigan breeders have been striving for years to have their dogs carry the tail in an attractive position not higher than the back. When the eye has been so accustomed to the neat finish of the Pembroke's tailless rear, it will be strange at the very least to see a long, bushy addition. Will there be prejudice in the ring, inadvertent or otherwise?

The question of exports is another factor. Corgi breeders around the globe traditionally have brought in fine English dogs. Very few would be willing to go to the expense and trouble of importing a dog to show in countries where docking is the norm. Almost no one would be willing to export an adult with the spectre of docking in mind. Bringing suitable dogs back to England always has been a problem due to the lengthy quarantine restrictions. At this point, the ultimate ramifications of England's new docking ban can only be surmised. There will unquestionably be major repercussions throughout the Pembroke Corgi world. We can only watch and wait.

Appendix

W HEN PREPARING the original manuscript for the publisher the two chapters "Breeding On" and "Tracking Today's Trends" called for a comparatively large number of photographs in a specific sequence to illustrate the theories advanced in the text. It was expected that in order to balance the book, inevitably some of these pictures would have to be placed in other chapters where fewer pictures were assigned. In the first edition, more than half of the illustrations for "Breeding On" were scattered throughout the book, no longer in the proper sequence, and not necessarily grouped according to family as planned. Fortunately this second edition did not have the same problem.

In order to assist the reader to locate and compare the pictures and better understand the thrust of the chapters on bloodlines in both editions, the chart below has been prepared. It shows family affiliations and lists the page on which each dog's photograph can be found.

Many of the pictures in the first edition had to be eliminated to make room for illustrations of the prominent dogs since 1978. Dogs which do not appear in this book are in parentheses, and their page number applies to the first edition of *The Complete Pembroke Welsh Corgi.*

Chapter 5   Breeding On

Eng. Am. Can. Ch. Lees Symphony, CDX/36

(Eng. Ch. Kaytop Maracas Mist/*63*)
      Eng. Ch. Kaytop Marshall/*39*

(Ch. Redclyffe's Tonic of Trafran/*2*)

Eng. Ch. Maracas Masterpiece/*38*
    (Am. Can. Bda. Ch. Maracas Monarch of Cleden, ROMX/*65*)
    (Ch. Gladiator of Rode, UD, Can. CDX/*65*
       (Ch. Rover Run Minstrel Man/*65*)
          Ch. Cote de Neige Derek/*40*
          (Five generations of Derek's descendants/*67*)
    (Eng. Ch. Crowleythorn Snowman/*64*)
        (Eng. Irish Am. Ch. Crowleythorn Ladomoorlands, ROM/*221*)
          (Am. Can. Ch. Rosewood Dark Brandy/*221*)
        (Ch. Halmor Hi-Fi, ROM/287)
          (Ch. Bear Acres Two for the Road, ROM/287)
          Am. Can. Ch. Bear Acres Mr. Snowshoes, UD, ROM/*40*

        (Am. Can. Ch. Suzyque's Southern Snowbear/*287*)

South African Ch. Drumbeat of Wyldingtree of Wey/*41*
    (Int. Ch. Gayelord of Wey/*223*)
    (Sportsman of Wey/*223*)
    Pennywise of Wey/*42*
    Ch. Stormerbanks Big Drum, CDX/*43*
        Ch. Cote de Neige Sundew, ROMX/*43*
        Ch. Willets Red Jacket, ROM/*44*
    (Ch. Craythorne's Fleetfoot of Wey/*225*)
        (Ch. Cormanby Commotion/*225*)
        (Ch. Cormanby Cavalier, ROMX/*16*)
        Ch. Cormanby Cadenza/*45*

Ch. Kaydon's Anthony/*34*
    (Rover Run Romance, ROM/*227*)

(Am. Mex. Ch. Penrick Most Happy Fella/*271*)
    (Ch. Penrick Belle A'Ringing/*210* brace)
        (Ch. Penrick Flewellyn/*8*)

Eng. Ch. Knowland Clipper/46

Ch. Crawleycrow Coracle of Aimhi, ROM/*43, 98*
    (Ch. Kaydon Aimhi's Kate/*94*)
    (Ch. Kaydon's Eversridge Penny/*94*)
                      Ch. Cote de Neige Penny Wise/*99*
    (Ch. Erhstag's Gage/*72*)
    (Ch. Benfro Windjammer/*72*)
Eng. Irish Ch. Zephyr of Brome/*47*
    (Am. Can. Bda. Ch. Maracas Monarch of Cleden, ROMX/*65*)
    Am. Bda. Ch. Maracas Gale Force of Cleden, ROM/*47*

Ch. Cote de Neige Christmas Candy, ROMX/*47*
Ch. Cote de Neige Pennysaver, ROMX/*48*
(Ch. Stokeplain Fair Chance of Cote de Neige, ROM/*202*)
(Ch. Cote de Neige Chance of Fox Run, ROMX/*233*)
(Ch. Cote de Neige Instant Replay, ROMX/*233*)
Ch. Red Envoy of Brome, CD, ROMX/*49*
Ch. Larklain's Firebright, ROM/*22*)
(Eng. Ch. Barngremlin of Braxentra/*14*)

Stormerbanks Ambrose-Stormerbanks Supersonic/50 and *51*

Int. Ch. Broom of Ballybentra/*50*
Eng. Ch. Stormerbanks Dairymaid/*96*

(Eng. Ch. Stormerbanks Sabreflash/*77*)

Ch. Stormerbanks Winrod Fergus/*55*

(Eng. Ch. Stormerbanks Invader/*77*)

Am. Can. Ch. Stormerbanks Tristram of Cote de Neige, ROMX/*52*
Am. Can. Ch. Welcanis Adulation/*52*

Lees Jackpot/*53*
Eng. Ch. Lees Sunsalve/*54*
(Am. Can. Ch. Lees Briardale Midnight, ROMX/*79*)
Ch. Wicklow's Whizzer, ROM/*54*
(Ch. Menfreya's Classical Jazz, ROM/*45*)
(Am. Can. Ch. Lees Mynah, CD, TD, ROM/*140*)
Am. Can. Ch. Llanfair Night Owl, ROMX/*56*
(Ch. Cottleston Card of Fox Covert/*165*)

Eng. Ch. Lees Wennam Eagle/*55*
(Ch. Lees Craythorne's Golden Plover, ROM/*231*)
(Ch. Happiharbor Captain Midnite/*231*)
(Ch. Happiharbor Ramblin' Man/*231*)

Combinations: (Ch. Halmor's Winrod Spencer, ROM/*90*)
Ch. Larchmont's Golden Triumph, CD/*57*
(Ch. Midon's Billie The Kid/*90*)

Chapter 6   Tracking Today's Trends

In this chapter some dogs are mentioned in the text, but due to space allowances no picture appears. Consequently, a page number is not appropriate. However, the names are included in this listing, as they are important members of their family.

Eng. Ch. Hildenmanor Crown Prince/60

With Eng. Ch. Caswell Duskie Knight/*62*

Ch. Bekonpenn Count Doronicum, CD, ROMX/64
    Ch. Larklain's Redd Dandy, ROMX/63
Ch. Cappykorns Bach, ROMX/61

Direct line influence

Am. Can. Bda. Ch. Velour of Rowell, ROM/214
Ch. Hildenmanor Master Spy, ROMX
Ch. Master Major of Millerhof, ROM
Ch. Heronsway Free At Last/66
Ch. Heronsway Free Style, UDT, HT, RIMX, VC/67
(Eng. Ch. Lees Opalsong of Treland/276)

Eng. Ch. Penmoel Such Fun of Rivona/65

Eng. Ch. Belroyd Lovebird/106
Eng. Ch. Revelmere Cock-A-Hoop
Ch. Irisan Bengimum Boy of Rivona/68

Stormerbanks-Lynfarne

Eng. Ch. Lynfarne Pacesetter/68

    Eng. Am. Ch. Lynfarne Poldark, ROMX/69
        Ch. Stormerbanks Poetry/69
        Ch. Lamin Ross Poldark

    Ch. Martindale Butter Brickle, ROMX/70
        Ch. Trewhyl Lyric of Pennington/107
            Ch. Pennington Ramblin' Lad, ROM/71
            Ch. Pennington Gloriand/*cover*
                Ch. Pennington Glory Hallelujah
        Ch. Renefield Bunny Quite Funny/72
        Ch. Renefield Fancy Pants

Blands

Eng. Ch. Olantigh Christmas Gift/75
    Ch. Foxash Dawn Piper of Rowell, ROMX
                Eng. Ch. Fitzdown Dorian of Deavitte/86
                    Eng. Ch. Bymil Black Nymph/105
                    Eng. Ch. Bymil Gold Sylph
Eng. Ch. Olantigh Christmas Carol
    Eng. Ch. Apollinaris Angel Clare
(Eng. Aust. Ch. Kydor Cossack/119)

Eng. Ch. Kathla's Dusky Sparkler of Blands/*73*
    Eng. Ch. Blands Solomon of Bardrigg/*72*
        Eng. Ch. Blands Sonny Boy/*76*
        Eng. Ch. Blands Sweet Someday
        Eng. Ch. Evancoyd Mr. Wonderful/*76*

    Eng. Ch. Olantigh Black Diamond/*75*
        Eng. Ch. Blands Status Symbol

    (Am. Can. Ch. Spartan of Blands of Werwow/*269*)
                        Ch. Festiniog's Toby Two, ROM
              Ch. Festiniog's Moonraker, ROMX/*81*
                Ch. Festiniog's Linebacker/*82*
                Ch. Festiniog's Touchdown, UD, PT
                    Ch. Arbor Festiniog Rickover, CDX, PT/*82*

    Can. Am. Ch. Blands Lucky Lad/*114*
        Can. Am. Ch. Willoan's Lucky Lady/*115*
        Can. Am. Ch. Stonecroft Simply Sinful/*115*

    (Can. Ch. Blands Saga/*267*)
    (Can. Ch. Willoan's Sparticus/*267*)
    (Willoan's Windsong/*269*)

    Ch. Anzil Honey Dew of Blands/*77*
        Ch. Penways Town and Country/*78*
    Ch. Nebriowa The Blacksmith, ROMX
        Ch. Nebriowa Coco Chanel/*108*
            Ch. Nebriowa Christian Dior, ROMX/*79*
            Ch. Nebriowa Jordache of Fox Meadow, ROMX/*80*
    Ch. Anzil Elegant Lady, ROMX

Belroyd-Pemland-Blands

Eng. Ch. Belroyd Jacana/*105*

Pemland Royal Command/*85*
    Eng. Ch. Belroyd Nut Cracker/*83*
        Eng. Ch. Blands Limited Edition of Belroyd
        Am. Can. Ch. Blaizewood Hooray Henry, CDX
        Ch. Karenhurst Nut Crunch
            Ch. Dylan of Karenhurst
        Ch. Cinnonie Cavalier
            Ch. Tri-umph's Turning Heads
            Ch. Howbout Welsh Wonder Boy

Eng. Ch. Pemland Magnus/*84*
    Ch. Pemland Maestro, ROM
        Ch. Roughouse Pennington Daryl/*87*
            Ch. Pennington Pastel/*88*
            Ch. Pennington Portrait
            Pennington Parable
    Ch. Revelmere Bring Me Joy, ROMX/*89*
    Ch. Magnum of Vennwoods, ROMX/*90*
        Ch. Nebriowa Front and Center
        Ch. Nebriowa Center Line

Am. Can. Ch. Schaferhaus Yul B of Quanda, ROMX/92

Am. Can. Ch. Leonine Leprechaun, ROMX/*91*
    (Am. Can. Ch. Faraway The Magic Kan-D-Kid, CD/*88*)
    (Am. Can. Ch. Rryde Symphony, ROM/*138*)
        Ch. Schaferhaus Danielle, ROM/*frontispiece, 104*
            Am. Bda. Can. Mex. Int. FCI Ch. Vangard Jenelle/*frontispiece, 103*
    Ch. Schaferhaus Relindo's Pele
    Ch. Clayfield Paisley, ROMX
    Am. Can. Ch. Schaferhaus Aeroglend Tupnc. ROM
    Ch. Vangard The Last Chance, ROMX/*230*

Am. Can. Ch. Yul B of Quanda, ROMX
    Am. Can. Ch. Schaferhaus Quanda Trifle
        Am. Can. Ch. Caralon's Q-T Sequoya, ROMX/*93*
            Am. Can. Ch. Caralon's Q-T Hot Wheels, ROM/*94*
            Am. Can. Ch. Horoko Caralon Dickens, ROMX/*95*
            Ch. BluJor Dickens Desert Fox
            Ch. Gaylord's Bobbindobber, ROMX
            Ch. Beckridge Boy George
    Am. Can. Ch. Dellmoor Jelly Bean

Bibliography of Selected Reading

Books
Some of these books are out of print.

Albin, Dickie. *The Family Welsh Corgi*. A Popular Dogs Handbook. London: Popular Dogs Publishing Co., 1970. 126 pp. Paperback.

Albin, Dickie, ed. *Corgi Tales*. Margate: Thanet Press, 1976. 113 pp. Paperback.

Avebury, Diana. *Zelda and the Corgis*. London: Piccadilly Press, 1984. 56 pp.

Chance, Michael. *Our Princesses and Their Dogs*. London: John Murray, 1936. 60 pp.

Cole, Margaret A. *The Welsh Corgi*. Edinburgh: John Bartholomew & Son, Ltd., 1981. 96 pp.

Combe, Iris. *Herding Dogs, Their Origin and Development in Britain*. London: Faber & Faber, Ltd., 1987. 253 pp.

Cox, Dora H. *Keeping Up With Jones*. Pittsburgh, PA: FEB Company, 1979. 26 pp.

Elias, Esther. *Profile of Glindly, A Welsh Corgi*. North Quincy, Mass.: The Christopher Publishing House, 1976. 128 pp.

Evans, Thelma. *The Welsh Corgi*. London: Watmoughs, Ltd., 1934. 89 pp. Out of print in 1939; later revised and enlarged by Thelma E. Gray.

Forsyth-Forrest, Evelyn. *Welsh Corgis*. Edited by S. M. Lampson. London: Ernest Benn, Ltd., 1955. 128 pp. Also A. S. Barnes & Co., New York; Wyman & Sons, London.

Gray, Thelma. *The Corgi*. London: W. & R. Chambers, Ltd., 1952. 60 pp.

Gray. Thelma. *The Welsh Corgi*. London: Watmoughs, Ltd., 1936, 226 pp., and 1946, 245 pp. Revision of earlier work by Thelma Evans.

Guillot, Rene. *Little Dog Lost*. New York: Lothrop, Lee & Shepard Co., 1970. 64 pp.

Haight, Mrs. Robert W., ed., *Welsh Corgies, A Guide to the Training, Care and Breeding of Welsh Corgies*. Jersey City, N.J.: T.F.H. Publications, Inc., 1956. 24 pp. Paperback.

Hubbard, Clifford L. B. *The Pembrokeshire Corgi*. The Dog Lover's Library. London: Nicholson & Watson, 1952. 126 pp.

Illustrated Study of the Pembroke Welsh Corgi Standard, An. The Pembroke Welsh Corgi Club of America, Inc., 1975. 32 pp.

Johns, Rowland, ed., *Our Friend the Welsh Corgi, Pembroke and Cardigan*. London: Methues & Co., Ltd., 1948, 1951. 96 pp. Second edition, 1954, 1960. 103 pp.

Kierstead, Caroline H., Ph.D. *Pembroke Pictures and Pedigrees*. An annotated index. Part I English Publications, Part II United States Publications. Northampton, Mass.: Gazette Printing Company, 1984. 115 pp. and 71 pp.

King, Dorothea. *Rex Q.C.* London: Pavilion Books, Ltd., 1983. 27 pp.

Lister-Kaye, Charles. *The Popular Welsh Corgi*. London: Popular Dogs Publishing Co., Ltd., 1954, 1956, 1959, 1961, 1965. 224 pp. In 1968 it was revised and enlarged by Dickie Albin, with a 7th edition in 1970 of 235 pp., and the volume was retitled *The Welsh Corgi*. An 8th edition was printed in 1974. 237 pp.

————. *Welsh Corgis*. A Foyles handbook. London: W. & G. Foyle, Ltd., 1957, 1958, 1961, 1964, 1966. 87 pp. Revised by Mario Migliorini, now published by Arco Publishing Co., Inc., New York, 1971. 90 pp.

Niccoli, Ria. *How to Raise and Train a Pembroke Welsh Corgi*. Jersey City, N.J.: T.F.H. Publications, Inc., 1964. 64 pp. Paperback.

Osborne, Margaret. *Know Your Welsh Corgi*. New York: The Pet Library, Ltd., 1970. 64 pp. Paperback.

Perrins, Leslie. *The Welsh Corgi*. (Also titled *Keeping a Corgi*.) Middleburg, Va.: Denlinger's, 1958. 131 pp. Printed by Wyman & Sons, Ltd., London.

Smith, Arthur. *"Shorty," Story of a Boy and His Corgi*. Grand Rapids, Mich.: AKA Publishers International, 1985. 64 pp.

Tudor, Tasha. *Corgiville Fair*. New York: Thomas Y. Crowell Co., 1971. 47 pp.

Handbooks

Available from the clubs that publish them.

Golden Gate Pembroke Welsh Corgi Fanciers, Inc. *Handbook*. Phyllis Young, ed., 1962. 148 pp.

Golden Gate Pembroke Welsh Corgi Fanciers, Inc. *10th Anniversary Handbook*. Phyllis Young, ed., 1967. 300 pp.

New Zealand Welsh Corgi Handbook. Various editors and years.

New Zealand & Australian Welsh Corgi Handbook, The. Various editors and years.

Pembroke Welsh Corgi Club of America, Inc. *Corgis in America*. Ronald H. Shakely, ed., 1970, 1971. *Pembroke Welsh Corgis in America*. Caroline Kierstead, ed., 1972–1978; Mary A. Miner, ed., 1979 on.

Welsh Corgi Club of New South Wales, The. *Handbook—The Welsh Corgi in Australia*. Various editors and years.

Welsh Corgi League, The. *The Welsh Corgi League Handbook*. Margate: Thanet Press, 1946 and yearly thereafter.

Newsletters
Information on club publications available through the secretaries.

Cascade Pembroke Welsh Corgi Club, Inc.—Pacific Northwest. *Corgi Clan Tales*. Mimeographed. Articles. 6–8 pages.
Central Florida Pembroke Welsh Corgi Club. *Central Themes*.
Columbia River Pembroke Welsh Corgi Club—Oregon. *Corgi Currents*. Quarterly.
Corgi Quarterly, The. Wheat Ridge, Colo. Hoflin Publishing, Ltd. A professionally prepared magazine, photographs, articles. 60+ pp.
Gaitway Pembroke Welsh Corgi Club Newsletter, The. St. Louis, Illinois area.
Garden State Pembroke Welsh Corgi Club. *Toplines*. New Jersey. Quarterly.
Golden Gate Pembroke Welsh Corgi Fanciers, Inc.—Northern California: *Corgi Tracks*. Monthly offset magazine. Articles and pictures. 20–30 pages.
Greater Houston Pembroke Welsh Corgi Fanciers. *Corgi Chronicle*. Quarterly.
Lakeshore Pembroke Welsh Corgi Club, Inc.—Great Lakes area. *Corgi Capers*. Quarterly offset magazine. Articles and some pictures. 15–20 pages.
Mayflower Pembroke Welsh Corgi Club. *The Corgi Cryer*. New England. Quarterly, offset. Pictures and articles.
Mile High Pembroke Welsh Corgi League. *The Good Companions*. Colorado.
North Texas Pembroke Welsh Corgi Fanciers. *The Review*. Monthly offset. Articles and some pictures. 12–16 pages.
Ohio Valley Pembroke Welsh Corgi Club. *Ovation Newsletter*.
Pembroke Welsh Corgi Club of America, Inc.—U.S.A.: *Pembroke Welsh Corgi Newsletter*. Quarterly offset magazine. Articles and pictures. 30–60 pages.
Pembroke Welsh Corgi Club of the Carolinas. *Carolina Corgi*.
Pembroke Welsh Corgi Club of Greater Atlanta. *Corgi Chatter*.
Pembroke Welsh Corgi Club of the Potomac—Mid-Atlantic states. *The Tide*. Bi-monthly offset magazine. Articles and some pictures. 10—15 pages.
Pembroke Welsh Corgi Club of the Rockies Newsletter. Colorado. Quarterly.
Pembroke Welsh Corgi Club of Southern California, Inc. *The Guardian*. Bi-monthly, mimeographed. Articles, some pictures. 8–10 pages.
Pembroke Welsh Corgi Association, The—Canada: *The Corgi Courier*. Quarterly offset magazine. Articles and pictures. 20–30 pages.
Southeast Pembroke Welsh Corgi Club Newsletter, The. Southern Tier states.
Welsh Corgi League, The—England: *Our Corgi World*. Semiannual, mimeographed. Articles. 8–10 pages.

Many clubs in other countries have similar newsletters. For information, contact the Kennel Club of that country.

Brochures

Golden Gate Pembroke Welsh Corgi Fanciers, Inc. *Pembroke Welsh Corgi Puppy Brochure*. 8 pp. *The Welsh Corgi*. 4 pp. Both illustrated.
Pembroke Welsh Corgi Club of America, Inc. *An Introduction to the Pembroke Welsh Corgi*. 8 pp. Illustrated.
———. *Judge's Pictorial of the Pembroke Welsh Corgi*, 1990. Photographs and the Standard. 8 pp. Not available to the general public.

Videos

The Pembroke Welsh Corgi Standard AKC Video/Slide Show. Published by the American Kennel Club in 1983.

Pembroke Welsh Corgi Specialty Videos. Various photographers and sponsoring Corgi clubs. (These videos may be available directly from the individual clubs. Inquiries should be made to the current secretary.)